SAUDI WOMEN WRITERS

Saudi Women Writers: Sociopolitical and Literary Landscapes details the achievements of Saudi women fiction writers from the 1960s up to the present day, many of whose works have yet to be published in English translation.

This book explores how various Saudi women writers' works reflect deep social, religious and political changes over several key phases: the secularism of the 1960s and 1970s; the 1980s religious revival, or saḥwa; the post-saḥwa period; and the era of globalization. Engaging with intersectional feminism, the book studies women's texts as a multifaceted space of identity, power and agency, with the capacity to critique, and possibly dismantle, traditional hierarchies, especially amidst evolving social, religious and political landscapes. By examining the works of Samira Khashugji, Qmasha al-Olayyan, Omima al-Khamis, Zaineb Hefny, Badriya al-Beshir, Raja al-Sanea, Saba al-Herz and Warda Abdul Malik, this book charts a fresh course in literary criticism, moving beyond restrictive and monolithic perspectives.

Saudi Women Writers: Sociopolitical and Literary Landscapes is an important and unique text which will be of use to both students and scholars of Gender Studies, Literature, Middle Eastern Studies, and Politics.

Basma A. Al Mutlaq has a Ph.D in comparative and feminist literature from the School of Oriental and African Studies, University of London. She was a Visiting Fellow at the Department of International Development, Queen Elizabeth House, University of Oxford, and was an assistant professor for two years at Prince Muhammad Bin Fahad University in Saudi Arabia.

SAUDI WOMEN WRITERS

Sociopolitical and Literary Landscapes

Basma A. Al Mutlaq

Routledge
Taylor & Francis Group
LONDON AND NEW YORK

Designed cover image: Mahmoud Saleh, via Getty Images

First published 2025
by Routledge
4 Park Square, Milton Park, Abingdon, Oxon OX14 4RN

and by Routledge
605 Third Avenue, New York, NY 10158

Routledge is an imprint of the Taylor & Francis Group, an informa business

© 2025 Basma A. Al Mutlaq

The right of Basma A. Al Mutlaq to be identified as author of this work has been asserted in accordance with sections 77 and 78 of the Copyright, Designs and Patents Act 1988.

All rights reserved. No part of this book may be reprinted or reproduced or utilised in any form or by any electronic, mechanical, or other means, now known or hereafter invented, including photocopying and recording, or in any information storage or retrieval system, without permission in writing from the publishers.

Trademark notice: Product or corporate names may be trademarks or registered trademarks, and are used only for identification and explanation without intent to infringe.

British Library Cataloguing-in-Publication Data
A catalogue record for this book is available from the British Library

Library of Congress Cataloging-in-Publication Data
Names: Al Mutlaq, Basma A., author.
Title: Saudi women writers : sociopolitical and literary landscapes / Basma A. Al Mutlaq.
Description: Abingdon, Oxon ; New York, NY : Routledge, 2025. | Includes bibliographical references and index. | Contents: Saudi Women Writers : Sociopolitical and Literary Landscapes – Rethinking the Patriarchal Discourse – Feminizing History : The Female as a Repository of Memories – Narratives of Violence : Communicating Corporeal Anxieties – Travel, Women and the City : The Literature of Encounter.
Identifiers: LCCN 2024037230 (print) | LCCN 2024037231 (ebook) | ISBN 9781032887821 (hardback) | ISBN 9781032855127 (paperback) | ISBN 9781003539681 (ebook)
Subjects: LCSH: Arabic literature–Saudi Arabia–Women authors–History and criticism. | Arabic literature–Social aspects–Saudi Arabia. | Arabic literature–Saudi Arabia–20th century–History and criticism. | Arabic literature–Saudi Arabia–21st century–History and criticism. | Women and literature–Saudi Arabia. | Women in literature.
Classification: LCC PJ8005 .A83 2025 (print) | LCC PJ8005 (ebook) | DDC 892.7/09928709538–dc23/eng/20241029
LC record available at https://lccn.loc.gov/2024037230
LC ebook record available at https://lccn.loc.gov/2024037231

ISBN: 9781032887821 (hbk)
ISBN: 9781032855127 (pbk)
ISBN: 9781003539681 (ebk)

DOI: 10.4324/9781003539681

Typeset in Sabon
by Newgen Publishing UK

To the memory of my father, who continues to inspire me, and to my mother, who shared every step of my journey.

CONTENTS

	Introduction	1
1	Saudi Women Writers: Sociopolitical and Literary Landscapes	17
2	Rethinking the Patriarchal Discourse	50
3	Feminizing History: The Female as a Repository of Memories	77
4	Narratives of Violence: Communicating Corporeal Anxieties	103
5	Travel, Women and the City: The Literature of Encounter	122
6	Protest and Self-orientalizing Texts	145
	Conclusion	159
	Index	*167*

INTRODUCTION

The Woman Issue: Reconciling Western and Local Discourses

Not too long ago, issues surrounding women and their rights in the Kingdom of Saudi Arabia were of particular interest – both locally and internationally. Despite the attention on the ongoing conflicts in the Middle East, Saudi women and the issues that concern them were still making headlines in the West. Certainly, the apocalyptic divide between 'Us' and 'Them' following the 9/11 attacks has amplified the West's criticism of Muslims around the world generally, and of Saudi Muslims specifically. The media in the West often uses sweeping generalizations and stereotypes about women in Arabia that bear witness to the intersection between gender-related and Orientalist discourses, with the latter's particular fascination with Arab and Saudi women. In fact, most discussions on Saudi women have been coloured by a combination of Orientalist and imperialist discourses, both of which continue to use the 'woman issue' as a vehicle to consolidate images of Western superiority in contrast to a perceived Eastern inferiority.[1] As such, Saudi women post-9/11 and the Gulf wars – especially, the war on Iraq beginning in 2003 – have figured prominently in the Western media along with Muslim women from Afghanistan and Iraq.[2]

In the kingdom, as in other GCC countries,[3] the struggle for female emancipation has been problematic due to existing tribal social structures that regard women as representing the collective identity and honour of the tribe. This has helped to promote a political culture that idealizes women's domesticity through a configuration of what Eleanor Doumato dubs 'ideal womanhood' perceived as a symbol of national identity, the appearance and behaviour of which represents the 'tribal family'.[4] Such concepts have proved

DOI: 10.4324/9781003539681-1

to be frustrating for women because when modernists in the region probe the issue of women they are accused not only of being Westernized and at odds with their culture but also of actively serving a foreign agenda. This resonates with Alanoud Alsharekh's more general observation that 'the issue of female emancipation is plagued with apathy, controversy and, one cannot avoid saying it, fear'[5] – a fear of being alienated from the people and, most importantly, the tribe. Ali al-Tarrah further explains, 'After more than a half century of independence [in] most Arab countries, tribalism and sectarianism remain the main allegiances underpinning Arab societies especially in the GCC countries.'[6]

The rise of the *saḥwa* ideology (a puritanical version of Islam that swept the whole region following the Iranian Revolution) in the late 1970s[7] thwarted the female-emancipation project in the kingdom, in the sense that, between the years 1979 and 2015, anti-modernists under its sway focused on Western economic and cultural encroachment as a conspiracy to push Muslim women out of their homes.[8] This was a time of 'critical social transformation and ideological rupture', to borrow the words of Saddeka Arebi, which privileged one particular gender based on mere biological difference. For instance, it has generated images of mythological figures: the woman as the 'queen of her home', the 'princess bride', the 'pearl in a shell' and so on. Arebi notes how 'women were of great [enough] concern to the various forces in society to warrant this dramatic collective theorizing in which they were key images, to the point of obsession'.[9] Such images, projected into public discourse, engaged with a network of cultural, religious and political signifiers to embrace a regressive web of power relations. This helped to form a biased social consciousness, and hence the exertion of power and control. The normalization of these images meant that female agency and subjectivity were gradually and unconsciously cancelled out. The damaging outcome would be seen in the years to come – more precisely, those between 1979 and 2000 – when a combination of religious and tribal laws not only impeded women's overall participation in public life but also led to their absence from leadership positions and decision-making processes.[10]

Saḥwa saw the world through a binary lens; thus, it was no surprise to see 'Awaḍh al-Qarni, an ultra-conservative writer, launch an attack on modernism in his 1988 book *Al-Hadātha fī Mīzān Al-Islām: Nazrāt Islāmyya fī Adab Al-hadātha* (Modernism in the Scale of Islam). Observers like Ali al-Shadawi among others agree that this volume was one of the most dangerous books to be published during the 1980s, because it presented modernity as inherently secular and ethically void, and conflated it with atheism and conspiracies against Islam and the Arabic language in general.[11] Personal attacks levelled at women who dabbled with modernism – like the poets Fouzia Abu Khaled and Khadija al-'Amri, and author Raja Alem – ranged from accusations of 'heretic Sufism' and 'sensual connotations' to 'conspiring against the Arabic language and Islam'.¹² Such attacks and the pressure on writers (at the time) indicated a deep cultural and sociopolitical rupture in the collective consciousness of the nation. They also posed the very important question of whether these phenomena were reflective of a misogyny inherent in the *saḥwa* or if they in fact comprised tribal values. What concerns me here is how incidents like this reveal the fragility of the dominant discourse in the face of women's marginal discourse. Such incidents also function as a reminder that women's discourse, no matter how marginalized it might be, is in fact an intersectional space of 'identity', 'power' and 'agency'.

Transversality in Women's 'New Texts'

Saudi Women Writers: Sociopolitical and Literary Landscapes examines the feminist, gender, identity and literary aspects raised by the works selected. I examine Saudi women's fiction in terms of what Stuart Hall describes as 'a space of weak power, but [...] a space of power'.¹³ I follow Roland Barthes' notion of 'punctum'¹⁴ – a point of memory that, in spite of being personal, intersects with layers of cultural and historical significance exposing what is not expected and rendering it visible for the reader. I also use the term 'transversal' to describe identity and resistance in women's marginal discourse and the alliance created in this space between art and social, political and activist practices. This draws on Gerald Raunig's theory of 'transversality'¹⁵ and what he terms 'transversal concatenation' – that is, the power of a 'new text' to demolish traditional hierarchy¹⁶ and 'produce different forms of [collective] subjectivity that break down the oppositions between the individual and the group'.¹⁷ In subsequent chapters, I examine such 'new texts', as I refer to the genuine Saudi women's novel, from Saudi women writers and their (at times) 'flagrance' – not only as a dialogue between female writers and the patriarchal tradition, which maps out a hitherto anxiety-ridden terrain, but also as a site for feminist, if not nationalistic, debate. The mission of transversality in this context is to create an alliance between these 'new texts' and protest, and to augment the messages that these women writers are trying to pass on to their audience. The creation of such an alliance is not new: historically speaking, the 'Arabian peninsula reflects a unique interconnection between the poetic and political [and more so, when it involves an ideology such as that of *saḥwa*] in which the symbolic organization of society is based on coordinating cultural affairs in words'.¹⁸ Thus, recurrent forms of self-expression and the exploration of love and desire surface in Saudi women's texts alongside evaluations of social, tribal and patriarchal practices, registering a 'punctum' of sorts that yields a profound cultural resonance.

For instance, a look at how Saudi women writers have been drawn to chatter about 'love' and 'passion' since the 1960s reveals how this was equated with a 'soft' anger towards tribal and cultural mores at the time. Their chatter, however, evolved over time into what many critics dub 'daring' and 'revolutionary' voices, breaking fiercely maintained cultural taboos surrounding self-expression, religion, love and intimate relationships. The 'daring voices' of these Saudi women novelists would provoke a controversy in the Arab world and accusations over the 'obscenity' of their subject matter. For example, Mahmoud Tarawri of the Saudi *Al Watan* daily complained of 'the tyranny of sex in the Saudi novel', claiming that 'it falls to those without talent to slap some sex onto the page and call it a novel'.[19] Similarly, Kuwaiti novelist Layla al-Othman – who herself was accused by radical Islamist groups in her home country of using indecent language and defamatory expressions in *The Departure*,[20] and sentenced to one month in prison for 'moral and religious offences' – said of the new Saudi novels, 'the trend towards increasing explicit content can be understood by the love of fame and the fact that publishing houses race to have new female writers who aspire to make hasty career jumps'.[21] What those levelling these charges fail to see is the fact that the female writers of a younger generation are using their pens to contest and negotiate dominant representations of their womanhood. In the process, they are collectively interrogating futile cultural laws – which burgeoned during the *saḥwa* years – in order to redefine gender roles, nationhood and belonging. For this reason, I argue throughout this book that these high-pitched, revolutionary voices and the chaos that they cause actually resonate with Hélène Cixous' and Catherine Clément's opinion:

> What would happen to logocentrism, to the great philosophical systems, to the order of the world in general if the rock upon which they founded this church should crumble? [...] So all the history, all the stories would be there to retell differently; the future would be incalculable; the historic forces would and will change hands and change body – another thought, which is yet unthinkable, will transform the functioning of all society.[22]

By retelling the whole story differently, these women are smashing Cixous' and Clément's 'rock' – that is, the (quite literally) 'master' narrative or the male-dominant discourse. In this book, I attempt to read women's struggles from within their fiction, focusing on their resistance to established narratives of society whereby the *saḥwa* is transformed into a marker of political and social memory that is, in turn, transformed into a shared historical memory. So, instead of simply analysing the negative effects of the *saḥwa* on women as an oppressive dogma, I examine the transversal nature of their texts in questioning its futile cultural values and the small but significant space of power that women writers have collectively cultivated in resistance to the dominant discourse. I also look at how they have adopted a subjective feminist tone – merging the private with the public, personal and cultural – and taken issue with the agents of patriarchy (the religious clerics, the father figures) and persistently questioned the mother – a figure often complicit in the exercise of patriarchal power. Overall, I examine how Saudi women writers are intentionally or unintentionally transgressing old, established boundaries. Thus, the recurrence of certain themes and patterns that revolve around women's quest for identity and individuality strengthens the assumption that resistance is not a conceptual language external to women writers but rather a primary prism embedded in their stories, choice of protagonists, settings and literary tropes. Hence, certain potentially misleading notions about women writers' silence need to be reconsidered.

Conceptual and Theoretical Framework

As in other parts of the world, the empowerment of women has gained 'buzzword' status in today's Saudi Arabia, with a surge in initiatives and leadership projects – all functioning in the context of 'reform', 'renewal' and 'change'. Within this framework, academics, activists, feminists and progressives are trying to combat female marginalization by reclaiming women's achievements in the disciplines of science, medicine, art and even feminism itself. The use of literature, and novels in particular, as a source of inspiration in the various areas of social science, research, policy making and so on has been a reliable method since the 1970s. Drawn from Michel Foucault's *The Archaeology of Knowledge* (1972), the concept of 'counter memory' aims to resist and subvert the dominant 'master narrative' (discourse). It also attempts to rewrite and retrieve history from the male-dominant point of view that has hitherto played a significant role in overshadowing, if not actively trivializing, the accomplishments of prominent women. Engaging counter memory has been a successful strategic tool in decolonizing people's collective imagination and in remembering the long-forgotten history and tradition of women (in Egypt, this concept has given birth to the Women and Memory Forum, which was founded in 1995).[23]

When I began thinking about voices that represent shifts in female identity, writers like Samira Khashugji, Qmasha al-Olayyan, Omima al-Khamis, Zaineb Hefny, Badriya al-Beshir, Raja al-Sanea, Saba al-Herz and Warda Abdul Malik came to mind immediately as being reflective of deep social, religious and sociopolitical changes. In addition, they mark the different schools of thought, belonging successively to the 1960s and 1970s era of secularism; the 1980s religious revival, or *saḥwa*; the post-*saḥwa* age; and, finally, the era of globalization. However, these phases are not set in stone; they overlap and coexist depending on the writer's proximity to the various influencing cultures (secularism, *saḥwa*, etc.). While the connection between these authors has nothing to do with their literary aesthetics or political leanings, the sum of their works nonetheless functions as an intersectional space of women's agency, identity and power – the aim of which is to exercise 'cultural memory' of women's overall engagement with the dominant discourse. I consider the aforementioned writers' texts as a counter memory comprising unevenly distributed multitudes of points, which correspond to the ideas of 'power' and 'defiance' that shift women's space from the private and silenced to the public and voiced.

Hence, through the works of these Saudi women writers, which I have mostly translated myself, I hope that the reader will be able to recognize a body of writing that tirelessly questions futile cultural laws while pushing back the old boundaries of *'awra*, or the 'shameful', that have been attached to them for so long. I also argue that by virtue of their contribution to literature, and by their sheer disruption of the patriarchal discourse or master narrative, these women are creating a counter memory that is forcing change in cultural and social attitudes and values. Thus, placing Saudi women's writing in its cultural, social, political and historical context over the span of almost 50 years, from the late 1960s to 2015, will help us to understand how Saudi women have responded to the institutionalization of their womanhood. It will also show the gradual process of change in social attitudes in the kingdom, and the transformation in women's perspectives – a development that defies established male representations; patriarchal language; and, above all, male apathy towards the 'woman question'.

Reading Saudi women's literature within this concept of counter memory or 'cultural memory' has been a valuable tool in the process of the cultural inclusion of female voices, and in understanding the accumulative impact of women's writing in freeing the Saudi female from the shackles of religious and tribal discourses. Examining the persistent struggle for the rights of women and their defiance of the prevailing patriarchal culture highlights the fact that in Saudi Arabia gender is traditionally a fixed constituent of identity. For this purpose, incorporating the first generation of Saudi women writers into this book is, in a way, a feminist attempt to exercise the 'cultural memory' of women's early engagement with the kingdom's dominating patriarchal narrative. This is especially so given the circumstances – i.e. that these early female fiction writers were few in number and that their works were mostly published outside the kingdom at a time before the dawn of mass communication, which meant that their influence was limited if not dispersed and their voices ignored. (This also explains why finding primary sources and scholarly work from this period proved to be such a challenge). Although a great amount of their work is, to our eyes, too rhetorical and emotional – and lacking major plot and social, psychological or political dimensions – nevertheless, it demonstrates an ardent desire to emancipate women and bring about social change. This view is further emphasized by the opinion of critics who believe that it was an experimental period that does not merit extensive study.[24] Although this latter verdict may sound too simplistic, if not outright biased, it nonetheless holds true to an extent – with a few exceptions, like the works of Huda al-Rasheed's novel *Ghadan Sa-yakūn Al-Khamīs* (Tomorrow Will Be Thursday), published in Cairo in 1979, which Ali Zalah describes as the 'closest to showing skill and artistry' of all Saudi novels of the period;[25] and Amal Shaṭā's novel *Ghadan Ansā* (Tomorrow I Shall Forget), published in 1980. No matter what critics say about the literary merits of their works, I regard them as a genuine sign of women reclaiming their identity, agency and position in Saudi public discourse. Thus, writing about the self; about the inner workings of the mind; and about familial issues, no matter how trivial they might be, shifts women's space from the realm of the private and silenced to that of the public and voiced.

To investigate this 'cultural memory', I adopt the tools of feminist literary criticism, which privileges the novel form over other literary genres. This partly explains why I have excluded the poems and prose works of a number of well-known Saudi women authors. I will, however, mention short-story collections in order to further examine certain themes or styles that occur in the works of some writers. This choice (to exclude other genres) was influenced by a previous groundbreaking ethnographic work that has been undertaken on this subject by Libyan-American author Saddeka Arebi, *Women and Words in Saudi Arabia*, which focused on newspaper articles, prose, poems, plays and short stories but avoided analysing any novels – perhaps due to the unpopularity of the novel form at the time of its writing in 1994. By conducting interviews with the writers in question, Arebi examined Saudi women's texts and voices as a force that challenged the language of patriarchal power, drawing on a plethora of anthropological and cultural theories but avoiding feminist literary criticism.[26] In justification, Arebi explains that these writers do not necessarily conform to Western feminists' ideas of resistance or their definitions of patriarchy.[27] In a previously published paper, she had cited Western feminism and its various schools of thought – Marxism, socialism and colonialism – as incompatible with the nature of both Libyan and Muslim women in general. Her argument advocated an end to a debate that many Islamic feminists like Leila Ahmad and Lila Abu-Lughod identified with – that there exists a conflict between feminism and the core values of Islam. What Arebi called for resonated with the views of many prominent women writers and activists in the region, whose attempts to reinterpret Islamic texts may have been liberating but were still incomplete.

Cynicism about Western feminism and its applicability to Arab women's narratives is not new, however. Feminist reading of women's texts has sometimes been charged by critics with being 'one dimensional' – for example, Elizabeth McKee warns against readings that attempt to 'centralize' the discourse of Arab women writers, which, she explains, have 'marginalized and ostracized both the producer of that discourse and their work'.[28] While these factors remain more or less relevant, I find that Western feminism has, as Joseph T. Zeidan puts it, 'a built in allowance for the contextualization of theory, theorists, and subjects of study'.[29] Casting doubt on the role of feminism as both a movement (Western, Islamic or intersectional) and a literary-critical canon is, therefore, unproductive.

Since its publication over four decades ago, Elaine Showalter's book *A Literature of Their Own: British Women Writers from Charlotte Brontë to Doris Lessing* has been an important landmark in the development of feminist criticism. Now a classic text, its initial importance lay in its analysis of women's literary traditions in the patriarchal society of nineteenth- and twentieth-century Britain. My original objective for the current volume was to assess the literary tradition of Saudi women novelists through Showalter's notion of the three stages of female, feminist and feminine – of imitation, of protest and of self-discovery, a turning inward to search for an identity freed to some extent from the dependency of male and female binary oppositions. However, the rapid pace of development in women's writing and the estimated 40 years' duration for each phase, as suggested by Showalter, makes Julia Kristeva's typology more relevant in terms of chronological order – allowing a greater degree of overlap and coexistence.[30] I have to admit, furthermore, that there are limitations to Showalter's concept of 'gynocriticism' as a feminist literary canon; in this, I agree with Susan Friedman's argument that its followers' 'foregrounding of gender has also produced [a] certain blindness that has left them seriously out of step with advances in theories of identity and subjectivity concurrently developing in many different fields'.[31]

For this reason, I rely rather on intersectional feminism as developed by Friedman, and I try to use it appropriately in the context of Saudi women's writing. Friedman, in her book *Mappings*, adopts a more pragmatic transnational and cultural theory that moves gender away from the paralyzing preoccupations of the binary oppositions of us and them, men and women, black and white that are found abundantly in gynocriticism and 'Third World feminism'. This approach has allowed me to move beyond gender into the new geographics of identity – particularly in examining women's agency and subjectivity in the context of shifting social, religious and political times (in this case, the aforementioned Gulf wars, the events of 9/11, globalization and the nearby revolutions of the western Arab world). It offers an alternative, more pragmatic, discourse, through which 'different aspects of identity move fluidly from the foreground to the background'[32] depending on changes in the situation of the subject. Many of the discourses suggested by Friedman foster an intersectional analysis of identity that sits at the crossroads of several different formations of power and powerlessness and identity confusion – shifting power relations that are complicated by ethnic, cultural and class divisions. The strength of Friedman's *Mappings* lies in the way that it develops a multicultural, international and transnational feminism in which the borders and boundaries established by feminists are not set in stone but rather 'shift with changing cultural formations, conditions, and alliances'. In other words, *Mappings* attempts to recreate a singular feminism that 'incorporates conflicting cultural and political formations in a global context'.[33] Friedman proposes a remapping of feminism and women's studies in which she replaces the emphasis on sexual difference and identity politics with what she calls 'cultural narratives of relational positionality', adding, 'these narratives redefine identity as a "positionality, a location, a standpoint, a terrain, an intersection, a network, a crossroads of multiply situated knowledges"'.[34]

In doing so, Friedman provides a full genealogy of the historical production of this new geography of identity, delineating six related but distinct discourses of identity within this new positionality – all of which have seriously undermined or complicated the projects of gynocriticism or gynesis as they were originally formulated. These are the discourses of multiple oppression, multiple subject positions, contradictory subject positions, relationality, situationality and hybridity.[35]

Furthermore, Friedman's concept of 'multiple oppression' offers a comprehensive analysis, in which women's oppression is recognized as a multilayered discourse that varies in intensity and configuration. For example, if women face prejudice, it is important not to overlook other forms of discrimination based on religion, race and class. In other words, women can be doubly oppressed by both society and sectarianism – by, among other things, belonging to the Shi'i religious minority, by being a black woman or by being underprivileged. Most importantly, both Friedman's *Mappings* and Foucault's concept of 'power-knowledge'[36] show how both discursive and non-discursive practices of oppression and violence have a built-in allowance for generating their antithesis – that is, power. In the course of this process, by textualizing and archiving moments of violence against women, female writers are collectively subverting the dominant, patriarchal, male discourse.

Exploring my chosen texts from the standpoint of these various feminist theories has enabled me to better understand the patriarchal politics and social structure embedded in Saudi women's discourses, and to identify an abundance of material through which to investigate an emerging *Khalījī / Saudi* feminism (see the following chapter). Examining the shifts and transformations in Saudi women's novels cannot but be illuminating, in the sense that the sum of their literary output serves to chronicle a (dare I say?) suffrage movement in the making. From the pioneering generation to contemporary and 'chick-lit' works, one can discern a persistent quest for social change, reform and individuality. A good example of this is the way in which all these works intensively use the first-person narrative and internal-monologue techniques to express their mounting frustration/ anger at the patriarchal system. And in a manner recalling Virginia Woolf, who chose death by drowning herself in a river, women writers in Arabia often choose fictional suicide as an answer to some of their troubled female protagonists' problems. This represents a trend via which writers project their feelings of despair and gloom at hopeless situations while also expressing a freedom of choice denied them in the real world, suicide being outlawed in Islam.

Other disciplines relating to cultural studies have also been used in this book. They range from Marxism, structuralism, modernism and deconstructionism to postcolonialism, and are represented by a plethora of theories such as those of Swiss semiotician Ferdinand de Saussure regarding binary oppositions found in comparisons between 'home' and 'city', 'self' and 'other', 'man' and 'woman', and so on. I read the theme of gender identity along the lines of Michel Foucault's and Judith Butler's theories; these texts will help to ground this argument in a more rigorous feminist framework. This has been a difficult task because in the realm of Islamic culture 'gender theory' is perceived to be destructive to the very concept of women and families, just as it is to the Catholic Church. This explains the lack of Arabic studies on gender identity within Muslim societies – a reminder of a recurring resistance to the theoretical in relation to its perceived foreign origin, whether that origin is Western philosophy or feminist theory. Similarly, Henri Lefebvre's and Thomas Bender's theories on the city and urban life offer a profound understanding of how the city can be a space for negotiating issues of identity, agency and social change. Finally, Cora Kaplan's work on gender and transnational feminism, drawn from postcolonial theories, has enriched this work in terms of the ways in which globalization and capitalism affect people across nations, races, genders, classes and sexualities.[37]

Chapter 1 of this book, 'Saudi Women Writers: Sociopolitical and Literary Landscapes', briefly reviews the phases of Saudi women's literature and the sociopolitical and cultural landscape of writing in Arabia from 1958 to 2015, paying special attention to the beginning of the women's struggle for rights and the emergence of a specific *Khalījī* / Saudi feminism. In it, I also seek to understand the reasons for the three-decade lag between the two author genders with regard to debut forays into literary fiction, throwing light on women writers and the social, political and global factors that opened the gates for their writing in 2000.

Chapter 2, 'Rethinking the Patriarchal Discourse', examines the works of Saudi women writers who are united by their unequivocal attempts to subvert and transcend male-dominant culture but who are divided according to the ways in which they inscribe feminist grievance. For example, I look at how Qmasha al-Olayyan uses the 'ugly plot' to contest women's gendered roles in marriage and motherhood juxtaposed with the external forces of aesthetic ideals that the protagonist has to navigate while debating women's futures outside these traditional gender roles. Omima al-Khamis, in *Sea-wafted Women*, engages in a critique of two cultures – the Najdi and the Levantine[38] – that label women as either 'queens' or 'nymphs', depicting female characters as either agents of power and change in their society or submissive to patriarchy. Badriyah al-Beshir explores how a mother figure can become complicit in the exercise of patriarchal power, and blames her for reproducing new forms of oppression. Finally, Maha al-Jahni, in her novel *The Cloak*, turns the eponymous garment into an emblem of women's resistance to the male-dominant social order with functions such as invisibility; mystery; wrongdoing; and, most importantly witchcraft – deployed in this book as a feminist fantasy of empowerment and a tool of solidarity.

Chapter 3, 'Feminizing History: The Female as a Repository of Memories', explores the concept of the female as a repository of memories and its potential to feminize history. Deeply rooted in feminist theory, literature and cultural studies, this perspective suggests that women carry the physical and emotional scars of historical events such as childbirth, violence, labour and oppression. These embodied memories offer a counter-narrative to the master male narrative.

While Raja Alem's *Khatem* distinguishes itself by its powerful and poetic language, its emphasis is on the inherent problem of male favouritism in the Arab nuclear family. And in Laila al-Juhani's *Barren Paradise*, I analyse how complicating the issue of pregnancy out of wedlock is by itself an act of subversion and resistance to the patriarchal social structure. Finally, in Nora al-Ghamdi's *Wejhat al-Bouṣlah* (Compass Direction), I show how the author registers a feminist grievance towards tribal laws in rural areas of Arabia by staging the protagonist's hideous stillbirth as a totem of society's sin.

Chapter 4, 'Narratives of Violence: Communicating Corporeal Anxieties', surveys how three authors have used the female body as a site to expose the cultural politics of gender and to capture the way in which Saudi women have breached taboos and developed a feminist discourse of their own. This chapter dwells on the female experience, incarcerated in the prison-like 'space' of the home, and the mutilated characters that it produces. Through the prism of the female body and 'gender politics', I examine how Saudi women writers have succeeded in exploiting these spaces and bodies in order to deconstruct an existing female identity and construct another, new one – capturing the change, renewal and resistance building within women.

In this chapter, I look into Laila al-Juhani's *The Days of Ignorance*, Badriya al-Beshir's *The Swing* and Hana Hejazi's *Two Women*. And I analyse how protagonists face obstacles resulting from prejudiced family dynamics. Allowing the reader to encounter stories of domestic abuse, confinement and punishment, these stories capture the level of resistance and change in Saudi female authors who, by tackling taboo issues, are collectively challenging stereotypical accusations of muteness on Saudi women's long and arduous road to gender equality.

Chapter 5, 'Travel, Women and the City: The Literature of Encounter', seeks to examine how large, cosmopolitan cities like London, Paris and Toronto act as mediators for Saudi women's consciousness, and how female writers from the kingdom have used these cities' spaces to cast doubt on their own.

The urban imaginary and its cognitive mappings of values, including concepts of culture and identity, play out differently in the various works of fiction by Saudi women. While cities such as Beirut, Cairo, London and Paris are correlated with romance and freedom in the imagination of many writers, especially those with Western leanings, the same cities challenge the values and identities of others. Through an inquiry into several texts and locations, Chapter 5 examines the ways in which the space of the city has been used as a feminist tool and a mediator between women's consciousness and their identity among the mature works of Omima al-Khamis and Zaineb Hefny, as well as the later daring and revolutionary voices of millennials such as Raja al-Sanea and Samar al-Megrin.

Chapter 6, 'Protest and Self-orientalizing Texts', examines how religious and cultural norms have turned women into markers of identity – a role that has not only shaped their writing but has also impacted on the author's decision to either disclose her identity or conceal it behind a pseudonym. I discuss the works of three women writers who use pseudonyms to broach taboos and subvert the implicit systems of patriarchal power. Temporally, these three novels were published in the same period: Saba al-Herz's *Al-Akrūn* (The Others) and Warda Abdul Malik's *Al-Awba* (The Return) both in 2006, and Taif al-Hallaj's *Al-Qaran al-Muqadas* (The Sacred Marriage) in 2007. All three writers depict a context to which they belong and which they know very well. They present an image of their social structures and their intersection with gender politics. These texts are deeply related to and reflective of the diverse social, religious and cultural realities in which their authors have lived. What they have in common is their shared, crushing anger and – on many occasions – the obscenity with which they express themselves.

Note on Translation

The translation of most quotations from Arabic-language stories or interviews have been undertaken by the current author.

Notes

1   For further reading on the subject, see Rana Kabbani, *Europe's Myths of Orient* (Indiana University Press: Bloomington, 1986). Also, Rosa Vasilaki, 'Reconstructing Gender, Race and Sexuality after 9/11', paper presented to the British International Studies Association, Manchester, 27–29 April 2011.

2 Nadje al-Ali believes that this is partly in an attempt to convince the public to support military interventions in those areas but chiefly because liberating women has become one of a number of 'selling points, in addition to delivering human rights and democracy': 'The Iraqi Women's Movement: Past and Contemporary Perspectives', in Pernille Arenfeldt and Nawar Al-Hassan Golley (eds), *Mapping Arab Women's Movements: A Century of Transformations from Within* (American University in Cairo Press: Cairo, 2012), p. 93. Also, Gayatri C. Spivak's theory of 'white men saving brown women from brown men': Gayatri Chakravorty Spivak, 'Can the Subaltern Speak?', in Cary Nelson and Lawrence Grossberg (eds), *Marxism and the Interpretation of Culture* (University of Illinois Press: Urbana, 1988), pp. 271–313; Antoinette Burton, 'The White Woman's Burden', in Nupur Chaudhuri and Margret Strobel (eds), *Western Women and Imperialism* (Indiana University Press: Bloomington, 1992), p. 145. See also Leila Ahmad's remarks on the use of the woman's issue in *A Quiet Revolution: The Veil's Resurgence, from the Middle East to America* (Yale University Press: New Haven, CT and London, 2011), pp. 222–4: Ahmad remarks, 'Many academics, as I noted, were shocked at the blatant coopting of the issue of the "oppression of women in Islam in the service of imperial wars and dominations", its use of the issue of women to justify the occupation and political subjugation of Muslim countries.' These sentiments echo Saba Mahmoud's words, '[d]iscourses of feminism and democracy have been hijacked to serve an imperial project': Mahmoud, 'Feminism, Democracy, and Empire: Islam and the War on Terror', in Joan Wallach Scott (ed.), *Women's Studies on the Edge* (Duke University Press: Durham, NC, 2008), p. 100; and Nina Power: 'feminism is something merely to invoke to convince the fence-sitting, morally-minded voters that war is the only option on the table [...] feminism has become so broad that it can be used to justify almost anything, even the invasion of other countries': Power, *One Dimensional Woman* (Zero Books: London, 2009).

3 'GCC' denotes the Gulf Cooperation Council, the political and economic alliance of six Middle Eastern countries: Saudi Arabia, Kuwait, the United Arab Emirates, Qatar, Bahrain and Oman.

4 Eleanor Doumato, chapter 9 in Abbas Abdelkarim (ed.), *Change and Development in the Gulf* (Macmillan Press Ltd: London, 1999); the term 'ideal womanhood' was coined by Doumato. It charts how women became the symbol of national identity; their appearance, behaviour and role in society at large symbolize the leadership's commitment to protecting its 'tribal family' from Western influences and challenges to patriarchal control during times of social change.

5 Alanoud Alsharekh (ed.), *The Gulf Family: Kinship Policies and Modernity* (Saqi Books: London, 2007), p. 3.

6 Ali al-Tarrah in Alsharekh, *The Gulf Family*, p. 47.

7 The *saḥwa* ideology affected every single aspect of life in the region (to varying degrees, of course) with the aim of turning its nations into Islamic states following the alleged model of the early periods of Islam, in which women were concealed from the public eye and men were encouraged to grow beards, to participate in *jihad* and to challenge 'Western hegemony' and foreign influences.

8 The greater pressure, however, was exerted on the country's education system and security services, which were recruited to fight the 'war on terror' alongside their strategic ally, the United States. So the use of the woman issue is not new and continues to be a 'battle flag' in wars and times of conflict. Leila Ahmad

points out how 'soon after 9/11, as the United States prepared for war, the women of Afghanistan began to figure prominently in the administration's rhetoric with Laura Bush's famous words "the fight against terrorism is also a fight for the dignity of women"'. Hence, the reaction to Western hegemony and the 'West's participation in governmental processes of, various countries in the region, was – and will continue to be – the formation of a number of nationalist movements'. In this sense, occupation, colonialism or any form of intervention in the Arab world resulted in growing anti-Western sentiments there. It may be too simplistic, however, to say that dormant *jihadi* movements – a ticking bomb that can be used and abused by many political parties and states – were suddenly reactivated in the region, but this nonetheless served as a reminder of earlier occasions on which nationalist and Islamic movements first emerged in the 1950s and had a huge impact on the Arab world at that time. A good example is the secular pan-Arabist nationalist movement the 'Nasserites' – named after Egyptian President Gamal Abdel Nasser – along with the Muslim Brotherhood and al-Qaeda among others. Ahmad also notes in her book *A Quiet Revolution* that Nasserism and Arab nationalism were countered in the 1960s by the creation of the Muslim World League, to promote to the *umma* (global Islamic community) Muslim identity and loyalty – rather than ethnicity – as the true grounds of identity and community for Muslims. With this development, Islamic groups gained power – including the legalized Muslim Brotherhood movement, which Khaled Hroub, director of the Media Programme at the Gulf Research Centre, Dubai, and the Cambridge Arab Media Project, rightly defines as '[t]he mother of most, if not all, movements of political Islam'. Other groups branched off from the Muslim Brotherhood, including al-Qaeda, which used political Islam as a way to lure millions of Muslims into a utopian vision of the world. Al-Qaeda emerged with a vengeance; its followers were indoctrinated with antagonistic sentiments towards the West and Western burgeoning hegemony in the wider Muslim world. ISIS (so-called Islamic State) and *al-Nusrah* are simply al-Qaeda 'brand names' that have emerged in recent years and claim to be Islamic. Many of these groups are working under the pretext of Islam, yet their actions are in line with an imperialistic project of expansion in the region and they certainly serve the interests of a new colonial agenda of hegemony. It is not my intention here to discuss the political aspect of such movements, but it is of great importance to see the interplay of this radicalism with global ideas and its rejection and doubt over anything coming from the West – including women's rights and Western feminist theories.

9 Saddeka Arebi, *Women and Words in Saudi Arabia: The Politics of Literary Discourse* (Columbia University Press: New York, 1994), p. 1.
10 For further reading on the subject, please see Hanan al-Ahmadi, 'Challenges Facing Women Leaders in Saudi Arabia', *Human Recourse Development International*, Vol. 14, Issue 2 (2011).
11 Ali al-Shadawi, *al-Hadāthah w'al Mujtama' al-Suūdī* (Riyadh Literary Club: Riyadh, 2009).
12 Awadh al-Qarni, *Al-Hadāthah fī Mīzān Al-Islām: Nazrāt Islāmyyah fī Adab Al-hadāthah* (Hajer: Cairo, 1988).
Also, see Saddeka Arebi, 'Other Examples of Critique: Questioning Women's Morality', in Arebi, *Women and Words*, pp. 260–4. For further reading, see Abdullah al-Ghothami, *The Story of Modernity in Saudi Arabia* (Arab Cultural Center: Beirut, 2004), pp. 30–47. Al-Ghothami points out, 'Those who wage a

war against modernists are in fact too afraid of change because they believe it will negatively impact religion, politics and culture.'
13 Stuart Hall, 'The Local and the Global: Globalization and Ethnicity', in Anthony D. King (ed.), *Culture, Globalization and the World-System: Contemporary Conditions for the Representation of Identity* (University of Minnesota Press: Minneapolis, 1997), p. 183.
14 Roland Barthes, *Camera Lucida: Reflections on Photography*, translated by Richard Howard (Hill and Wang: New York, 1981), p. 44.
15 Gerald Raunig, *Art and Revolution, Transversal Activism in the Long Twentieth Century* (Semiotext(e): New York, 2007), p. 18.
16 Raunig, *Art and Revolution*.
17 See Gary Genosko (ed.), *The Guattarri Reader* (Blackwell: Oxford, 1996), pp. 14–16.
18 Arebi, *Women and Words*, p. 9.
19 Yaser Ba-Amer, *Jadal al jins fi alriyywaya al arabiyya* [Sexual Debate in the Saudi Novel] (Aljazeera.net, 8-5-2010; www.aljazeera.net/news/cultureandart/2010/5/8/جدل-الجنس-في-الرواية-السعودية). The article also quotes cultural critic Mohamed Al-Menkeri saying that it is 'regrettable that some people think sex is the most important component' of this conservative society, and ignore issues like the search for religious freedom, class divisions, educational failures or gender.
20 Layla al-Othman, *The Departure* (Dar Al Madā le tebā'ah w'alnaśer: Beirut, 2000).
21 arablit.org/2010/02/27/kuwaiti-novelist-says-too-much-sex-in-new-saudi-womens-lit (accessed 21 April 2022).
22 Sandra Gilbert, 'Introduction', in Hélène Cixous and Catherine Clément, *The Newly Born Woman*, translated by Betsy Wing (Manchester University Press: Manchester, 1986), p. 65.
23 See website of the Women and Memory Forum: www.wmf.org.eg/en (accessed 21 April 2022).
24 Sultan S. M. Al-Qahtani, Introduction, 'The Novel in Saudi Arabia: Emergence and Development 1930–1989, an Historical and Critical Study', PhD dissertation, University of Glasgow, 1994. See also Ali Zalah, 'The progress of the novel in Saudi Arabia', *Banipal*, No. 20 (2004).
25 Zalah, 'The progress of the novel'.
26 Abdulrahman Muhammad al-Wahabi, 'Women's Novel in Saudi Arabia: Its Emergence and Development in a Changing Culture', PhD thesis, University of Manchester, 2005, pp. 34–5.
27 Saddeka Arebi, 'Gender Anthropology in the Middle East: The Politics of Muslim Women's Misrepresentation', *Journal of Islamic Social Sciences*, Vol. 8, No. 1 (1991).
28 Elizabeth McKee, 'The Political Agendas and Textual Strategies of Levantine Women Writers', in Mai Yamani (ed.), *Feminism & Islam: Legal and Literary Perspectives* (SOAS: London, 1996), p. 134.
29 Joseph T. Zeidan, *Arab Women Novelists: The Formative Years and Beyond* (State University of New York: New York, 1995), p. 3.
30 Kristeva's three phases of feminist writing focused on deconstructing the binary opposition between male and female; they concentrated on a 'unified' human experience, as shown by the androgyny in Virginia Woolf's *Room of One's Own* and *Three Guineas*. Kelly Oliver (ed.), *Ethics, Politics, and Difference in Julia Kristeva's Writing* (Routledge: London, 2013).

31 Susan Friedman, *Mappings: Feminism and the Cultural Geographies of Encounter* (Princeton University Press: Princeton, NJ, 1998), p. 87.
32 Friedman, *Mappings*, p. 90.
33 Friedman, p. 47.
34 Friedman, p. 19.
35 Friedman, p. 20.
36 In this neologism (in the original French, *savoir-pouvoir*), coined by Foucault, the most important part is the hyphen: this links the two aspects of the integrated concept together.
37 David Glover and Cora Kaplan, *Genders: The New Critical Idiom* (Routledge: London and New York, 2009).
38 Referring respectively to the Najd (the territory forming the geographical centre of the Arabian Peninsula) and the eastern Mediterranean region.

1
SAUDI WOMEN WRITERS
Sociopolitical and Literary Landscapes

In 2011, Raja Alem's *Ṭawq al-Ḥamama* (The Dove's Necklace) became the first Saudi novel to win the International Prize for Arabic Fiction, a literary event that attracted international headlines and drew attention to the voices of Saudi women writers. Similarly, in 2004, when she was only 24 years old, Raja al-Sanea had created an international buzz when her book *Banat al-Riyadh* (Girls of Riyadh) inspired a new wave of Saudi mass-market, 'chick-lit' novels with suggestive and enticing titles. This international fame and acclaim for Saudi women writers within the larger, male, literary corpus raises questions about the origins of such writing.

It is remarkable that the first novel accredited to a Saudi woman, Samira Khashugji's *Wadda't Āmālī* (Farewell to My Hopes), did not see the light of day until 1958, a good 28 years after the publication of the first novel by a Saudi male author: Abdel Qodous al-Ansari's *Al-Tau'amān* (The Twins) in 1930.[1] It is not my intention here to discuss the Saudi male literary tradition so much as to correlate the literary modes that distinguished men's novels from those of women's fiction. Salma Jayyusi, in *Beyond the Dunes*, observes men's writing and the beginnings of Saudi literature in general, saying, 'it would be wrong to expect that any of these writers had profound knowledge of the finer techniques of story writing […]. This new and attractive art form was still in its infancy in Saudi Arabia and had not fully matured even in Egypt, the country whose writers were seen as "role models" for our own young writers'.[2]

Hasan Namy, in his book *al-Riyywaya al-Suū'dia: Wāqeuhā wa-taḥwolātahā* (The Saudi Novel: Reality and Transformation), discerns the period following *Al-Tau'amān* – more precisely, that between 1930 and 1954 – as a long period of scarcity and stagnation in the development of a real

Saudi novel. And indeed it was not before 1959 that another shift took place in the male novel through Hāmed Damanhourī's pioneering work *Thaman al-Tathya* (The Price of Sacrifice). Damanhourī's literary skills were evident in his distinctive social and psychological preoccupations, which incorporated the delineation of his protagonist 'Ahmad's internal conflict and his feelings of being torn between his love for his cousin Fatma, to whom he was engaged, and his love for the beautiful and educated Egyptian Fa'izah, the sister of his friend in Cairo. This conflict only ended with 'Ahmad's resolution to honour his word and return home to marry Fatma, an ending that marks the triumph of tradition over modernity and the issue of women's emancipation.

Damanhourī, considered the father of the Saudi novel, was educated and influenced by the Egyptian writers Muhammed Hussein Haikal and Naguib Mahfouz. It is no wonder, therefore, that there are similarities between *Thaman al-Tathya* and Haikal's *Zainab*: both debate modernity and tradition within their authors' respective culture, revealing features of the romantic novel in their plot, settings and autobiographical elements. Although young Saudi male writers were echoing progressive Egyptian calls for women's emancipation and education at the time, their writing nonetheless lacked empathy with the 'woman question' in the sense that they were more focused on the difference between East and West and the importance of Islamic values and tradition in the face of modernity. Such themes are typical of postcolonial writings anywhere in the world. Rashad Al Areqi examines the first Saudi novel (*The Twins*), saying,

> it is very simple in its form and context. It does not reach the anticipated standard of art. It attempts to educate the people [in] the significance of adhering to the Islamic and oriental values. It is about the civilization[al] relations between orient and occident. The novel eventually attempts to glorify the orient[al] culture and values and simultaneously exposes the corruption of the occident as it seems the main aim and the message of the novel.[3]

This postcolonial element would intensify and become a trend in the kingdom with the onset of the *sahwa*. Mansour al-Hazimi observes that 'the conflict between modernity and tradition [*taqlid wa tajdid*] was becoming a trend in the 1980s'. Soraya Altorki further explains that 'as time progressed "renewal" came to be manifested in women's fiction writing'.[4] This trend for renewal in women's fiction would proliferate over the years and become a struggle of sorts – especially with the increased spread of women's education and greater exposure to the wider world.

To fully understand the lag of nearly three decades between debut forays into literary fiction between the two sexes, one should look at the complex interplay of history, politics, religion and tradition that had such a significant impact on women's education and their social standing. Hence, I investigate in this chapter the circumstances that have made it possible for Saudi women to write, often transcending the concept of 'art for art's sake', and will also seek to identify the political and historical phases that have impacted on these women's literary journeys.

The Three Phases of Saudi Women's Fiction

What I find striking about Saudi women writers is their unrelenting resistance to patriarchal gender politics, a theme that was 'softly' ignited in the 1960s when Saudi female writers were not even close to being feminists but were nonetheless exposed to other cultures that were more open to women's emancipation and rights than their own. For example, Samira Khashugji, among others, wanted to see social changes happening on her own soil, and challenged the tribal-based negativity towards women and girls that was rife at the time. These writers subtly criticized misogynistic attitudes, not only through the realm of storytelling and poetry – traditionally seen as a 'safe' (i.e. non-political) bastion of 'art for art's sake' – but also through other legitimate channels such as academic and journalistic writings and contributing to the public discourse. This aspect has been partially analysed and documented by Saddeka Arebi in her 1994 work, *Women and Words in Saudi Arabia*.

What seems to be missing, however, from previous examinations of Saudi women's fiction authors is a gender-based scrutiny of how women have been objectified by the cultural dynamics and the different phases through which Saudi women have passed since the establishment of the kingdom in 1932. These phases saw women's position in society ebb and flow depending on a set of shifting laws. Mai Yamani defines the role of Saudi women between 1932 and 1950 as one of serving traditional female roles, mainly as mother and nurturer of the family. The secular period of the 1960s and 1970s marked an openness to change – especially during the reign of King Faisal, when women enjoyed semi-equal opportunities at work and scholarships abroad. The third phase, the 1980s, saw women's roles suffer a setback resulting from *saḥwa* (Islamic revivalism).[5] In this book, I also look at the fourth phase of change and reform, which started from the mid-1990s and ran until 2016, and I investigate how, during that time, women writers 'invaded' the kingdom's extremely gendered spaces.

There is little doubt that it was the literary icon Samira Khashugji who broke the monopoly of male writing and publishing in the kingdom when her debut novel, *Wadda't Āmālī* (Farewell to My Hopes), came out in the year 1958. Her subsequent works include *Thekrayāt Dām'ah* (Tearful Memories), 1963; *Warā' al-Dabāb* (Beyond the Clouds), 1971; *Qaṭrat Min ad-Dumu* (Teardrops), 1979; and *Barīq 'Aynaik* (The Sparkle of Your

Eyes) in 1963 – the latter being turned into an Egyptian film. One cannot adequately appraise Khashugji's contribution to Saudi women's literature, however, without taking into account her very glamorous and privileged life. As the daughter of the Saudi Minister of Health, Muhammad Khashugji; the sister of the tycoon Adnan Khashugji; and the first wife of another 'up-and-coming' figure, the future owner of Harrods department store in London, Muhammad Fayed, and the mother of Emad (Dodi) al-Fayed, Samira's upbringing and life shaped the way in which she both perceived and presented herself to the world.

Being a Saudi citizen yet living and growing up in Alexandria, Egypt, impacted on Samira Khashugji's literary output and gave her the courage to write freely about love, relationships and other social issues. Her continuous (narrative) chatter about love, for example, especially love outside of marriage, was seen as bold – in fact, too bold for the tribal mentalities of the time. While most of her novels reflect the popular secular thought of the 1960s and 1970s, which idealized the Western model of female emancipation and liberation, her writing triggered widespread criticism for being transgressive, over-Westernized and out of tune with Saudi culture. As a result, there is a huge gap between her standing in the West and in her own country, a point that reminds me of Egyptian writer Nawal el-Sadawi's comparative popularity among Western and Arab readers.

Other Saudi women authors who emerged at a later stage – to be precise, in the late 1970s and 1980s – included Huda al-Rasheed, who published four novels, among them *Ghadan Sa-yakūn Al-Khamīs* (Tomorrow Will Be Thursday) in Cairo in 1979 and *'Abath* (Vanity) in 1980. The 1980s also saw the publication of writing by more Saudi women who had been educated in Egypt, like Intisar 'Agīl,[6] who mostly wrote short stories – a good example is her collection *Mawāni' Belā 'Arṣefah* (Ports without Pavements), from 1988 – and Safia al-'Anbar, who published a total of four novels, with her debut work, *'Afwan Ya'Adam* (Excuse Me, Adam), published in 1986. Another outstanding writer of that period is Amal Shaṭā, who published a total of five novels that mostly dealt with Hejazi culture, including *Ghadan Ansā* (Tomorrow I Shall Forget) in 1980.

This pioneering generation was scant in number simply because girls' education was not available in the kingdom, so they were sent to boarding schools in neighbouring countries like postcolonial Lebanon and Egypt.[7] According to Soraya Altorki, the first generation of Saudi women to attend those boarding schools came from elite families.[8] Madawi al-Rasheed further explains that these girls belonged specifically to the first generation of merchants and bureaucrats in Saudi Arabia, who 'dared to send their daughters abroad because [previously] the stigma was too high'.[9] It is not surprising, therefore, to see that this education impacted on the way in which those writers engaged with their own culture, and how they returned with different experiences and a different perspective from those of their audience back home.

This fact is evidenced by the extent to which many works of this period were characterized by elements of alienation, displacement and romanticism, and by the openness with which they tackled issues surrounding love, marriage, family dynamics and divorce as well as calls for social reform and women's emancipation – all a far cry from the self-absorbed approach of 'art for art's sake'. In fact, certain works of this period capture the cultural chasms between the first generation of such students – that is, those who experienced a secular education in the postcolonial state of Egypt – the second, who underwent a mixture of private schooling (like that offered by Dar al-Hanan in Jeddah, Saudi Arabia, as in the case of Zaineb Hefny), and those who were the fruit of a standard, national education system. The latter witnessed the peak of *sahwa* or Salafist ideology, which lasted from the late 1970s to the mid-1990s. I intentionally use the word 'witnessed' because, for various reasons, many writers of the first, second and third literary phases discussed in this book did not succumb to the pressure of extremism. This is clear in their collective scepticism of, if not outright rebellion against, its biased laws.

The First Gulf War in 1990–1 was a major turning point in the history of the Gulf states, as it politicized people who had never before taken an interest in politics. This contact with the West brought aspects of another culture and selective Western ideals to otherwise sheltered and isolated Arab Gulf communities. One consequence of this contact was that the West sought to expose the poor status of women in the Gulf states to international scrutiny. With the involvement of the West in the Gulf conflicts, however, opposition to women's rights has only grown more vehement, creating a radical backlash against values that are dismissed and vilified as unwelcome 'Western' imports.[10] The Saudi people's engagement with the 'woman question' also coincided with the arrival in the kingdom of satellite TV and, later, internet communication-technology tools, which played a huge role in the opening up of society.

This has resulted in the birth of the genuine Saudi women's novel, which I refer to throughout this book as the 'new text', which started in the 1990s and peaked in the year 2000 with a remarkable total of almost 100 novels written by women (some of which were debut efforts), with an average of 20 to 30 new releases per annum.[11] Hasan Namy, a university professor and critic, observes, 'I see *Girls of Riyadh* [by Raja al-Sanea] as a turning-point for readership in Saudi Arabia'. He further notes that around 50 novels were published in 2006 compared with 26 in the previous year (exact numbers are not available, since the majority of these works were published outside the kingdom).[12] Of course, these statistics not only attest to the popularity and growing readership of women's novels but also mark their authors' increased appetite for fame and status in a global economy that is ready to consume and translate works about the mystical Saudi Arabia.[13]

This proliferation of the novel form in general and women's writing in particular, as well as the burgeoning book-club groups in most regions of the kingdom, has raised questions about the reading habits of people in recent years. A survey conducted by the King Abdulaziz Center for National Dialogue in 2017 showed that 21 per cent of people read on a regular basis whereas 53 per cent were sporadic readers.[14] Another study, conducted in 2019 by the General Survey Commission in Saudi Arabia, showed that between 55.4 and 61.7 per cent of adults read books.[15] More recently, the Saudi Center for Opinion Polling (SCOP) presented and led a seminar titled 'Have Saudis Abandoned Books?' at King Saud University. They concluded that:

> Reading books constituted the favourite pastime activity for 11% of Saudis over 18 years of age, this in line with many European countries. 34% of Saudis read books in various fields, regardless of demographic factors. The analysis also found that 33% of readers in the study considered themselves as 'intellectuals'. Overall it was interesting to see that many of the international trends in book reading were mirrored in the kingdom.[16]

This interest in reading justifies the popularity of international book fairs in the kingdom and their attraction of over half a million visitors to both Riyadh and Jeddah. These book fairs are usually accompanied by a cluster of literary and cultural activities, forums, workshops and competitions, paying special attention to fiction writers and their works. This celebration of literature was reason enough for me to examine the novel form as a legitimate channel that attempts to destabilize traditional boundaries by expressing women writers' feminist views away from socio-religious and political limitations. I argue throughout this book that the cumulative effect of these texts leads to the formation of a new 'geographics of identity'.[17] This is evident in their plots and discursive practices, which take women from a place of marginality to one of centrality, from the private and silent to the public, and from powerlessness to power – recalling Donald Hall's words: 'the semantics of power and powerlessness [embedded in their texts] offers infinite surprises and rich opportunities for both personal reflection and reflections on culture – specifically, on performances of subjectivity'.[18]

No longer oblivious to the world, people were experiencing a relative freedom that they had never previously enjoyed. This was when the Saudi novel came of age through the more mature works of male authors such as Turki al-Hamad and Ghazi al-Gosaibi, and female authors such as Laila al-Juhani and her 1997 novel *Al-Ferdūs al-Yabāb* (Barren Paradise); and Zaineb Hefny and her controversial novel *Nesā' 'End Khat al-'Estewā'* (Women on the Equator) from 1996 and *Al-Raqs 'Alā al-Dufūf* (Dancing to the Sound of Drums) from 1998. These writers benefited from the changing social and political milieu, which allowed them to be more open than their predecessors in challenging their social and political realities.

It is no exaggeration to say that by the mid-1990s, the purpose of Saudi women writers was being redefined. From representing collective voices, hitherto used to assert patriarchy and gender hierarchy, it was now focusing on individual voices set on dismantling the patriarchy and pursuing the female author's serious quest for individuality and a new identity amidst a wider renaissance that swept the entire region. Voices challenging patriarchal discourses grew louder around the end of the 1990s and the turn of the millennium, when the late King Abdullah bin Abdulaziz, a reformist, had implemented policies and strategies to emancipate and empower women. There was an awakening on all levels to the lack of women's civil and political rights, and the kingdom's media freely debated the rights denied women – as could be seen in the guardianship issue, violence against women, the prohibition of women's driving and the harassment laws.

Rights initiatives and female-empowerment projects became essential components in a nascent Saudi feminism. Abdulrahman al-Wahabi verifies that feminism in Saudi Arabia as a political and cultural movement began immediately after 9/11.[19] This feminism coincided with a boom in internet communication technology, smartphones and social media that created a space of virtual liberty for cross-class and cross-gender communication. The pace of change in the kingdom was at full tilt – for instance, the country ratified the Convention on Elimination of all forms of Discrimination Against Women (CEDAW) in August 2000, and in 2003 it established the King Abdulaziz Center for National Dialogue. This was followed by other modernizing steps, such as the increased visibility of women in the media and, later, the appointment of 30 women to the country's Shura Council (parliament) in 2015. This move signalled a significant shift in the political landscape, granting women a voice in the legislative process and underscoring the kingdom's commitment to reform. It was indeed an exciting period for everyone – but especially for women authors, who were living in a time of real change, reform and renewal. The momentum of change continued to accelerate under the leadership of King Salman bin Abdulaziz and Crown Prince Mohammad bin Salman. Their focused efforts on improving women's status led to more progressive policies and reforms. This included lifting the ban on women driving in 2018 and easing guardianship laws, granting women greater autonomy and freedom.

Overall, the period marked by these modernizing steps was a time of renewal and reform, significantly altering the societal landscape and empowering women to participate more fully in public life. The excitement of this era was palpable, especially among authors who found themselves in a time of profound change. They could express their perspective and experiences in ways previously unimaginable, contributing to a broader cultural and intellectual renaissance.

This general mood of freedom and change did not occur in a vacuum; it is deeply embedded in the texts and works that were committed to the debates on national issues and identity. Fiction writers, for instance, were grappling with the ideologies of *takfeer*[20] and *jihad* in their pejorative meanings of killing innocent people, as in al-Hamad's 2005 novel *Al-Ṭareeq ela al-Jannah* (Winds of Paradise). This issue was also broached by women authors, such as Badriya al-Beshir with her *Hend we al-'Askar* (Hend and the Soldiers). Samar al-Megrin wrote about oppressive laws in her debut work *Nesā' al-Munkar* (Women of Vice) in 2008. Other serious works by Omima al-Khamis, Raja Alem, Nora al-Ghamdi, Munira al-Subai and Laila al-Juhani, among others, were written in the same spirit of 'self-criticism', 'change' and 'reform'.

For this reason, I examine women's writing as a 'collective action by non-collective actors'.[21] By turning the personal into the public, and sometimes by opting for explosive and scandalous narratives, these individual writers have unintentionally collaborated to express a collective defiance of the patriarchal culture. In this, they have teamed up to question their own reality, burdened by repressive social and religious norms.

A good example is Wafa Abdulrahman's 2011 novel *Raghabāt Shayṭānyah* (Satanic Desires).[22] It explores the life of a divorcee within the culture of Islamic patriarchy, or *saḥwa*, that has created gender hierarchies and exclusions. It does so through its protagonist, Amal, who has been forced by her oppressive family to endure a miserable marriage to a suspicious and alcoholic husband. Her mother, as a typical guardian of the patriarchy, locates female worth in the role of wife and mother, and denies her daughter the right to a divorce. Eventually, Amal returns to her family house, adamant to leave her husband. Her mother follows, and scrutinizes her daughter's every move. The novel marks the shift in Amal from total submission to her mother and family to rebellion when she falls in love with Ṭalāl. Through this relationship, Amal becomes a symbol of the power of love, forgetting about the strict social laws of her society in the sense that she goes out with Ṭalāl, ignoring harsh social codes and the prospect of being held accountable for her transgression. Her sense of personal autonomy, however, does not last long because she is soon caught red-handed on her return to the house by her foreign chauffeur, who acts as yet another agent of the patriarchy or guardian of morality. He admonishes her in broken Arabic, demanding of her, 'Who is this guy you went out with?' The chauffeur immediately judges her a criminal, although there is no proof or justification for the scandalous rumours that he spreads around the neighbourhood. Amal is shunned by her ex-husband, family and society. Her young son is shattered by the news and, as a reaction, joins a Muslim *mujahdīn*. Her married daughter is warned against seeing her, and the youngest girl is forced to stay with her father. The narrative attempts to expose how society turns a blind eye to male transgressive behaviour – her husband is portrayed as a heavy drinker who cheats on his wife – whereas Amal, as a woman, is ostracized.

Upon her return to her own family home, Amal actually feels liberated by her new title of 'whore' and thinks of travelling abroad to escape her dilemma, to flee her reality. However, she cannot because she needs written consent from her *maḥram*, a male family member. Eventually, she goes mad, hallucinating and hearing her son's voice calling her name. She ends up wandering the streets looking for him. By choosing a different path than many others and refusing to meet society's expectations of enduring a miserable marriage, Amal challenges biased cultural morals that seek to normalize patriarchal tyranny. Her defiance of the marriage contract and subsequent pursuit of love outside marriage lead not only to social stigma but also to the loss of her family's support and love, ultimately resulting in her final 'fall' and madness. This insanity indicates a social malice of sorts, with hysterical women acting as mirrors of their society. In the context of Saudi women's discourse of resistance, this serves as a metaphor for the 'stalemate' experienced by women who are locked into miserable situations in which their struggle for selfhood, identity and social justice are met with (literally) man-made obstacles.

Abdulrahman's narrative can be criticized for being too eventful, too crowded and artistically flawed; it tries to do too much, with its failed attempts to shock the reader with statements like 'liberated by the name of a whore' and the protagonist ending in madness – situations that are meant to create a force and a momentum for change, if not shift the reader's view of the world. I find that it should be read as part of an entire crop of writing, whether in serious form or that of 'chick lit', that challenges cultural stereotypes about the identity of Saudi women, with writers unanimously trying to deconstruct the issue of violence and reveal the rift between genuine Islamic values on the one hand and, on the other, the now nullified, biased laws such as the guardianship system, the nuisance of the religious police and other forms of intimidation that only weaken women's overall status in society.

The Struggle for Women's Rights in Saudi Arabia

So, we might ask, why has it taken Saudi women several decades to find their voices?

And was it a coincidence that at a time when the kingdom was striving to introduce women's education, female pioneers were already contributing to public discourse? As we shall see below with Samira Khashugji (*Beyond the Clouds*), these pioneers were igniting 'soft' calls for change. One could venture to say that this was no coincidence, as there was an elite class that believed in women's education. Since education was not available in their homeland, they sent their daughters to study in neighbouring countries like Egypt and Lebanon. Some of these students returned home and played a major role in breaking the monopoly of an otherwise male-dominated Saudi literature. This fact was reason enough for me to devote special attention to particular works by the pioneer Samira Khashugji, with her feminist leanings, while underlining the different socio-religious and political phases that had a direct effect on women's overall struggle for rights.

After girls' education had (latterly) been introduced in the kingdom, in 1960, some high-school graduates in the 1970s pursued higher-education degrees in the United States and many other countries around the world – in the hope that the future would be promising, as Saudi Arabia was witnessing a boom on all levels. However, their hopes were soon dashed by a religious narrative that swept the region and made it difficult for women to participate in public life. In her book *A Society of Young Women*, Amélie Le Renard chronicles that shift in public life, saying, 'Among the Saudi women I met, perspectives diverged regarding the general enforcement of gender segregation that took place in the 1970s and 1980s. It was considered a regression by those who had pinned their hopes on the changing practices of certain intellectual, economic, and political elites of the late 1960s.'[23]

Of course, the 1960s and 1970s also represent a time when Saudi women had freedom of choice and could move around the country unveiled, when local and expatriate women had the choice of wearing what they wanted without interference from the *muṭaween* (religious police). In fact, many expats enjoyed private beaches, wearing sarongs, shorts and even bikinis despite the presence of men. In her book *In The Land of Invisible Women*, Qanta Ahmad describes how amazed she was on realizing that there had been a time when Saudi women were uncovered, no *'abayas* (cloaks) or headscarves at all; as Ahmad notes, 'Riyadh wasn't always so difficult [...] when I was newly married in the '50s, we never covered! No abbayahs, no scarves. I could go out alone without my husband.'[24]

King Faisal's assassination in 1975 was a national tragedy that disrupted the momentum of women's emancipation. Although his predecessor, King Saud bin Abdulaziz, had been the one who initiated girls' education in 1960 and established 'The General Presidency for the Education of Girls', it was King Faisal and his wife, Iffat al-Thunayan, who took up the challenge of sustaining women's education amidst harsh defiance from tribes around the kingdom. This vanguard of young female students would also face another obstacle in the 1980s, also known as the 'setback years', during which time, as we have seen, a radical form of religion came into prominence, with entrenched religious laws that weighed heavily on women and gender barriers that impeded the full integration of female jobseekers into the workforce.

On the 'home front', resistance to female participation in public life was strong at the time. It was felt in the official discourse as well as in women's religious groups that flourished in the 1980s and played a powerful role not only in marginalizing women but also in reshaping the public discourse. The accompanying narrative emphasized the domestic and traditional roles of women as mothers, wives and daughters, stressing their duties rather than their rights. Indeed, despite the fact that fertility and reproduction actually empower women with a sense of agency and control over their families in the majority of Arab and Muslim societies, they were nonetheless used to define and limit women's roles in Saudi society at the time.

In fact, discussions about women's rights in the kingdom were often framed within a Muslim family context. Even Khashugji – a trailblazer and social reformer, who led the *al-Nahḍa* Philanthropic Society, the first women's organization in the kingdom, and was among the few educated Saudi women of her era – wrote, 'Islam mandates that women receive education.' She emphasized that 'educating women is essential for their husband's happiness, for the proper upbringing of their children, and for fulfilling their religious obligations'.[25]

Khashugji's emancipatory project started back in 1963 with her book *Yaqthat al-Fatat al-Arabiyah al-Saudiah* (The Emergence of Saudi Young Woman), a groundbreaking work that attempted to establish a framework for women's emancipation on the Arabian Peninsula with themes of liberation and emancipation familiar from the articles that she wrote and published in her glossy *al-Sharqya* magazine. In what appears to have been an equally emancipatory and collaborative project in 1962, a year before the publication of her book, Khashugji, along with Muthafer Adham (King Faisal's brother-in-law) and princesses Sara al-Faisal and her sister Latifa al-Faisal, founded the Saudi *al-Nahḍa* organization – which later became known as the *al-Nahḍa* Philanthropic Society – and also the Peninsula Female Cultural Club. Ahmad al-Wasil claims that these groups were created as the foundation for a 'Saudi Woman's Union'.[26] There is no more evidence to document the history of the *al-Nahḍa* organization, or explain why the emancipatory project mentioned by al-Wasil failed to materialize on the ground. However, many would agree that these societies did not serve the cause of women in particular so much as they did the needy and disadvantaged factions of Saudi society. Omima al-Khamis further elaborated on this perspective in 2017, 'awareness of feminism has come a long way in the Gulf; however, it is still lacking the infrastructure for organized work, collective action and long-term goals that would have an impact on decision makers: that would be through associations and unions'.[27]

Although women's rights in Arabia have come a long way, one cannot overlook the historic struggle of those who took the risk to make a difference nor ignore the frustration felt by those who lived through the process.[28] For our purposes, it is important to see how women writers textualized and archived their struggle for rights and freedom, and how neighbouring revolutions disseminated a sense of excitement that women generally were becoming more politically engaged and vocal.

A particularly remarkable feature of women's struggles at that point was their ability to organize and mobilize using social-media tools alone while also fuelling the rise in feminist activism in Arabia. In fact, women's protests against the ban on driving were a major shift for women's rights in the religiously and culturally conservative kingdom, and a milestone on the generally obstacle-strewn road to female emancipation. Their attempts in 2011 and 2013 to reverse the laws regarding the guardianship system and the decades-long ban on driving through many initiatives – such as 'Women2Drive', 'My Right, My Dignity' and 'Balady' – were thwarted. With the arrival of HRH Ibn Salman, discrimination of all sorts against women was annulled in a matter of two years. This proved beyond doubt that stagnation in women's rights is, as Haya al-Mughni states in her book *Women in Kuwait*, 'by no means the result of Islam alone but rather a combination of political, economic, and patriarchal forces – in other words, the politics of gender'.[29]

Given the above, it should come as no surprise that Saudi women remain openly divided on the issue of women's rights. Le Renard, in *A Society of Young Women*, believes that the *multazimat* (conformist Muslim female voices) do, contrary to what is often claimed, encourage women to have a life outside the family and home. In a chapter entitled 'An Archipelago of Women-Only Spaces', in reference to the burgeoning number of religious women's groups within the kingdom in the 1990s, she explains,

> While remaining fairly consensual and unquestioning, the discourse developed by women for women differs thematically from the religious discourse of official institutions. Its goal is to respond to [the] specific needs of women. They [the groups] often discuss woman's rights and encourage women to commit to religious and charitable activities, which, incidentally, imply having a life outside of the home and family.[30]

Le Renard raises a very important issue: that these *multazimat* are in a way 'incidentally' encouraging women to have a life outside the home. A controversy, no doubt, that is deeply embedded in the religious public discourse. It is not 'incidental', therefore, to see these *multazimat* echoing patriarchal public discourse and encouraging women to attend religious gatherings and to participate in charity work while rejecting the introduction of the very laws that would grant those same women basic personal and family rights. For example, few women preachers spearheaded both the anti-harassment law, drafted by the Shura Council in 2012, and the CEDAW while simultaneously reiterating the male discourse that challenged that law, asserting that it would pave the way for gender mixing and women's 'abomination'.

By highlighting here such divisions among Saudi women on the issue of women's rights (before the onset of reforms in 2017), I have tried to prepare the ground for ambiguities that may arise in the following chapters. It is important to pay attention to the ways in which Saudi women have reacted to such regressive voices by either concealing or revealing their views, feelings and desires without fearing definitions of a 'good Saudi woman' or succumbing to a culture that has – at some point in history – mythologized the beauty of the silent women, which is central to Saudi women's discourse of power.

Moral Geographies and the Private Sphere

Investigating gendered spaces is key to understanding how sociopolitical and religious forces have impacted on the overall literary journey of Saudi women – often in unexpected ways. For example, literary clubs, several of which were founded in 1975 by prominent intellectuals and writers in the main cities of Saudi Arabia, created a cultural 'buzz' for men more than for women; the number of women fiction writers in the country was small due to educational and social circumstances that made their contribution to literature difficult. It was a prosperous time for the country in all walks of life, including the arts. Over the years, these clubs would multiply in number: there were 12 such establishments as of 2015, following their integration into the Ministry of Culture. They were remarkable in terms of giving women the opportunity to participate in shaping the public discourse and, more recently, in taking leadership roles as board members and speakers – something that would have been unthinkable in previous decades.

However, women's participation in those male-dominated clubs was never easy, and this leads us on from a discussion of historical phases to a consideration of space. The literary-club scene prompted Saudi author Omima al-Khamis,[31] at a literature event in 2010, to say that 'more room should be given for women', suggesting that 'Saudi women's participation in the literary clubs should be supported with specific membership quotas'.[32] Indeed, Saudi women's struggle for a 'room' in public spaces is central to any arguments on gender, identity and resistance in the kingdom. In this regard, I find that Marilyn Booth's remarkable work *Harem Histories* makes a great contribution to previous discussions on space, and particularly (female) *harems* – 'used in this context as metaphor: a hovering, implicit institution that signified women's relations to domestic and public space'.[33] Booth contemplates spatial thinking as a key concept if the *harem* is to be 'humanely formed, and [...] a powerful shaper of human identities and understandings'.[34] Such female – and, indeed, male – spaces have certainly negatively impacted on Saudi women's social status between 1980 and 2000, which, to quote Daphne Spain, has 'distanced women from the valued nodes of knowledge that underwrite social hierarchies'.[35]

I explore here how such dramatic fluctuations in Saudi women's rights and their struggle to enter the exclusively male-dominated spaces – in the past – have led to an entire genre being shaped by the various voices and themes that different generations of female authors have used to subvert patriarchal laws. One such theme relates to how the 'private sphere' has been used by women writers to draw the reader's attention to the 'limitation of women's mobility, in terms of both identity and space, [that] has been in some cultural contexts a crucial means of subordination'.[36]

Therefore, the central thread linking most of the chapters in this book is represented by the role of what Muslim feminists dub 'moral geographies' – how women's freedom and mobility has been shaped by social norms and 'the spatialization of moral codes of behavior'.[37] This is true in the sense that women in Muslim-majority societies are expected to adhere to 'modesty codes' of behaviour: *'urf* – that is, a set of verbal and non-verbal boundaries, the observance of which is passed down from mother to daughter. Fatima Mernissi, in her memoir *Dreams of Trespass*, recalls how as a girl she was taught to respect *ḥudud*, the 'sacred frontiers', and a myriad of invisible boundaries that she always dreamed of transgressing. Mernissi warns, however, that '[h]armony exists when each group respects the prescribed limits of the other; trespassing leads only to sorrow and unhappiness'.[38] She further explains, 'you could be powerful, and still be a prisoner of a frontier',[39] indicating both the dangers of stepping across spatial boundaries and the significance of such frontiers in both Morocco – her home country – and the societies of the wider Muslim world. It is hardly surprising, therefore, to see that Saudi women's fiction has also been shaped by these 'sacred frontiers' and 'private spheres'.

Thus, throughout this book there will be an exploration of the interrelationship between women's geography and power relations, in which 'space' and 'place' are gender-loaded concepts that greatly influence cultural formation and gender relations. Saudi women writers have often used the themes of 'place' and 'space' to (de)construct gender relations in society. The confinement of Saudi women to the private sphere has been accompanied by an evolving feminist discourse of power, an aspect that will be investigated throughout the book. I focus on 'space' not only because it has a deep-rooted social, religious and symbolic significance in traditional Muslim culture but also because it is an important feminist tool. Women's designated space signifies concepts of the 'forbidden', 'shame', 'honour' and the 'hidden', by means of which the woman is considered one of the *maḥārem*,[40] and therefore deserving of seclusion from the outside world. The practice of *ḥedād* (the mourning period of four months and ten days following the death of a husband)[41] is just one example of how profound the connection can be between space, gender and identity in Muslim societies.

Such spaces also mark a further leap, from the historical and the spatial to the personal. In them, veiling, which is adopted at puberty, signifies the leap in a girl's life from childhood to womanhood, ushering her into a new era of seclusion from the rest of society while further rigid boundaries are established, the transgression of which is – like that of Mernissi's spatial 'sacred frontiers' – unthinkable. This is clearly shown in Badriya al-Beshir's 2006 novel *Hend we al-'Askar* (Hend and the Soldiers), which depicts the mobility limitations and moral codes of behaviour placed upon the protagonist, Hend, who is surrounded throughout the narrative by what feels like policemen or soldiers (*'Askar*) – a loaded term that suggests a process of being closely watched by male members of the family in a situation that amounts to living in a police state in microcosm.

The physical restriction placed on the lives of women explains the centrality of 'place' as a key narrative element in Saudi women's writing, and seems to contradict Virginia Woolf's plea for 'a room of one's own'. Hence, confinement to the house and restrictions on women's mobility are broken in many of the novels by the use of a public place, such as a hospital; by the protagonist's journey to neighbouring countries; or by migration to the West – each of which seems to give women writers a much-needed freedom to negotiate space in relation to their identities. Their protagonists thus benefit from connecting with the world beyond their rooms and quarters, adding a new layer of depth and drama to the narrative.

Arab *Khalījī* / Saudi Feminism in Women's Fiction

The themes of gender and activism in Saudi women's fiction has prompted me to engage with Western feminism as a mediator and influencer of a developing Arab *Khalījī* / Saudi feminism. *Khalījī* refers to the people of GCC states who share a similar social, political and religious background, and I have chosen to address it because of the distinctive cultural situation that these people share: their tribal traditions and wealth; the rapid pace of globalization that their societies are undergoing; and, most importantly, women's rights and family law. The guardianship law was a specific Saudi issue until 2019 and, at the other end of the spectrum, Kuwaiti women's personal status in law was amended in 1984 and again in 2005 to grant them full political rights. In between these two poles, however, the Gulf states do have many aspects in common – for example, a form of family law based on the old *sharī'a* code. And, in spite of the aforementioned gains, Kuwaiti women, in common with their counterparts in other GCC states, continue their struggle to pass citizenship on to children of non-Kuwaiti husbands and to combat violence against women and discriminatory custody and inheritance laws. Women's family law thus has a long way to go in most GCC states, as Munira Fakhro explains in a paper entitled 'Gulf Women and Islamic Law':

> whether they come from rich or poor families, conservative or modern, they confront the same restricting regulations under the *sharī'a* law, which ensure segregation of the sexes and discrimination against women

in matters such as inheritance, divorce, child custody and other family issues.[42]

It is, however, important to point out that Kuwaiti and Bahraini women have experimented with feminist activism since the 1960s under the umbrella of the British consulates at that time, which meant that their participation in public life also came earlier than in the rest of the Gulf states.[43] Zaineb Hefny emphasizes,

> it is very difficult to define what Khaliji feminism is in women's fiction, even more difficult is putting them in one basket. Bahraini, Kuwaiti and Omani women were ahead of Saudi and UAE women in terms of feminist activism due to the early socio political mobility in their countries. Saudi feminism came at a later stage. However, they all share the same paternal systems.[44]

This early activism and social interaction fostered a women-friendly attitude in the Kuwaiti and Bahraini public spheres. It is also proof that social interaction is crucial in matters relating to gender roles. This is not just a matter of identity or status but more of a continual process of negotiation – between male and female roles;[45] over the establishment of male and female domains; and in freeing women from the old, limiting, patriarchal roles assigned to them of mother, wife and daughter.

In this volume, mapping women's novels, the themes of gender and activism transpire along with a search for individuality and a challenge to cultural and tribal laws that continue to confine women to traditional and domestic roles. Joseph Zeidan observes that this individuality can be automatically read as feminist in the context of Arab culture because the latter's power structure values conformity to the collective, ethnic religious identity.[46]

Taking my cue from Foucault's theory of resistance and the notions that 'where there is resistance there is power' and of how 'to use resistance as a chemical catalyst so as to bring to light power relations, locate their position, find out their points of application and the methods used', I find that it is imperative to locate the various forms of resistance to existing power structures in women's everyday life as portrayed in their fiction. On the one hand, analysing all sorts of resistance, including minor acts of defiance, and 'what they reveal about the historically changing relations of power in which they are enmeshed as they are incorporated into [in this case Arabia] and its economy,' as Lila Abu-Lughod puts it.[47] For instance, examining the alliances made by women as friends, neighbours and kinfolk, sharing little secrets that they would never reveal in the presence of men or mothers who, in most texts, are depicted as guardians of the patriarchy. Another way is looking at how women subjugate the dominant male discourse by ridiculing masculinity, through woman-to-woman talk and through their cathartic fiction writing, which I discuss in Chapter 6. Further forms of resistance include women's blocking of marriages, either by going on hunger strike, crying or fleeing a bad marriage. In this respect, I examine the mother–daughter conflict, with the former often cast as a guardian of patriarchal values; the daughter displaying hostility towards males, including brothers; and criticism of the religious establishment as a purveyor of discrimination against women.

On the other hand, I explore major acts of resistance evident through the recurrent themes of violence, abuse, rape, hysteria, suicide and incarceration/ imprisonment embedded in the discourses of women writers in Arabia as a reflection of a profound battleground between both women and the power structure, and between women and men – to highlight the unbalanced gender power relations. Of course, this outcome did not arise in some sort of social, religious or political vacuum; on the contrary, patriarchal power, as Sabry Hafez observes, 'has acquired a divine dimension through the religious ratification of the supremacy of men'.[48] This is the result of a centuries-old history of biased male interpretations of religious texts, which has enabled continuing patriarchal power.

With the oil boom in the Gulf states – and, especially, in Arabia – these unbalanced gender power relations were reinforced during the *sahwa* years. Salwa al-Khateeb discerns that Gulf affluence has contributed to isolate females through the importing of foreign labourers and the implementation of further restrictions that have reduced women's need to venture outside the home.[49] Technological advances and the building in Saudi Arabia of separate institutions for men and women – such as banks and universities – have helped to preserve the 'invisibility' of women and regulate female marginalization.

The year 1991 marked a phase of openness to the world and the beginning of GCC states' serious efforts to improve women's position in society. Of course, Western feminist notions of an equal right to education and health services were not alien to the Arab/Muslim world, and its achievements in these fields were widely recognized. However, as Lila Abu-Lughod observes, at that time, 'the only true model of emancipation was the Western model of feminism'.[50] Yet Western feminism often spurs feelings of discomfort, if not actual antagonism, because it has been identified with Western imperialism. It reawakens in many Muslims memories of colonialism in Egypt, and of Europeanized Egyptians such as Qasim Amin, the Alexandria-born lawyer, and his call for women's liberation in his homeland – a call that, in spite of initial resistance, spread in Egypt and found its way into other relatively advanced Arab countries.[51] Amin's admiration for European civilization and 'European man' is evident throughout his writings. It was this admiration and the desire to emulate the West, and particularly his calls to abandon the veil, that infuriated Islamists of the time and left a mark in the Muslim consciousness, which cannot easily be erased, against any calls for reform that would follow a Western model. This negative association between feminism and colonialism in the Arab and Muslim worlds stemmed from the Western colonial mission in the East, which projected notions of inferiority onto the colonized and saw the *neqab* (full-face veil) and veiling generally as the fundamental expression of Muslims' 'backwardness' and a major obstacle to their 'civilization'. Veiling, which was to Western eyes, as Leila Ahmad says, 'the most visible marker of the differentness and inferiority of Islamic societies,' now 'became the symbol [...] of both the oppression of women and the backwardness of Islam, and it became the open target of colonial attack and the spearhead of the assault on Muslim societies'.[52]

Veiling, Silence and the Anonymous Writer

Although 'veiling' is part of Arabia's tradition, with the *'abaya* being an integral feature of women's appearance in public life, it is the oscillation that Saudi women's veiling has been through – between moderation and extremism – that denotes deeper, parallel shifts in female identity. It is important, then, to read the veil as a metaphoric signifier of women's shifting identity, agency and individuality that also directly relates not only to women's levels of resistance but also to their choice of whether to reveal their true identity or hide behind a pseudonym, as the three authors discussed in chapter 6 choose to do. It also serves as the basis for reading the change in women's fiction, focusing on their 'rebellion' against established codes of honour and narratives of society with particular attention paid to the binary of 'voice' and 'silence',[53] which, I contend, is directly linked to their literary 'veiling' and 'unveiling' of both form and feelings. The application of this binary comes in response to culture, religion, feminist and postcolonial discourses.[54]

Until 1979, the battle that Saudi women faced was that against tribal laws, but the subsequent shift in legislation would turn this battle into a particularly tenacious struggle because it became entrenched in everyday life.[55] The rise of the *sahwa* changed everything as it strove to ensure that women were 'properly' covered in public places – gendering thereafter space and society, and creating what Foucault terms 'discourse' or, more precisely, the 'knowledge that structures the constitution of social relations through the collective understanding of the discursive logic and the acceptance of the discourse as social fact'.[56] This explains a kinship between culture, religion and *sahwa*, with the latter regulating the tribal and patriarchal laws through a 'discourse that took control of individuals in the name of modesty and honour'.[57] Soraya Altorki observes the modality of veiling and voice in her 1986 book *Women in Saudi Arabia*:

> Veiling is viewed by men and women as a religious injunction; any lapse is seen as sin, punished by Allah [...] veiling is also a social norm,

enforcement of which is monitored by the most important male affecting a woman's behavior; namely a husband or father. It is therefore instructive to view the practice of veiling not only in terms of the religious rationale but as an expression of male authority over women's behavior, specifically their mobility outside the house [...]. The pitch of a woman's voice is not discouraged because of its seductiveness to men; rather, it is because women's voices should not be heard.[58]

It is not surprising, therefore, that mandatory veiling in the 1980s carried meanings of concealment and marginalization into other cultural realms aside from literature. It included notions of 'silence' that burgeoned during the *sahwa* years – endorsing complete control not only over women's dress but also over their voices.

Against such a backdrop, Saudi critic Ahmad al-Wasil explains how women perhaps found an outlet in literature because, whether in poetry or novel form, it gave them the space needed to express their social concerns. Censorship was particularly strong on lyrics intended for audio broadcasting because they had to be declared appropriate for a male-dominated space and audience[59] – unlike the more private, individual consumption of literature.[60] Al-Wasil's view emphasizes a space for women in literature not found in lyrics – yet textual evidence actually points to a scarcity of women's fiction at the time, with few works published abroad and others being deemed illicit and shameful, which explains their authors' excessive use of symbolism and metaphors. Indeed, it was a difficult period for both female fiction and lyric writers to flourish. Within such limiting concepts, few women writers were capable of resisting what were considered feminine properties when even the simple act of writing and communicating with the public was regarded as denoting their unveiling of face and voice. A good example of this attitude is given by the way in which Sohila Zain Al-'Abedin, a Saudi Islamic writer and thinker, wrote in 1985 criticizing the female columnist Juhair al-Musa'id for expressing her feelings, stating that 'unveiling emotions [...] is no less dangerous than unveiling the face'.[61]

This criticism of al-Musa'id's self-expression is a reminder of Foucault's idea of the 'implicit systems' in Archaeology of Knowledge, which refers to the making of subjects and to restrictions placed on that subject production, and how the individual is not regulated by an exterior relationship to power – on the contrary, the 'individual is formed or rather, formulated through his discursively constituted "identity"' shaped by social constraints.[62] Veiling in this case is extended to women's expression of their emotions, desires and sensibilities, reflecting how writers and commentators in such high-walled societies regulate and reaffirm the meaning enacted by the dominant discourse. Foucault further notes that this 'reiterative process discourse normalises and homogenises, including upon the bodies and subjectivities of those it dominates'.⁶³ He explains the concept of the 'subjection' in 'Rituals of Exclusion':

> My problem is essentially the definition of the implicit systems in which we find ourselves prisoners; what I would like to grasp is the system of limits and exclusion which we practice without knowing it; I would like to make the cultural unconscious apparent.⁶⁴

It is remarkable therefore to observe how Saudi women express themselves and navigate these implicit systems, illustrating how the dominant discourse has influenced their resistance to patriarchal power. Additionally, it is crucial to examine how women writers have articulated their desires despite the cultural and religious constraints surrounding them. Muhammad al-Abbas, the Saudi critic, recognizes the significant impact of such restrictive discourse on women's creativity:

> Until the present day there [have been] no Saudi women writers who are capable of changing the reader's world: the crux of the problem lies not [only] in state bans and censorship, but in self-censorship that is fraught with wariness of the illicit, shameful and *ḥarām*, although fiction writing in its simplest form demands gnawing away at feelings of embarrassment and shame. Women writers do not have the narrative skills and real life experiences that usually provide writers with ideas; most of their novels lack imagination due to the chronic idleness of aesthetic values that [have] been killed in the female who is bombarded with oppressive laws. Such laws are not necessarily state laws, rather they are a variation of futile social traditions that are endorsed by religious mandates and intellectual imprisonment against women writers who dare to – relatively speaking – disclose themselves or disrupt the otherwise patriarchal literary tradition.⁶⁵

Indeed, the issue of physical veiling and veiling one's true feelings has been a controversial matter, and one that novelist Laila al-Juhani felt compelled to address during the annual Abu Dhabi Book Fair in a lecture entitled 'Love Issues in Saudi Female Novels'. In it, al-Juhani argued, 'The social strictures put on women are of course more severe than [those] put on men, especially for those who try to cross red lines', thus confirming that writing about sexual issues is not forbidden *per se* but appears to be unacceptable for women authors alone.⁶⁶

It is within this dynamic interplay of veiling and unveiling that many Saudi women writers have either responded with complete silence or with ambivalence to the 'woman issue', or have broken moral codes in defiance of a patriarchal culture that favours their 'silence' and 'invisibility'. Miral al-Tahawy explains a further aspect of this interplay:

> Male Arab critics have often reduced the aesthetics of female writing to the acts of 'revealing' and 'undressing.' Therefore, female writing of any kind connotes 'undressing,' a word often used as a synonym for writing. Even the writing itself is often described as 'naked' or 'revealing.' Such texts are often praised as 'a rebellious body of writing that reveals and exposes society by exposing itself.' Critical praise idolizes the act of undressing in both its social and psychological aspects. Good writing is writing that performs its role of 'revealing the unspoken in Arab society,' and sometimes 'unveiling what is hidden,' 'baring what was covered,' 'stripping reality,' 'dropping the veils of historic fear of disclosure and revelation,' or 'stripping bare the reality enveloped in a cloak of modesty.'[67]

For the sake of unveiling what is hidden, I argue that the act of writing itself has put these women back into the public place to which they had been denied access, giving them the opportunity to address critical issues using their voices and experience in the hope of creating a change in society. The sum of their works represents the dynamic transformation and negotiation of boundaries that define women in terms of *'ār* (scandalous) and *'aib* (shameful). Such definitions, in fact, directly contribute to some women writers' use of pseudonyms; as al-Wasil notes, 'if they were to reveal their real identity, it would be considered *'awra* [scandalous], in effect exposing what is private, one's name'.[68]

This fear of revealing 'one's name' or identity, of exposing 'what is private', and the fear of the 'implicit system', to borrow the words of Foucault, has encouraged Saudi writers across the board – men and, more so, women – to write under a pseudonym.[69] Like many at the beginning of their literary journey, for instance, the winner of the 2010 international Arabic Book Prize, Abdo Khal, wrote under the female name 'Nevine Abdo'. Ghazi al-Gosaibi used the names 'Ibn Abdrabbuh' and 'Muhammad Al-'Elynī'. Less surprisingly, perhaps, women writers also used aliases: to name but a few, Juhair al-Musa'id adopted the name 'Alanoud Al-Essa'; Khryiah Al-Saggaf wrote under seven different pseudonyms, some of which are male names like 'Waḥīd' and 'Ensān'; and the poet Fouziah Abu Khaled assumed the moniker 'May Al-Sagirah'.[70]

While the aforementioned writers used a false identity for fear of crossing cultural boundaries, author Samira Khashugji wrote under her first name, Samira, followed by 'Daughter of the Arabian Peninsula' – albeit for a different reason. Being the provocative writer that she was, a picture of her unveiled and in Western-style dress was emblazoned on the cover of the ten novels that she wrote between 1958 and 1973. Having both a picture and no pseudonym proves beyond doubt that she had no real issues over revealing her true identity, although the description of her identity ('Daughter of …') was meant to confirm Khashugji's integration and sense of belonging to her country of origin, Saudi Arabia.[71]

A Fragmented Memoir: Samira Khashugji – *Beyond the Clouds*

> If we go back to the 60s and 70s of [the] last century, one could say that Samira Khashugji and Huda al-Rasheed were the only two Saudi women fiction writers, who dared to broach the woman question, albeit shyly, due to paternal and religious hegemonies at the time. Which resulted, in both writers choosing self-imposed exile to avoid people's taunting.[72]

Although this book is about Saudi Arabia's 'new text' and 'revolutionary' voices (discussed earlier, in the Introduction), it cannot by any means ignore the fact that without the achievements of the pioneering generation Saudi women's fiction writing would not have had the high importance that it holds in the epistemic view of activists, feminists and scholars. Hence, the discourse on Saudi women's early contribution to literature is just as important as their later discourse, because it helps us to understand the main constructs that have influenced feminism in Saudi women's fiction. This explains why I have devoted attention in this chapter to Samira Khashugji, whose contribution to the Saudi novel cannot be overlooked.

As we have seen, the early crop of Saudi female writers were educated in neighbouring Arab countries – mainly Egypt. Their contribution to literature coincided with the belated beginnings of education provision for women in Saudi Arabia – a national event that shows how female pioneers were making great strides at a time when the government of the kingdom was battling tribal backwardness. On reading their works, one can see that they had different struggles to those of their successors – chiefly, because the majority of them opted to live outside their home country. Thus, the 'battles' that they chose to fight were hybridized; they were waged from the 'borderland' – that is, the space where two identity discourses blend or clash. This hybridity, which Friedman defines as branching out of 'positional identity' or 'cultural grafting', was the result of a 'geographical migration'[73] that basically 'configures identity as the superposition of different cultures in a single space often imagined as a border; a site of blending and clashing'.[74]

The concept of positional identity developed most directly out of postcolonial and diasporic studies, and has been a helpful tool in understanding the blind spots, fragmentations and dead-end texts that accompany binary narratives. It is significant therefore, but not surprising, to see that the works of Samira Khashugji, Huda al-Rasheed and Safia al-'Anbar among others bear some resemblance to the major literary trends of the Arab world that operated according to 'residual' colonial logics in both Egypt and Lebanon.[75] By 'residual', I mean that the work produced in the 1960s–1970s cannot be labelled as belonging to either a colonial or a postcolonial literature *per se*, but rather fits into a process in which values, thoughts and concepts are mediated by these two poles. As Krestin W. Shands, in his anthology *Neither East Nor West*, suggests, postcoloniality 'is a time period and condition marked by the challenges of difficult change and complicated continuity within an unpredictable mix of pre-, ant-, post-, and neo-colonial elements'.[76] Khashugji's texts embrace this mix in the sense that she openly broached love and relationship issues while also critiquing the tribal thinking that was then rife in the kingdom and the double standards of its male-dominated society – issues that many of these first-generation writers had not, in fact, experienced first-hand. This explains why her writing reflects a romantic streak and yet a 'soft' anger of the kind celebrated as a feminine phase in the Anglo-American feminist theories that were popular in Egypt and the Levant at the time.[77]

Most importantly, this borderland identity planted the seeds of the feminist project in the kingdom because these authors' hybridity gave rise to a 'third space' through its mimicry of Western culture, to borrow the language of Homi Bhabha.[78] The result was neither completely Westernized nor indigenous, generating a 'third culture' and a new semi-feminist discourse that attempted to subvert patriarchal literary forms. As Ashcroft et al. further explained,

> this subversion may not be a conscious aim of the authors. It may be generated, inescapably, by the ideological conflict that inevitably takes place in the text. On a wider scale, there has also been a radical questioning of the basic assumptions of dominant systems of language and thought.[79]

Near the beginning of Samira Khashugji's 1971 novel, *Warā' al-Dabāb* (Beyond the Clouds), the author says of its protagonist, 'When Sakinah went to her room an hour ago, in the monastery where she decided to spend the rest of her life, she felt an urge to write.'[80] There is a confession of sorts here, and images of a Christian 'monastery' and a 'nun' that complicate the presentation of ideological beliefs and religious boundaries in this particular work. Specifying that Sakinah chose to be a 'nun' and 'give her life to God' in the first few pages of the book is, in a way, a challenge to anti-postcolonial models and the religious establishment of the author's home country. The omniscient narrator further complicates the idea of faith and tolerance among believers, contending, 'she knows that by being a nun she is protecting herself from corruption'.

Like other Arab intellectuals at the time, Khashugji was perhaps trying to imagine a secularist, pan-Arab identity that disrupted Islamists' stereotypes of Arabs as united only by faith. This point is further strengthened by the imposition of the ongoing conflict with Israel on two occasions in the novel: in the first chapter when Sakinah recalls how she lost her brother in the 1948 war and in chapter 2 when her beau, Wafiq, joins the Arab troops in the 1967 war. Recurring terms of 'war' and 'nuns' were definitely foreign to the average Saudi back home, but were part of a modernist trend led by Egypt's prominent figures (Rifaa al-Tahtawi and Taha Hussein among others) who embraced ideas of secular pan-Arabism.

Although not wholly representative of this writer's varied output, *Beyond the Clouds*, Khashugji's second work, calls for an accountability of action because the author fails to establish the 'real-ness' of her story on many levels – those of social norms and traditions, and a legitimate interaction between men and women (kin, brother, father). The protagonist, Sakinah, is depicted as escaping her miserable marriage in Jeddah for Beirut after discovering her husband's betrayal with another woman in their own house. Her jet-set lifestyle and travelling to Beirut to join her family, who live there, and then on to live in Paris for no obvious reason calls into question legal, tribal and patriarchal laws that were rife in the kingdom around 1979. True, the guardianship law was not formally enforced back then; nonetheless, there were cultural constraints that the author overlooked. Similarly, Sakinah's out-of-wedlock relationship with Wafiq would have been religiously and culturally unacceptable at the time, and it was these deviations from cultural norms that brought the author a great deal of criticism.

This deviation would, however, have not even been possible without Khashugji's adoption of travel as a literary tool – not only to speed up events but also to give the protagonist the freedom needed to interact with other characters. Saddeka Arebi – in her book *Women and Words in Saudi Arabia*, published in 1994 – observes, 'in order for the writer to introduce any unfamiliar mode of interaction between characters that is not socially sanctioned, or to portray rebellious, profane, or perverted characters, especially females, they utilize madness. Sane characters, however, can only do so by "traveling"'.[81] Sakinah is definitely a rebellious soul, eager to explore the world, and it was only through this character and the technique of travel that Khashugji was able to give her protagonist a space through which she could break with both the metaphorical, ancestral silence of women in Arabia and the symbolic veiling of both emotions and verbal expression.

If Khashugji thus had control over space, she equally had control over time. The use of techniques such as stream of consciousness and flashbacks allows the protagonist to broaden her memories and to make sense of the present by looking at the past. In fact, the excessive use of monologues and flashbacks in the book makes it difficult to assess to what extent there are parallels between reality and fiction – in the sense that Sakinah freely travels between the East and the West just like the author, who had a lavish and cosmopolitan lifestyle setting her apart from the average Saudi woman at the time.[82] Sakinah's consciousness is analysed through the first-person narrative that occupies the greater part of the text, alternating with a third-person account from the all-seeing narrator – thus creating space for both the subjective world of Sakinah and the outer world. The countless monologues and the 'I' of the first-person narrative invite the reader to understand her individual struggle as a woman. It is no secret that Khashugji's protagonist's disappointment in men mirrors the author's own misery with her husband; it raises questions about the emotional stability and inner peace of both, and it is an ever-present lens through which Khashugji was compelled to view the world and interpret it in a memoir-like narrative. This autobiographical feature in Saudi women's fiction is quite common: Nadje al-Ali, in her book *Gender Writing/Writing Gender*, asserts, 'All the writers interviewed emphasised the close relationship between their personality, their personal experiences and their social environment and the content of [their] literary works.'[83]

Mapping the borders of public/personal lives enables the author to have agency and power over past events. Despite fragmentations in the construction of past memories, one should credit Khashugji for using her pen to resist the male discourse that condones the betrayal of women in a marriage. In a way, autobiographical writing is conducive to the theme of fragmentation, which Judi M. Roller views as common among Western feminist novelists as well as Arab women writers because of 'the schizophrenia of modern culture's views of women and the battle in women themselves between the old ways and the revolutionary spirit'.[84] These 'battles' between old and new, self and society on the one hand and the ensuing fragmentation on the other are especially discernible in the work of émigré Saudi women writers of this generation, like Khashugji. They were advocating female emancipation and education, and wanted to see improvements in the status of women in society similar to those that they and other women had experienced in neighbouring countries. They were, however, suppressed by the many cultural restrictions back home, having to imagine a setting in which their characters could freely interact with others and negotiate gender-related issues. Their texts bear witness to what Gloria Anzaldúa defines as invisible 'borders',[85] and they thus comprise borderland-identity discourses – a space in which, in this context, Egyptian or Saudi identities meet with varying degrees of the other culture prevailing in the text. This is an encounter between a plurality of cultures within the self, which involves contradictions, fragmentations, ambiguities and oscillation between two or more cultures.

Khashugji's protagonist's 'borderland' cultural identity is negotiated and conflicted with many times in the narrative, through statements that negate and contest the validity of a nuclear family against the backdrop of patriarchy and religion. Sakinah questions marriage, and undermines it – 'If love is a concrete thing why do people marry? They marry because they do not trust their feelings to last'[86] – and such argument stands in opposition to the culture in her home country, which values the concept of marriage and family. Hers is an opposition stemming from a borderland identity that is also discernible in the author's oscillation between two cultures and sets of religious/secular beliefs. Contradictions in the novel culminate in the writer's solution for the protagonist's doubt about marriage when faced with betrayal: she leaves her second husband, Sameh, and later still, when she is frustrated with further disappointments in her life, Sakinah opts to become a nun ('taking the veil' in another sense). Such cultural fragmentations, however, risk fostering the production of colonial texts in which ideas and images of the colonial 'White' take centre stage in opposition to the uncivilized 'Other'. In fact, the entire narrative of *Warā' al-Ḍabāb* is permeated with a sense of displacement that manifests itself in its countless dissimilarities and binary oppositions – for instance, between the snowbound Lebanese Cedar Mountains and the desert, in a subtle reference to 'home' and 'native' as opposed to modern and civilized. The writer also goes on to compare men who represent two different cultures. Majed is Sakinah's not-so-pleasant Saudi ex-husband and Khamer is her more polished Lebanese boyfriend, whose description recalls that of a sophisticated English gentleman (he even kneels and kisses Sakinah's hand, making her shiver with pleasure) and evokes a colonial characterization *per se*.

Notes

1 The early beginnings of literature in Saudi Arabia attest to the fact that male writers were well versed in the literature of Egypt, the Levant and the diaspora or the Americas, and had been exposed to these countries' diverse intellectual and literary movements. Many of their writings demonstrate an awareness of works beyond the kingdom's borders – such as the translations by the Lebanese author Jurji Zaydan of Western literature, the liberation of women in Egypt by Qasim Amin (the spiritual father of feminism in Egypt) and the renowned literary salon of Palestinian May Ziadah. The pan-Arabism sparked by the Nasserite movement was also a development that many Saudi young men engaged with while studying in Egypt, but it was intellectually diffused and unarticulated in their literary output until the 1990s, when Turki al-Hamad and Ghazi al-Gosaibi broke their long silence and delved into political expression in their novels (mentioned in the main text). Before that, Saudi writers had mostly been onlookers of the mesmerizing and enthralling movement because of their state's anti-Nasserite sentiments at that time, and its restrictions on freedom of expression. The sole exception was the remarkable Saudi novelist Abdul Rahman Munif, who lived between Amman and Baghdad and, hence, could afford the freedom to express his opinion.

2 Salma Jayyusi, *Beyond the Dunes: An Anthology of Modern Saudi Literature* (I.B. Tauris: London, 2006), p. 20.
3 Rashad Mohammed Moqbel Al Areqi, 'Hybridity and Problematic of Identity in Gulf States Narrative', *European Journal of English Language and Literature Studies*, Vol. 3, No. 4 (September 2015).
4 Soraya Altorki, 'Struggling for the Centre from the Periphery: The Fiction of Zaynab Hifni', *Contemporary Arab Affairs*, Vol. 3, No. 3 (July–September 2010), pp. 352–61. DOI: 10.1080/17550912.2010.494410 (accessed 21 April 2022).
5 Mai Yamani, 'Some Observations on Women in Saudi Arabia', in Yamani (ed.), *Feminism and Islam: Legal and Literary Perspectives* (SOAS: London, 1996), p. 278.
6 Intisar 'Agīl was educated in Lebanon but went back to live in Jeddah, Saudi Arabia, where she regularly contributed to local papers and magazines. This had an impact on her writing, keeping it more in touch with reality than the work of many other authors who had, like herself, been educated abroad. 'Agīl's work fluctuates between traditionalist and modernist values, critiquing her culture for treating women as mere commodities while also raising questions about women's participation in public life. In her collection of stories *Mawāni' Belā 'Arṣefah* (Ports without Pavements), published in 1988 at the peak of the *saḥwa* era, 'Agīl consolidates patriarchal norms and practices by reinforcing the image of the nurturing mother and by highlighting women's careers as a threat to the nuclear family. In this collection, a short story entitled 'My Lady Doctor' concerns a successful female doctor who cannot leave her job when her husband is relocated to work abroad. A separation follows, and their daughter is depicted as growing up to be an unhappy young woman in desperate need of love and care. The story opens with the maid revealing a secret: 'I think Amal (the daughter) is in a relationship with a man'. After some interrogation, the busy mother is shocked to learn that her daughter has actually been talking to her father and that she has decided to go and live with him. Here, the writer asserts a male-dominant discourse that pushes women back into the private sphere by emphasizing their role as nurturers of the family, constantly occupying the kitchen and absorbed with trivialities.
7 Christian missionary institutions were established in Egypt as well as other parts of the Middle East. They were dubbed *rahbat* ('nuns') and transmitted a body of European literature, along with all the cultural images contained therein, in colonized countries. Many of those schools were created in the context of colonialism as 'civilizing missions', intended to consolidate Western hegemony in the region and to privilege one culture over the 'other' – see Melvin Eugene Page and Penny M. Sonnenburg (eds), *Colonialism: An International, Social, Cultural, and Political Encyclopedia*, Volume 1 (ABC-CLIO: Oxford, 2003); and Heather J. Sharkey, *American Evangelicals in Egypt: Missionary Encounters in an Age of Empire* (Princeton University Press: Woodstock, Oxfordshire, 2008).
8 Soraya Altorki, *Women in Saudi Arabia* (Columbia University Press: New York, 1986), p. 19.
9 Madawi al-Rasheed, *A Most Masculine State: Gender, Politics and Religion in Saudi Arabia* (Cambridge University Press: New York, 2013), p. 86.

10 The radicals saw the invasion of Kuwait, and the ensuing permanent presence of US military forces in the Gulf, as hostile interference in Muslim people's affairs; this became a major turning point in world politics, igniting an antagonism that would culminate in the events of 9/11. Because the 9/11 suspects were mainly of Saudi nationality, strict measures were subsequently imposed on the countries of the region to ensure that they implemented genuine reform.
11 Dr Ahmad Sabrah, in a seminar discussing 'Saudi Women Fiction Writing Boom; Origins and Consequences', Dar Alhayat, 11 January 2011. See also al-Rasheed, *Most Masculine State*, p. 22, which explains that the real reason behind the boom in the Saudi novel market was the absence of legal restrictions and rules on fiction writing, unlike the clear legal prohibition on demonstrations, organizations and civil-society activities; a novelist is not required to apply for a licence – hence, more and more intellectuals choose to express themselves in fiction.
12 Andrew Hammond, '"Girls of Riyadh" Spurs Rush of Saudi Novels', Reuters, 2007. Available at www.reuters.com/article/idUSL0824250120070724 (accessed 21 April 2022).
13 For further reading on the subject, see Marilyn Booth, '"The Muslim Woman" as Celebrity Author and the Politics of Translating Arabic: Girls of Riyadh Go on the Road', *Journal of Middle East Women's Studies*, Vol. 6, No. 3 (Fall 2010); al-Rasheed, *Most Masculine State*.
14 Al-Watan online, 5 May 2018, https://www.alwatan.com.sa/article/374874 (accessed 18 July 2022).
15 'The Saudi family: A Reader in a Non Reading Milieu', *Eqtesadyah Daily*, 8 August 2019.
16 Saudi Center For Opinion Polling (SCOP), 8 October 2023.
17 Friedman, *Mappings*.
18 Donald E. Hall, *Fixing Patriarchy: Feminism and Mid-Victorian Male Novelists* (Macmillan Press Ltd: London, 1996), p. 1.
19 Al-Wahabi, 'Women's novel in Saudi Arabia'.
20 *Takfeer* in Islam is directed to Muslims who deviate from their faith.
21 Asef Bayat, *Life as Politics: How Ordinary People Change the Middle East* (Stanford University Press: Stanford, CA, 2010), p. 97.
22 Wafa Abdulrahman, *Satanic Desires* (Faradis Publishers: Bahrain, 2011).
23 Amélie Le Renard, *A Society of Young Women: Opportunities of Place, Power, and Reform in Saudi Arabia* (Stanford University Press: Stanford, CA, 2014), p. 33.
24 Qanta Ahmad, *In The Land of Invisible Women: A Female Doctor's Journey in the Saudi Kingdom* (Sourcebooks: Naperville, IL, 2008), p. 56.
25 Ahmad al-Wasil, 'Samira Khashoggī, *"al-mara wa al-talim"'* [Women and Education], *Huqul*, No. 5 (2007), p. 81.
26 Al-Wasil, *'al-mara wa al-talim'*.
27 Email interview with Omima al-Khamis, February 2017 (current author translation).
28 In their memoir, *The Sixth of November*, Aisha al-Mana and Hessa al-Shaikh talk about their experience as pioneers who led the first protest against the unwritten driving ban and how frustrated they were with the stalemate over women's rights in the kingdom. They note, 'The huge tribal resistance against girls schooling was not followed by big shifts and changes in women's emancipatory movement[s],

with the exception of women's welfare philanthropic societies that were found by elite women, and revolved around eradicating illiteracy [...] and helping the needy.' Aisha al-Mana and Hessa al-Shaikh (eds), *The Sixth of November: Women Driving 1990* (Jadawel: Beirut, 2013), p. 22.
29 Haya al-Mughni, *Women in Kuwait: The Politics of Gender* (Saqi Books: London, 2001), p. 184.
30 Le Renard, *Society of Young Women*, p. 40. Yet, perhaps unintentionally, she (Le Renard) overlooks the fact that the sort of controversies described above are deeply embedded in the religious public discourse, and are proof that women's rights will always be compromised for socio-religious gain.
31 Al-Khamis' novel *The Leafy Tree* was long-listed for the 2010 International Prize for Arabic Fiction (IPAF).
32 'Should There Be Quotas for Women in Saudi Book Clubs?' *Arabic Literature and Translation*, 30 December 2010.
33 Marilyn Booth, 'Introduction', in Booth (ed.), *Harem Histories: Envisioning Places and Living Spaces* (Duke University Press: Durham, NC and London, 2010), p. 10.
34 Booth, 'Introduction', p. 7.
35 Daphne Spain quoted in Booth, *Harem Histories*, p. 7.
36 Doreen Massey, 'A Place Called Home', in Massey, *Space, Place and Gender* (Polity Press: Cambridge, 1994), p. 157.
37 Amy Freeman, 'Moral Geographies and Women's Freedom: Rethinking Freedom Discourse in the Moroccan Context', in Ghazi-Walid Falah and Caroline Nagel (eds), *Geographies of Muslim Women: Gender, Religion, and Space* (Guilford Press: London, 2005), p. 147.
38 Fatima Mernissi, *Dreams of Trespass* (Perseus Books: New York, 1994), chapter 1.
39 Mernissi, *Dreams of Trespass*, chapter 3.
40 A word that literally translates as 'close relatives of the opposite sex', and so able to mix together without sin; these are usually the father, husband and son, and the male offspring of a woman's sisters and brothers.
41 Part of a body of Muslim culture dictating (without penalizing those who do not adhere) that the new widow must not be seen by any man except those who are related to her – i.e. *maḥārem* – or, in matters of urgency, by a doctor or lawyer.
42 Munira Fakhro, 'Gulf Women and Islamic Law', in Yamani (ed.), *Feminism and Islam*, p. 256.
43 Fakhro, 'Gulf Women and Islamic Law', pp. 256–7.
44 Email interview with the author Zaineb Hefny, March 2017 (current author translation).
45 Jean Anne Sutherland and Kathryn Feltey, *Cinematic Sociology: Social Life in Film* (Sage: London, 2013), p. 110.
46 Zeidan, *Arab Women Novelists*, p. 3.
47 In her analytical study 'The Romance of Resistance: Tracing Transformations of Power through Bedouin Women', in which she condemns the way ideologists have thus far romanticized resistance in their studies of the relationship between resistance and power, Lila Abu-Lughod argues instead that resistance should be used as a diagnostic of power. She raises a very important question of what the implications are of the forms of resistance that [studies] locate. What do these forms of resistance reveal about the historically changing relations of power in

which they are enmeshed as they become increasingly incorporated into [in her case] the Egyptian state and economy?
The first arena for resistance, Abu-Lughod suggests, is the segregated female world, where women daily enact all sorts of minor defiances of the restrictions enforced by elder men in the community. Women use secrets and silences to their advantage; they often collude to hide knowledge from men. The second and widespread form of resistance is the Bedouin women's resistance to marriage: how mothers sometimes successfully block marriages that their daughters do not want. The third form of resistance is woman-to-woman talk, an irreverence towards the mark of masculinity and the privileges that this automatically grants, which indicates the significance of the ideology of sexual difference itself as a form of power. The fourth is a kind of oral lyric poetry or little songs.
48 Sabry Hafez, 'Women's Narrative in Modern Arabic Literature: A Typology', in Roger Allen, Hillary Kilpatrick and Ed de Moor (eds), *Love and Sexuality in Modern Arabic Literature* (Saqi Books: London, 1995), p. 155.
49 Salwa al-Khateeb, 'The Oil Boom and Its Impact on Women and Families in Saudi Arabia', in Alsharekh (ed.), *The Gulf Family*.
50 Lila Abu-Lughod (ed.), *Remaking Women: Feminism and Modernity in the Middle East* (Princeton University Press: Princeton, NJ, 1998), p. 14.
51 Amin's major works were translated as *Liberation of Women* and *The New Woman*. The first public confrontation between feminism and Islam took place when, in 1898, Amin's book *Tahrir al-Marah* (Liberation of Women) provoked a furore because it called for women to abandon the veil – a symbol of their oppression and an obstacle to their fully fledged involvement in public life. Although Amin's call improved women's lives overall at the time by granting them education, work and marriage-related rights, people remained suspicious not only because it encouraged women to ditch the headscarf and *'abaya* – confirming, in the process, the superiority of Western civilization, which was being emulated on all levels – but also because it shook the very foundation of the patriarchal order, which was (and is) based on male dominance and superiority over the female. Leila Ahmad wrote, in her book *A Quiet Revolution*, 'Amin's text is grounded in the idea of the self evident and comprehensive superiority of Europe and its societies and civilization [...]'. The war of words waged against Amin by Islamists, and their anti-Western sentiments, were taken up by radical groups such as the Salafist Jama'at Islamiah. Although founded in 1941, Jama'at Islamiah spread its ideology and acquired an active form in 1971 through its deployment of *ḥisbah* (the divinely sanctioned duty of a ruler [government] to intervene and coercively engage in 'enjoining good and forbidding wrong' to keep everything in order according to *sharī'a*). The group attacked mixed couples seen in public, and at parties and music festivals – a practice that would later result in the policing of both men and women in public places, and would spread throughout the Arab and Muslim world to a varying degree.
52 Leila Ahmed, *Women and Gender in Islam: Historical Roots* (Yale University Press: New Haven, CT and London, reissue edition, 1993), p. 152.
53 Arab culture equates the desirability of women with silence, virtue and charm, as a code of 'chastity'. By speaking up and breaching silence, these women are resisting the dominant discourse.
54 Drawing specific parallels between the 'feminine' stage, or Victorian era, as discussed by Elaine Showalter, and Saudi women's storytelling is nothing but

inspiring – with parallels to the rigid Victorian moral structures that dictated how society dealt with everything from domestic to public life, to the use of pseudonyms. For example, Mary Anne Evans, the Victorian novelist, used the pseudonym George Eliot to avoid the stereotypes surrounding women writing in her time and to shield her private life from scrutiny.
55 A good example is the fight for women's personal rights – one such struggle being against the *mahram*, or guardianship law. Endorsement of the 2012 anti-harassment law would grant women safety in public spaces and lift the ban on women driving. (Some of these laws were endorsed in the late 1980s.) In more recent years – specifically, post 9/11 – veiling gained a different meaning of 'agency' and 'national identity' mediated through the market forces of consumer capitalism to become a 'kind of brand or label of a consolidated Muslim femininity'. The veil, or *'abaya*, became a symbol of defiance against previous ideological and patriarchal constructions of femininity that is reappropriated to signify an aesthetic value and individuality – lending credibility, or what Marilyn Booth dubs 'truth effect', to authors and their work among their readers. In fact, 'the *'abaya*-as-fashion notably disrupts its primary signification without ever fully displacing it, thereby constituting a form of passive resistance', explains Noor Al-Qasimi. By 'fashioning' the *'abaya*, women are in fact 'bargaining with patriarchy', which has come to signify 'a form of struggle' as opposed to 'pure domination'. Thus, the struggle over the *'abaya* form mirrors a deeper, parallel shift in women's identity. Veiling in this sense no longer signified women's segregation or subordination, or women's veiling of emotions; on the contrary, it facilitated women's access to public places and became a tool by which women could negotiate their spatial boundaries.
56 Michel Foucault, *The Archaeology of Knowledge* (Routledge: London and New York, 2002), pp. 135–44.
57 Michel Foucault, 'Subjection, Resistance, Resignification: Between Freud and Foucault', in Judith Butler, *The Psychic Life of Power: Theories of Subjection* (Stanford University Press: Stanford, CA, 1997), pp. 83–4.
58 Altorki, *Women in Saudi Arabia*, pp. 67–8.
59 Many restrictions and limitations were placed on female singers, who were suddenly prohibited from appearing on state TV and confined to segregated events like weddings and private parties. For example, the poet Thuria Qabel struggled, like so many others, to have her lyrics sung; famous Saudi female singers such as Ebtisam Lutfi and Etab had their public TV appearances suspended, eventually leading to Lutfi's withdrawal from the music industry and Etab's self-imposed exile in Egypt.
60 Ahmad al-Wasil, 'Noon al-Ghena' fi al-Jazirah al-Arabiah: al-Tajrebah Wa al-Mada' [Music in the Arabian Peninsula: Trial and Limitation], *Huqul*, No. 5 (2007).
61 Sohila Zain Al-'Abedin, in Arebi, *Women and Words*, p. 222.
62 Butler, *The Psychic Life of Power*, p. 83.
63 Foucault, *Archaeology of Knowledge*, p. 221.
64 Michel Foucault, 'Rituals of Exclusion', in Judith Butler, *The Psychic Life of Power*, pp. 83–4.
65 Muhammad al-Abbas in private email interview with the author, February 2012. The term *harām* denotes what is forbidden.

66 'Al-Beshir and al-Juhani, Two Novelists Addressing Social Taboo', Aletihad News Center, 14 March 2008.
67 Miral al-Tahawy, 'Writing the Body and the Rhetoric of Protest in Arab Women's Literature', *Journal of Levantine Studies*, Vol. 7, No. 1 (Summer 2017), translated from Arabic by Shoshana London Sappir.
68 Ahmad al-Wasil, 'Sat'ir wa aqlam sarikhah: takwin al-muthaqafah al-saudiyya wa tahawulatha' [Curtains and Sharp Pens: Saudi Women Intellectuals and Their Changes], *Idhafat* Vol. 7 (2009), p. 86. The danger of exposing 'what is private' is rooted in Arabic culture and codified in its literature. A good example is the legendary love story of the poet Qais Ibn al-Mullawah and his beloved Laila, Al Ameriah. Al-Mullawah broke the moral codes of his society by voicing his love for Laila and revealing her identity, eventually leading to hostility from Laila's father and her tribe. This hostility resulted in the loss of his love and eventually his mind, and the story shows him wandering the desert, living with wild animals and reciting beautiful love poetry until he turns insane – thus gaining the name *Majnun* (madman). Similarly, Jamil ibn Ma'mar al-Udhri – also known as Jamil Buthayna, a classic Arabic love poet during the Umayyad period – asked for the hand of Buthina, which was refused by her tribe because of his poems praising her; by voicing his love for her, Jamil, too, broke the moral codes of his society, and hence their love was doomed. Buthina was forced to marry someone else, but they continued to see each other even after her marriage although they never consummated their love because of the many obstacles placed between them.
69 For further reading on the subject, please see al-Tahawy, 'Writing the Body', in which she cites critic Abd Allah al-Ghadhdhami's explanation of women writers' fear of revealing their identity, which highlights the fact that

> [w]omen's writing is associated in Arab culture with many of the concerns raised by numerous traditional Arab texts, which associated writing with immorality [...] This made it forbidden to teach free women to write, on the assumption that the women would learn to write in order to correspond with men, which meant sending flirtatious letters to seduce them. In that sense letter writing became an instrument of moral corruption and obscenity, as expressed by Khair u-Din Ni'man bin Abi a-Thana' in his work 'The Purpose of Preventing Women from Writing.'

70 Documented by Saudi author Muhammad Abdelrazzaq al-Qash'amy in his book *Al-Asmā' al-must'arah le'l kutāb alsaudīn* (Dar almufradāt l'lenasher w'altawzī': Riyadh, 2005).
71 Confirmed by Ahmad al-Adwani in Hasan Namy (ed.), *The Narrative Discourse: Women's Fiction* (The Cultural Club: Jeddah, 2007), p. 98.
72 Zaineb Hefny in private email interview with the author, March 2017.
73 Friedman, *Mappings*, p. 24.
74 Friedman, p. 25.
75 Diana Taylor, 'Transculturating Transculturation', *Performing Arts Journal*, Vol. 13, No. 2 (May 1991), p. 91.
76 Krestin W. Shands (ed.), *Neither East Nor West: Postcolonial Essays on Literature, Culture and Religion* (Elanders: Stockholm, 2008), p. 9.
77 Alanoud Alsharekh, *Angry Words Spoken Softly* (Saffron Books: London, 2007).
78 Homi K. Bhabha, *The Location of Culture* (Routledge: London and New York, 2004).

79 Bill Ashcroft, Gareth Griffiths and Helen Tiffin, *The Empire Writes Back: Theory and Practice in Post-colonial Literatures* (Routledge: London and New York, 2002), p. 174.
80 Samira Khashugji, *Warā' al-Dabāb* [Beyond the Clouds] (Manshūrāt Sa'id Ba'albakī: Beirut, 1979), p. 11.
81 Arebi, *Women and Words*, p. 179.
82 Abdel Baqi in Namy (ed.), *Narrative Discourse*, p. 102. Baqi confirms the direct correlation between the writer's life and her output, and he raises the important parallel that Khashugji had endured anxiety, alienation, emotional starvation and lack of affection in the absence of a loving husband and family – something that is reflected in her stories.
83 Nadje Sadiq al-Ali, *Gender Writing/Writing Gender: The Representation of Women in a Selection of Modern Egyptian Literature* (American University in Cairo Press: Cairo, 1994), p. 113.
84 Judi M. Roller, *The Politics of the Feminist Novel* (Greenwood Press: Westport, CT, 1986), p. 68.
85 Gloria E. Anzaldúa, *Borderlands/La Frontera: The New Mestiza* (Aunt Lute Books: San Francisco, 1987).
86 Khashugji, *Warā' al-Dabāb*, p. 76.

2
RETHINKING THE PATRIARCHAL DISCOURSE

In this chapter, I examine the works of four writers – who are united by their attempt to subvert patriarchal discourse yet divided by the way in which they register their feminist grievances – through the symbols and metaphors that they, intentionally or unintentionally, use to express their views. Omima al-Khamis, for instance, in *Sea-wafted Women*, attempts to subtly resist the elitist Najdi discourse – if not destabilize that central region's tribal thinking entirely – by giving voice and fictional space to the displaced and émigré characters that she portrays. Qmasha al-Olayyan implicitly challenges gendered roles of marriage and motherhood using the 'ugly plot' to raise questions in her readers' minds about the fate of women who fall out of the marriage enterprise, raising questions about patriarchal values that objectify a woman's body by equating her worth with that of her appearance. Badriya al-Beshir, in *Hend and the Soldiers*, engages in a harsh critique of the mother figure for being an accomplice of patriarchal power and for reproducing forms of oppression and discrimination within the family, distancing the daughter character from her mother as a means of denouncing the set of masculine values reproduced and nourished by mothers in what amounts, in Showalter's words, to 'matrophobia'.[1] Finally, I look at Maha al-Jahni's *The Cloak*, about the *'abaya* – an emblem of Saudi women's identity, modesty and propriety – which in her book is turned into a symbol of feminist fantasy of empowerment and solidarity.

The 'Battlefield' between Nymphs and Queens: Omima al-Khamis – *Sea-wafted Women*

Omima al-Khamis,[2] in her novel *Baḥryāt* (Sea-wafted Women) from 2006,[3] explores and evaluates the dynamics of the traditional Najdi family – fetishized through the eyes of the omniscient narrator and three Levantine women who have come to Riyadh (the heart of Saudi Arabia) as, respectively, concubine, wife and teacher. The novel draws our attention to a number of relationships: women and tribal law, the conflict between local Najdi and the 'sea-wafted' women, and the latter's relationship with their mother countries. It also raises questions in the reader's mind as to what al-Khamis wants her novel to withhold and what she attempts to offer. Who is she siding with? Is she vindicating the sea-wafted women at the expense of the Najdis? Focusing on the latter part of the novel helps to answer this. I argue that, in documenting the traumatic journeys of the protagonists and those around them, the author critiques outdated traditions in Najd and the Levant, articulating a feminist critique of these societal norms.

This explains why a significant amount of narrative space is devoted to the second wife of Saleh Al-Ma'abal, Bahijah, who was thrust into a harem-like old mud house in pre-oil Saudi Arabia. Her early separation, as a concubine, from her mother and family in Syria brings to light elements of melancholy, alienation and a failure to assimilate into her new surroundings. The novel opens with the narrator's voice depicting Bahijah's alienation and difference from the others:

Riyadh 1954
She was glowing and radiant, her chestnut hair parting glimmered underneath her dark lace veil, which was draped lightly, brushing her high cheekbones. She was out of place, lacking harmony with her surroundings. Bahijah was a luminous alien, in a muddy brick house, located on the Almaable's farm at the southern tip of Riyadh. [...]
Bahijah's presence attracted onlookers. She was a magnet to the nosiness of the women surrounding her. The women stopped their faint feminine whispers, quiet burble, prayers, and mumblings. They became engaged by the festive colors that were fueled by Bahijah. The tones of her voice and her fair complexion were not in harmony with the earthy matt colors around her.[4]

Here, Bahijah is 'the axial point around which the actions of the novel circulate' in the sense that she 'attracts the main concerns and debates which the novel is meant to raise'[5] – mainly focused around her clash with patriarchal Najdi tradition. This makes the stream-of-consciousness technique that *Sea-wafted Women* adopts ideal for the purpose. Hence, going through Bahijah's thoughts with a fine-tooth comb produces what Gloria Anzaldúa calls *mestiza* or border consciousness: a 'third space' identity (Chicana in Anzaldúa's case; Levantine in al-Khamis') and what Norma Alarcon calls the 'site of multiple voicing'.[6] Anzaldúa's borderlands consciousness emerges from a subjectivity structured by multiple determinants – gender, class, sex – in competing cultures and racial identities.⁷ If we accept that Anzaldúa's *mestiza* 'third space' identity is crucial for the discourse of minorities by its exclusion of some women – mainly, the locals – and the inclusion of foreigners, we can read the discursive shifting of power and meaning within this narrative and how it is capable of 'reconfiguring and recentering itself depending on the forms of oppression to be confronted'.⁸ Curiously, al-Khamis skilfully transforms the pain of living in the borderlands and the resulting 'in-between-ness' into a discourse of power, if not change. More precisely, the 'third space' or 'contact zone' identities created in the novel provide a space for friction and social/cultural exchange. For instance, by choosing Bahijah to be a central character in *Sea-wafted Women*, the narrative attempts to chronicle her rebellion against both cultures (Levantine and, more so, Najdi) and what has been oppressed in each. For Bahijah, who lives with her family-in-law, 'being home' with them means repressing her pale-skinned, vivacious, Levantine self. The narrative records Bahijah's repressed consciousness, which is split between her refusal to remain silent in the face of the matriarch Um Saleh's censure and what was seen as inappropriate in Najdi traditions at the time. The narrator notes,

> Her mother in-law kept telling her to be quiet, to calm down and lower her voice, to blend with the muted background, but Bahijah was silent for few moments and then not so long after taking a deep breath, like a colorful fish thrown on a sand dune, she started to talk again.

Bahijah's momentary silence echoes Anzaldúa's words: 'Petrified, she can't respond, her face caught in the spaces between the different worlds she inhabits.' The repeatedly contrasted 'home' of origin and the new 'home' of the sea-wafted woman create a struggle in Bahijah, one that is aligned with a configuration of empowering motifs and an ironic representation. Thus, the passage above captures Bahijah's bewilderment, and then her attempt to shun the sharp surveillance of tribal society. For instance, the motif of a fish in most cultures denotes birth, rebirth and transformation; used in this context, it signifies the death and rebirth of Bahijah's spirit every time she is confronted with cultural limitations – preserved and regulated by her mother-in-law. This symbolic rebirth is transformed into a discourse of power, which transpires in the narrative through Bahijah's refusal to abide by Najdi traditions and by choosing to continue her chatter instead of 'blend(ing) with the muted group'.

The discourse of power is further emphasized by the alliances that Bahijah makes with other foreign women in Riyadh and the creation of a community within another, larger, community. Hence, the 'chorus' of women in al-Khamis' novel expands with others like the fellow-Levantine Souad, Bahijah's sister-in-law, who is trapped in a loveless marriage; Rehab, a Palestinian teacher who came to Riyadh with her father acting as her guardian (*maḥram*);

the German Ingrid; and the Abyssinian (Ethiopian) Mariama. This group of women is given voice to tell other stories that are capable of disrupting the dominant Najdi discourse and of shifting the characters' identities from powerlessness to power, and their marginality 'into a powerful space' in the dynamic interplay of local and global, as defined by Stuart Hall.[9] As such, problematizing Bahijah's difference and her failure to integrate with her in-laws produces a discourse that evades the binary split to construct a third element/space, through which the reader is familiarized with the struggle that Levantine women went through at various points in Arabia's history. This act of 'familiarizing' the reader is definitely a conducive narrative tool simply because, to borrow Melissa Wallace's words, it 'give[s] voice to minority cultures, bringing the silenced to the attention of the masses'.[10] Wallace's 'friction/contact space' is further avowed by the narrator's denunciation of Bahijah's mother-in-law, the 'first wife' in her new family, and other local women, creating a division between the local and the sea-wafted women.

In this way, al-Khamis stresses the difference between Bahijah and other women in the family and takes oppression/discrimination as the main constituent of her identity, which leads to the naming of other kinds of victimization (based on colour, class and culture). While piling up forms of oppression could be a weak point for a novel, this discourse finds its own strength in the dialectical analysis – that is, oppression generating its antithesis: multiple richness and power centred on difference.[11] Hence, Bahijah's difference is repeatedly underpinned by the narrators' remarks on her 'snow white' beauty and the way in which '[h]er white skin is too intense among the darker skinned women of Najd, while her cheerful and chattering personality makes her stand out among other less beautiful and dull women of the Ma'bal tribe'.[12] Not surprisingly, Bahijah is portrayed in the first part of the novel as someone who strives for cultural integration but whose attempts are doomed: she is still treated as the 'Other' and called *Shamyah* (a derogatory expression for Levantine woman) even after the birth of her son, Muhammad. However, her otherness intensifies with the arrival of her younger son, Musa'ad, who has inherited his maternal uncle's looks and complexion. She pities him when she hears the family call him names like '*Shawerma* vendor' and 'tomato' in reference to his red cheeks and foreign, Levantine looks.

If we read the novel more carefully, we can follow the sea-wafted women's insights into a multilayered network of cultural and gender relations – specifically when the narrator recounts what these women feel and what their tribal new surroundings have denied them or have left unspoken:

> They were the seafarers who enjoyed mastering the mermaid's private language and the hidden sounds of nymphs packed and exported to the desert in the middle of the Arabian Peninsula.[13]

We are told that what binds the sea-wafted women is the secret that they share of 'a private language' and a bumpy journey that no one understands but them; the narrator adds, 'the 'nymphs' were 'packed and exported' by their families, all the way to the desert'. In this paragraph, the authorial voice incriminates both cultures for treating these women as mere 'mermaids' or 'nymphs' – symbols of beauty and femininity that are turned into a commodity to be bought and sold in the more affluent marriage markets of Arabia.

Through the characters' multiple positioning, alienated from their 'mother culture', they are also 'alien in the dominant culture, the woman of *pale* color does not feel safe within the inner life of her Self'[14] (my italics). Caught in this 'third space' identity, or what al-Khamis characterizes as 'the upper layers of the atmosphere', the narrative chronicles Bahijah's alienation from, if not her rebellion against, her 'mother culture' too:

> She went to Syria several times with her children, but found she had become an alien, the eyes of her extended family always remaining fixed on her bags and those gifts that she may have brought from Saudi Arabia, for a queue of well-wishers who expected to have a place on her gift list.
>
> Her continuous bewilderment and alienation kept her suspended in the upper layers of the atmosphere that separate the Arabian Peninsula from the Levant. Always knowing that her grave will be in Riyadh.[15]

Similarly, her sister-in-law Souad recalls how she was hastily married to Sa'ad:

> When the bridegroom came from oil-wealthy Saudi Arabia, the parents did not ask much about his details. But her Uncle Ibrahim, seeing Souad's family busy preparing her bags to go, said in surprise 'Ask him about his background, his situation. To me the man looks old, used, and creased. So make further investigation about him before you pass Souad to him.'[16]

Al-Khamis uses the metaphors of 'gifts' and being 'oil-wealthy' in reference to the sea-wafted women in order to explore social injustices, commenting on how those women did not have the choice or freedom to reject their marriage proposals. In particular, Bahijah's and Souad's feelings of exploitation and alienation from both their 'home culture' and the dominant Najdi culture is unmissable, and only strengthens their exclusion and marginality. The latter state – known to be 'the most dangerous form of oppression',[17] as noted by Iris Marion Young – is a major narrative theme in this novel, evident in the sea-wafted women's powerlessness in the face of tribal laws.

The significance of space as a situational identity marker in the *Sea-wafted Women* is unmissable. Each situation in the novel foregrounds different aspects of Bahijah and Souad, a reminder of Fieldman's observation 'empowering or limiting [them] in ways that shift according to [their] location'. For example, when they first arrive in Riyadh, both women are depicted as inferior to the Ma'abal family, and the axis of class and colour vulnerability are foregrounded; while other constituents of their identity such as gender remain in the structural background. In contrast, when they are with their families in the Levant, both are portrayed as a source of financial relief; the constituent of wealth is foregrounded while other aspects of their identity such as gender and colour linger in the background.

More specifically, Bahijah was taken as a concubine and only elevated to the status of 'wife' after having her first son. The narrator explains that 'Saleh's passion for her was his secret, which was buried in the depths of his heart like a congenital defect or scar.'[18] The unequivocal image created of Saleh's love for Bahijah as a 'scar to be hidden' signifies a tension between desire and social norms. The author's use of the word 'secret' denotes a fantasy of sorts – and, here, I find Butler's analysis of Foucault's perspective on the psychic life illuminating:

> The social norms that work on the subject to produce its desires and restrict its operation do not operate unilaterally. They are not simply imposed and internalized in a given form. Indeed, no norm can operate on a subject without the activation of a fantasy and, more specifically, the phantasmatic attachment to ideals that are at once social and psychic.[19]

Butler goes on to explain that engaging in relations that might trigger social condemnation can sometimes be the reason for desire in a relationship, or what Foucault describes as the 'opprobrium it promises', which, as in the case of Saleh, 'acts as a defence against another sort of sexual practice that is feared or disavowed'.[20] The significance of this Foucauldian analysis for this novel lies in the fact that Bahijah acts not only as the fantasy for Saleh but also as the one who brings him joy. His first/current wife, Modi, is demonized; she is depicted as having 'black frizzy braid[s]' and 'stubby fat fingers, short legs, and quick, short steps that made her seem hesitant, her steps on top of each other like a timid hedgehog'.[21] Indeed, by staging Modi's ugliness in this scene, the author attempts to vindicate Saleh for taking up another wife, while also mocking patriarchal laws that attach a high value to women's desirability – the currency on which women rely to safeguard their marriages. For Foucault, there is no desire outside of discourse and no discourse freed of power relations. He writes, 'discourse can be both an instrument and effect of power, but also a hindrance, a stumbling block, a point of resistance and a starting point for an opposing strategy'.[22] Thus, the discursive shifting of power and meaning within such derogatory references in the narrative place Modi out of power's matrix, since desire cannot be inscribed without this 'power-relation'. No matter how much the pious Saleh tries to be fair between his wives, he drifts towards the Levantine beauty and, on Modi's night, he 'came in, sleepy and drowsy, threw himself on the bed beside her, keeping his body stiff and lifeless, away from Modi's fidgety body'.[23]

And just like Bahijah, the modern Souad was hidden from her in-laws until she had her first son; she was then allocated a small villa in the Ma'abal compound. If Bahijah rebelled against Najdi traditions, Souad on her part failed to love her drunken husband, Sa'ad al-Ma'bal, and surrendered instead to courtly love with the character Met'ib. But by turning the sea-wafted Souad into a site of conflict, following Met'ib's inappropriate advances towards her – and by having the third-person narrative in the novel interfere with the course of events – patriarchal power is not only questioned but also subverted. The narrator interferes, adding a layer of intrigue: 'Where has all the romance gone; the whispering and sneaking into her window and peeking at her. Despite her initial attraction, all Souad can see now is a primitive hungry animal; the hunger that she sees in the eyes of vegetable street venders.'[24] Staging Met'ib as a 'hungry animal' who resembles the 'street vendors' is, in a way, an attempt to disgrace the power that continues to marginalize Souad as both a foreigner and a woman. The symbolic value of such references registers the author's feminist critique of societal norms that condones poor behaviour in men and holds women accountable for everything. This feminist leaning is further injected into the narrative with Souad's unexpected visit to Met'ib's wife, Nawal – a visit portrayed as 'a battlefield', into which 'Souad was coming [...] with all her munitions, her fresh skin, shining hair, full lips, marble neck.'[25] In contrast, Nawal was like a queen:

> The queen commanded the space around her throne, with her elegant home, her dreams, the riots of her children, and her degree from the University of London; not only that but her long-standing dream of a high position, and the empowering of women, complaining about the lot of women of lower ranks, denigrating the dolls and concubines, who made their priority the winning of a man's heart.[26]

The authorial voice takes control of the narrative at this point to pass on its central message: the importance of women's education and empowerment in battling tribal issues and gender inequality. Each situation and space of the novel is employed to foreground the different axes of women's identity: beauty and commodification in the nymphs – Bahijah and Souad – and substance and power in the educated women – Rehab and Nawal. The author succeeds in constructing a new social reality that fosters the importance of women's rights to education, work and success outside the traditional gender roles of marriage by referring to Nawal as a 'queen'; a symbol that acts as a marker of a nascent Saudi female identity. This situation instigates a feeling of shame and inadequacy in Souad, which compels her to abruptly end her visit to Nawal.

Although *Sea-wafted Women* dwells on the dilemma of Levantine women who lived in pre-oil Najd/Riyadh, which by default means reproducing stereotypical and patriarchal gender norms, it nonetheless subtly produces a parallel feminist discourse, that is, the discourse of positionality, more specifically, what Susan Friedman calls 'situationality':

> Each situation presumes a certain setting as site for the interplay of different axes of power and powerlessness. One situation might make a person's gender most significant; another, the person's race; another, sexuality or religion or class. So while the person's identity is the product of multiple subject positions, these axes of identity are not equally foregrounded in every situation. Change the scene, and the most relevant constituents of identity come into play.[27]

This discourse of situationality culminates in the 'Battlefield' scene, to draw the reader's attention to the role of women's emancipation in producing healthier societies and communities. This notion is further avowed through the story of the third sea-wafted woman, Rehab, who has come to the Saudi capital as a teacher after a failed love affair in Beirut. Her education, alertness and the choices she makes in her new life shape her destiny – from teaching in the desert-like Riyadh of the 1970s to accepting one-sided love with and, later, marriage to Omar al-Hadrami, the uneducated Al-Ma'abal chauffeur. Despite their differences, they are portrayed as 'mastering their harmonious life dance', of completing each other. With Rehab's help and encouragement, Omar becomes a successful businessman. The narrative explains, 'Omar was able to open five branches of his stores in Riyadh, Jeddah and al-Khobar. At the same time, Rehab taught six generations of young women, who conquered the illiteracy demon.'[28]

This new text transforms the relation between art and sociopolitics from instrumental to transversal and demolishes the traditional hierarchy that turns art into a mere support for a specific discourse. Although the content of *Sea-wafted Women* is critical of futile cultural laws, destabilizing, as it is, the elitist Najdi discourse, it is neither celebrated nor endorsed for its subtle feminist properties. It remains in the margins, as a 'space of weak power, but it is a space of power', a reminder of Stuart Hall's words: 'Anybody who cares for what is creatively emergent in the contemporary arts will find that it has something to do with the languages of the margins, and this trend is increasing.'[29]

'Mirror, Mirror on the Wall ...': Qmasha al-Olayyan and the 'Ugly Plot' – *The Virgin Wife*

For many readers, the turning point of Qmasha al-Olayyan's 1993 collection of short stories, *al-Zawjah al-'Athra'* (The Virgin Wife), comes when Sara, one of her principal characters, is gazing at her reflection and seeing nothing but ugliness. She invokes the name of God to express her despair: 'God, why am I this ugly, why didn't you give me a touch of beauty, why do I look like a disfigured monkey next to my sister Maryam, why is she beautiful and I am not?'[30] This mirror scene is crucial, not only because it forces Sara to face her body and scrutinize her looks alongside those of her sister but also because, from a Lacanian standpoint, the mirror has the psychological symbolic value of alienation of the subject from itself – resulting in rejection of one's self. This rejection can be found in the language of hatred, the dramatic staging of Sara's appearance and the freakish images in the text that reduce her identity to that of a 'disfigured monkey' and 'ugly Sara'. Such fictional devices underline the author's take on women's gendered roles in marriage and motherhood, juxtaposing them with the external forces of aesthetic ideals that the protagonist has to navigate while debating women's futures outside the traditional gender roles. The author effectively chooses the spatial and temporal thresholds of the mirror scene to mark the conflict brewing within Sara. It forms a climactic point in the narrative, depicting Sara as anxiously getting ready to attend a wedding and signalling, there and then, extreme hostility towards her reflection. Jacques Lacan's concept of the 'mirror stage' is illuminating:

> Repeated and reinforced by the subject in his/her relationship with the external world. The imaginary, therefore, is not a developmental phase – it is not something that one goes through and grows out of – but remains at the core of our experience. As the sense of original unity and coherence in the mirror phase is an illusion, there is a fundamental disharmony regarding the ego. The ego is essentially a terrain of conflict and discord; a site of continual struggle.[31]

Freud further explains that when the ego is split, it creates a 'critical agency' that keeps judging the subject and diminishing their self-regard, the ego debasing itself and raging against itself.[32] Thus, in a gesture of melancholy, which includes the prospect of reclaiming agency, Sara is portrayed as questioning the justice of God, voicing her bitter complaint and adding another dimension to the protagonist's general expression of pain, helplessness, hopelessness and suffering. This presents what Freud defines as melancholia: 'a form of grief that differs from mourning in that it is a "morbid pathological disposition" with the potential to create harmful and even dangerous consequences for the melancholiac'.[33] Al-Oayan in this short story manages to assert multiple subject positions not only through storytelling but also through establishing a relationship between fiction and sociopolitics. Sara in this regard is turned into a site of 'multiple subject position' which emerged gradually from the discourse of 'multiple oppression' in the late 1980s. Friedman defines this discourse

As the intersection of different and often competing cultural formations of race, ethnicity, class, sexuality, religion, and national origin, et cetera. Within this paradigm the self is not singular; it is multiple.[34]

In *The Virgin Wife* the author succeeds in documenting the misery and confusion of a woman against the backdrop of a conservative religious discourse. Sara, the protagonist, is categorized not only as an 'ugly woman', but also a 'Third World woman', who 'grew up in Arabia at the height of *saḥwa*'; she suffers from 'low self-esteem' and 'unaffectionate parents'. Through a God-directed soliloquy, Sara's ugliness is amplified and her vulnerability is exposed to the reader – revealing a yearning for love, selfhood and a meaningful life.

If we read the story carefully, we can identify that Sara's melancholy stems from her feelings of not fitting what de Beauvoir dubs the *eternal feminine* ideal, resulting in a loss that occurs on her subconscious level and dictates her conscious, damaging self-talk. In other words, the psyche of the melancholic Sara has been disfigured without her realizing it. This fear and hatred of the body locks the protagonist into a life of misery, negatively impacting on her judgement of herself and family as well as her choices in life because it is sustained by aesthetic ideals of the 'other' – or, equally, her sister – producing a tension and frustration in the self. This tension is problematized through the authorial voice that takes control of the narrative to pass on the central message: Sara's alertness to how her sister is favoured by their parents and treated as a prize of sorts. The narrator expounds, 'Maryam sits next to her father in the front seat of the car, so everyone can see his beautiful daughter, and she [Sara] sits with her mother in the back seat', remarking of Sara that 'her eyes are small, her nose is big and crooked just like that of a falcon' and concluding that 'her big mouth and thick lips, her pale face and kinky hair [ensure that there is] nothing beautiful about her face'.

Staging Maryam as the archetype for a patriarchy – the angelic daughter – in contrast to her ugly and monster-like sister is significant. At a first glance, one might think that those images resonate with 'paradigmatic polarities'[35] of 'angel' and 'monster' that are inherited from male literature (Saudi and otherwise) – images that could only generate a paralyzing subjection that goes against the feminist project of reclaiming the female body from the patriarchy. Such images were often reproduced by female writers who made no attempt to deconstruct or revise these polarizing representations of women. This surface negation of the feminist project is capable of producing an implicit meaning: which relies on the reader to infer the intended meaning or assumption lying behind the discourse. In this sense, 'paradigmatic polarities' are employed to serve the purpose of the narrative – and that is, to show the worth of Sara in the eyes of her family and their estimation of her value in the marriage market. As Julian Henrique puts it, 'the subject itself is the effect of a production, caught in the mutually constitutive web of social practices, discourses and subjectivity, its reality is the tissue of social relations'.[36]

According to the above excerpt, Sara had to negotiate the best options available to her in her specific familial/social situation. Such choices are sometimes forced on the subject, since the subject positioning (ugliness/jealousy/spinsterhood) makes her chosen action the only possible one. Thus, when Sara receives a marriage proposal, her family hastily agrees without taking the time to ask about the groom. After a few days of marriage and odd episodes, Sara is shocked to find out that her husband Sai'd has undergone female-to-male transgender surgery, a change that has left him miserable at not being able to cope with his new form and role as a man. The story ends with Sara getting a divorce and Sai'd reverting to his original sex; the two end up as girlfriends. If we agree that the author was simply echoing the dominant male discourse, then what do the excessively freakish images suggest? And what is the symbolic value of juxtaposing the 'ugly' Sara and transgendered Sai'd? I argue that the almost grotesque images created of Sara are conflated with her marriage to Sai'd, both described as outside the binary gender roles/framework. As such, al-Olayyan turns the bodies of the hypothetical husband and wife into a feminist discourse echoing Judith Butler's elucidation of Foucault's theory on subjection:

> For Foucault, then, the disciplinary apparatus produces subjects, but as a consequence of that production, it brings into discourse the conditions for subverting that apparatus itself. In other words, the law turns against itself and spawns versions of itself which oppose and proliferate its animating purposes. The strategic question for Foucault is, then, how can we work the power relations by which we are worked, and in what direction?[37]

The ability of ugliness and transgenderism to negotiate the thin line between spoken and unspoken social boundaries, and to produce a counter narrative – an exclamation mark – raises questions about social order that can be interpreted as resistance to the natural flow of social gender dynamics. In this sense, Sara and her husband are depicted as occupying the margins of society. Therefore, Sara's marriage to Sai'd functions as a double act of rebellion against radicalism, which insists on limited roles for women.

Reading al-Olayyan's short story within the historical context of the early 1990s – that is, the peak of the *saḥwa* – I would say that her use of the 'ugly plot' instead of the expected courtship or marriage narrative perhaps unconsciously flags a feminist concern over the terrible fate of that awaits women who fall out of the marriage enterprise and its supposed fairytale 'happily-ever-after' ending. Also, given the nature of melancholy, which is characterized by 'profoundly painful dejection [and] abrogation of interest in the outside world', it is not surprising to see a gloomy attitude in al-Olayyan and her representation of women. This is evident in the character of Sara, who is seen as a topos – a theme that is part of the literary engagement with the dominant discourse. Such representations, I argue, afford ways of criticizing oppressive traditions as a way of challenging normative culture. Thus, one could say that al-Olayyan 'speaks the unspeakable' through the trope of female ugliness, broaching it as a marker of social and familial failure, portraying her protagonist as doomed to punishment and a life of spinsterhood. Hence, ugliness functions as a marker of passive resistance to the dominant discourse, through which the author speaks back to power.

The Mother, an Agent of the Patriarchy: Badriya al-Beshir – *Hend and the Soldiers*

> In my mind, God assumed my mother's face, always angry, always threatening; the fire he promised was, on the whole, not much different from the pinches that her fingers burned on the insides of our tender thighs.[38]

Written in 2006, this notorious passage, in which Badriya al-Beshir[39] compares her mother's anger to that of God, caused a great deal of anger among Islamic hardliners – to the extent that she was refused entry into some Gulf states because of 'profanity'.[40] Daring to do the forbidden, the author's imagining of God's face and her hostility towards the mother figure has offended many religious groups who consider this to be un-Islamic. After all, God has commanded 'man' to show kindness to his parents in a verse from Hadith in which, in particular, Prophet Mohammad stresses total obedience to the matriarch: 'Your heaven lies under the feet of your mother'.[41] Al-Beshir, being the controversial writer that she is, breaks away from conformity and the official discourse – and never more so than in *Hend we al-'Askar* (Hend and the Soldiers), from which the passage above comes, in which she points a finger at the mother figure, blaming her for internalizing sexism and gender discrimination. Hend's relationship with her mother takes the form not of direct oppression that calls for resistance but more of a harsh critique, through which the author intends to expose the role of the matriarch in reproducing and consolidating the multiple faces of patriarchy and in propagating what Michel Foucault terms 'docile bodies' – that is, the control of women's behaviour to maintain existing gender hierarchies between men and women. This is accompanied by accounts of being continually watched by a male superior, of being pushed into the private sphere and of having a strange sense of fear of men and the outside world. Hend remembers,

> when I was young, I would dream of going to school because it was the only place to play. Men believe that houses are for women, and its fences are their borders. With time women got used to those houses, believing that it's the only secure place for them in the world. That men outside the house are monsters, and would attack them if they leave the house. That's why women in my country age prematurely, they get depressed, and fear illness; illness of husbands and children.[42]

It is worth noting that the image of the mother as victim as well as promoter of the patriarchal culture is a bonding factor between this novel and Hana Hejazi's *Emra'tān* (Two Women – Chapter 4). However, this work by al-Beshir problematizes the role of the mother within the family, giving it a larger textual space than the aforementioned works; here, the matriarch is held accountable for complicity in patriarchal tyranny. *Hend and the Soldiers* goes over the protagonist's life and her mother with a fine-tooth comb, using a retrospective narrative of past incidents in an attempt to evaluate social practices and tribal laws that weaken women's status in the family and society. The novel opens with the protagonist Hend expressing her sorrow:

> When rain falls on the thirsty Najd, people receive it with a frenzied joy. Najdi rain is by nature light and gentle and scarce. The smell of rain stirred the dried branches of my heart. It hurt to feel them breaking inside my ribs. As the parched leaves of memory fell, distant sorrows began to surface. My chest tight, I went to wash myself before a short prayer.
> As I opened my bedroom door, the smell of coffee wafted from the kitchen; it spread throughout the house like fire on a hot summer day to greet my nose.[43]

It is clear that the novel is rich in symbolism. In this text, the author uses spatial and temporal memories, shuttling the text between present and past, reality and romance using symbols such as rain and coffee – both cherished in Arabia's traditions. However, the author emphasizes the importance of coffee making in Arabian households and the habit of brewing and mixing it with cardamom to give it the desired colour and flavour. Coffee in this context thus serves as a symbol for both women and memory, with the former described as sharing stories and connecting around a cup of the beverage. This tradition is carefully maintained by the character of Amoush, the black servant – a former slave who, despite King Faisal's official abolition of slavery in the 1960s, has remained with the family, proving that laws can change but entrenched hierarchies take much longer to shift. Amoush is depicted as a repository of knowledge, telling stories and connecting the dots as she brews her coffee, making sure that a tale is tweaked and never told twice in quite the same way.

The tension between the protagonist, Hend, and her mother, Haila, is thus felt brewing throughout the novel. Hend recalls a poignant moment in her childhood when she tried to sing her mother a love song, a tune she had learned from school, thinking that she would have a connection with her mother. She remembers,

> I hoped my mother would throw her arms around me after she had heard the song; I even thought of putting the baby down so that she could hug me properly, with body and soul. Instead she took the big spoon out of the pot and brought it to my face. 'Get out of my way before I whack you on the head with this spoon'.
> My mind had learned to deny such events to protect me from pain. Later it did the same with all that was unromantic in my life by projecting the opposite image. On this occasion, it told me that Mother was not at all angry with me or my song; she was angry with Ibrahim and his silly crying. For she also said, 'May Allah not let you live one more day. Your brother has shattered my head with his screaming!'[44]

The mother's favouring of Hend's little brother Ibrahim in this paragraph is unmissable. Throughout the novel, there is censure for the mother, who fails Hend on many levels: as a daughter who is suppressed and denied the small pleasures of life and, later on, as a divorced mother who is forced to stay in a miserable marriage longer than she should have. Hend is surrounded by real and metaphorical soldiers – her father, a sergeant; her ex-husband Mansour, a lieutenant; and her little brother, Ibrahim, a potential *jihadi*, as we later see – all of whom impede her battle for agency and independence. These characters are part of an army of men surrounding the protagonist along with her male co-workers and members of the Committee for the Prevention of Vice and Promotion of Virtue menacing her throughout the novel. This web of power dynamics shows how gender is a cultural construct – a code that makes the female in certain social positions bear the social meaning of biological difference.

Al-Beshir skilfully draws a cycle of events that shows the mother Haila's negative impact on Hend, letting her down on multiple occasions – one being her relationship with her first love, whom she met through her friend Mudhi, a platonic affair that never gets beyond exchanges of flowers, pictures and midnight phone calls. The sole exception occurs when he returns from a trip to London and she can't resist seeing him. When he knocks on the door to see her, in the middle of the night, her sister stands guard in case a member of the family wakes and sees them. Hend recalls,

> I put on a green dress with white flowers and applied khol and lipstick. I waited behind the slightly open door, having turned the lights off so that no one passing by would recognize him. He drove around the house a few times to make sure there was no one who could see us. When he saw the light flicker on and off (the signal we had agreed upon), he slowly drove to our door. I heard his car hissing quietly as it drew nearer, so I opened the door a little wider and waited there as I heard the car door being closed and glimpsed a white thobe[45] approaching the door. [...]
> Everything about his presence blossomed with love. He looked alive and vibrant, as opposed to the stillness of his features in the photos, which I had hidden in a drawer in my room. [...]
> He placed his palms on my ears and turned my head toward the light to see my lip [...] Before I could look into his eyes to see his intent, his face had already shaded mine in a kiss.[46]

The author succeeds in staging the happiness of Hend on seeing her love, and the details of their first kiss, which proliferate alongside delineations of her fear, anxiety and worry about her family. The ubiquitous, subjective and personal 'I' of the protagonist is intertwined with the social and the political – pointing towards female–male interactions in a tribal and patriarchal culture, with the tribe functioning as a moral agency 'compelling individuals to limit the articulation of [their] desire'.[47] Through the resulting 'side glances', the author reinforces the idea that love and desire are governed by 'tribal and patriarchal laws [that] have regulated [their] rhetoric [...] since pre-Islamic times, so that the regulatory system can control the individual in the name of polity, modesty and honour', as Moneera al-Ghadeer observes.[48]

Hend in this love passage is presented as the site of multiple subject positions, in which the axes of adventure, love and beauty are foregrounded, while other constituents of her identity such as fear of her mother and of transgressing societal moral codes remain in the structural background. Categories such as a 'beautiful woman', 'Third World woman' are not by themselves parameters of a complicated multifaceted identity. But, just like Al-Olayyan's protagonist, Sara, Hend grew up in Arabia at the height of *sahwa*, she is also a divorced woman, a column writer and a woman who fell in love against the will of her family. Her identity sits at the crossroads of many different formations of power and powerlessness; forged through engagement of the self with the tribal order. The fact that her first kiss is remembered, following Hend's divorce, in a moment of longing for the good old days prior to her marriage to Mansour, emphasizes both the protagonist's feelings of loss and sorrow towards her first lover and her denunciation of social practices and tribal laws.

In fact, if we read the novel more carefully, we can follow its multilayered network of cultural and political gender relations. The narrative recapitulates what a girl like Hend desires and what her tribe/family/mother wants – that is, the thin line between the spoken and unspoken social boundaries, which Foucault sees as a 'power [that] cannot be made fully concrete even by analyzing the normative or punitive apparatuses of any complex relation of power and knowledge',[49] adding 'that one may sometimes transgress, and occasionally transform, but never escape'.[50] Following Foucault, then, the unspoken but 'always operative' regulating system represses love and desire for different reasons – one being issues of class, or *nasab* (lineage), a major cultural issue in Arabia. So, when Hend is caught by her mother flirting with a man on the phone, she is henceforth treated with suspicion and subjected to discipline and surveillance. The author describes how her protagonist is constantly being watched in case she is 'fooling around'; her mother Haila cautions her, saying, 'Don't even dream of being able to marry a man you've flirted with over the phone at night.'[51] Hend almost loses her position as a 'good' girl, and in order to retain this position she has to give up her love object and succumb to her family's choice of husband. By doing so, Hend – temporarily – becomes a prisoner of the patriarchal discourse, which produces 'docile bodies' and the definition of 'good girl'. In this regard, Butler provides an illuminating psychoanalytical angle on Foucault's formation of the subject; she notes,

> If, following Foucault, we understand power as forming the subject as well, as providing the very condition of its existence and the trajectory of its desire, then power is not simply what we oppose but also, in a strong sense, what we depend on for our existence and what we harbor and preserve in the beings that we are [...] subjection consists precisely in this fundamental dependency on a discourse we never chose but that, paradoxically, initiates and sustains our agency.[52]

For Butler, subjection is something 'done to us', and which we sometimes seek to escape or avoid. Much the same state has overtaken al-Beshir's protagonist, in the sense that she is embroiled in a discourse that she never chose yet cannot escape. This discourse reveals the wide generational division between mother and daughter, a division that is further exacerbated by the family's decision to marry Hend off to Mansour. She struggles, however, to forge any connection with him, and ends up as a divorced mother. The failure of Hend's marriage to Mansour is a challenge to the cruel matriarch and the oppressive cultural inheritance passed on from one generation of mothers to the next, teaching successive generations of young women to be obedient in the face of tribal laws. One could, however, view Hend's divorce as symbolizing the conflict between herself and established social paradigms.

By drawing the reader's attention both to her protagonist's breaking of tribal laws and to her mixed feelings of fear, excitement and joy over her first kiss, the author registers her disruption of a male discourse that has overlooked women's voices and feelings. It also points to the rise of new texts and voices that merge the private and public with the personal and sociopolitical; transgressing established gender boundaries.

Al-Beshir skilfully creates the image of the cruel mother figure who preserves patriarchal tyranny within her family. However, this character is also (partly) vindicated and assigned a reason for her cruelty and submission. As a little motherless girl, Haila was spotted by her distant cousin and future husband, Othman, while she was challenging other boys in their neighbourhood by counting numbers at a fast pace. When he asked the girl her name and she told him, this simple act of replying brought her the misery of an untimely marriage and what amounted to paedophilic treatment at the hands of her much older husband – causing a fundamental shift in her personality from being a bubbly and chatty girl to a silent and stern woman. As a result, throughout the novel Haila blames herself for having told Othman her name. The all-seeing narrator explains, 'It's her sharp tongue that is responsible for what has happened, and what her grandmother warned her of. Nothing would have happened if she [had] stayed silent. It is from that day that she started to hate talking.'[53] The morphing narrator – in this case, no longer anonymous but taking the form of Haila's best friend Amousha – succeeds in explaining the dark side of this mother figure; it is from her that we learn that Haila was an unwilling child bride. Oblivious to what was happening around her, she had been married off to a man 15 years her senior. The author's presentation of Haila's shock and consequent silence denotes not a submissiveness so much as a struggle to manipulate and control the marriage that she has been locked into. She tries to escape her husband twice but is forced to return in the name of tradition and religion, with her grandmother's words still ringing in her ears: 'a woman should be forbearing' and 'should obey her husband'. Haila's experience of what amounts to a marital rape has dramatically changed, if not mutilated, her consciousness and her view of the world.

Throughout *Hend and the Soldiers*, the narrator also keeps the reader attuned to how Hend's brother, Ibrahim, had grown up to be complex, violent and suspicious of everyone around him – especially his sisters. He thus becomes the final piece in the chain of '*Askar* – the 'soldiers' of the novel's title – who, as we mentioned in Chapter 1, are depicted as surrounding Hend like secret policemen in this domestic police-state-in-miniature. Alongside this, the cruel mother also acts as an apologist for her son's extremist behaviour, encouraging in him along the way a sexist attitude towards female members of his family – all in the name of culture and religion.

Hend is portrayed as a modern woman with relatively liberal leanings, who continually compares old conventions, modelled on the figure of her mother, with the new norms of life and rejects them – thus contradicting Virginia Woolf's famous statement, 'We think back through our mothers if we are women.'[54] Al-Beshir inscribes a feminist grievance through 'sidelong glances', in which she challenges the cruel matriarch and the oppressive cultural inheritance. Similarly, in eventually choosing death for Ibrahim the author registers not only her divergence from the dominant religious discourse, but also her prediction that this ideology could not survive. Indeed, it is important to recognize the dialectic between extremist discourse and feminist texts, and to refute the general claim that Saudi women's fiction writing and resistance are incompatible. Reaction to the *sahwa* ideology, and its negative impact on the lives of women, actually became a major theme in the works of female writers in the kingdom after the year 2000. Many Saudi novels of this period feature, somewhere in the background, the figure of a young *jihadi* brother or son – an extremist, who threatens the nuclear family. The fragmented episodes describing Ibrahim's secretive trips to Qassim – in central Saudi Arabia – and other undisclosed destinations progressively unfold a succession of evocative images that stand as a parallel to the authors' inner state, including resistance to all forms of patriarchal surveillance and subjugation. The powerful fragments generated in this fashion create a free space for the reader to identify something broken, suggesting a potential for the fragmented state to be made whole again. Thus, they prepare the ground for speculation on what is about to happen when Hend seeks salvation in Toronto, where she joins her elder brother Fahad, a man of moderate views. In the airport lounge, she glimpses a newspaper article about a terrorist attack that had taken place the previous day and, to her horror, she sees a photograph of the familiar face of Ibrahim – covered with blood but peaceful as never before.

Witchcraft, a Feminist Fantasy of Empowerment: Maha al-Jahni – *The Cloak*

In her 2008 novel *'Abaya* (The Cloak), the author and poet Maha al-Jahni scrutinizes the *'abaya* garment[55] as a marker of women's gender identity, on both metaphorical and functional levels. The *'abaya*, as a garment stipulated by cultural patriarchal hegemonic order, signifies a girl's leap from childhood to womanhood, marking her compliance with cultural and ideological constructions of femininity. In this novel, I argue that al-Jahni turns this emblem of Saudi women's identity, modesty and propriety into the symbol of a feminist fantasy of empowerment and sisterhood.

The narrative structure of *The Cloak* echoes that of Egyptian author 'Ala' al-Aswani's *'Imarat Ya'qubyan* (The Yacoubian Building) of 2002, in which the semi-private space of the eponymous apartment block allows readers to peer closely into its residents' lives, revealing what is normally hidden about a particular fragment of Cairene society. And if the scandalous and much-celebrated *Yacoubian Building* successfully portrayed the decadence and degeneration of postcolonial Egyptian society through the residents living or working in the building, *The Cloak* opts to document the lives of those victimized and underprivileged women – widows, single mothers and oppressed or despairing wives – who, at times of desperation, seek the help of fellow-resident Fetha as an experienced and wise woman, and as a mediator between them and an anonymous sorceress.

The aforementioned choice of setting and cultural narrative sets the stage for al-Jahni to portray Saudi society in microcosm, documenting the struggles that women have to face against the male-oriented, traditional social order of the noughties. Their struggles often take the form not of direct oppression, calling for outright resistance in response, but of reproducing forms of behaviour that consolidate patriarchal oppression and encourage notions of female subjectification – of creating what Foucault dubs 'docile bodies'. It must be noted that spatial dimensions in this novel are extremely restricted owing to the setting of a single apartment building, within which the action is tightly confined. In fact, a lack of movement or change of scene is one of the major disadvantages of this work, making it too monotonous – a dilemma that the author tries to resolve with her narrator's many intrusive comments about the characters and events.

The novel is, however, rich in symbols and metaphors – a point that is clear from the outset in its title (*'Abaya*) and the spatial features of the building depicted. The action opens with a scene involving Fouzia, a miserable wife who is treated disrespectfully by her husband: the omniscient narrator observes, 'she would be found sitting still on a sofa by the balcony, not making a move, for days and nights. Time flies by, and she would still be sitting there'.[56] The image created of Fouzia sitting on the couch, speculating on her husband's time of arrival, represents a point of convergence between the private and public space of her home and the street, between inside and outside, object and subject. She is positioned with her back to the private realm while looking, through an open window, away from her home towards the future as though across a threshold – a symbolic transitional zone across which she would need to move before engaging with the world. The openness of the window allows for both continual surveillance of the public space and a speeding up of events in the narrative: without it, Fouzia would not have spotted her husband's car parked in front of the building an hour before he entered their flat, raising her suspicions of an affair between him and their beautiful neighbour Ghaida. When confronted with what she saw, the husband is depicted as raising his voice and hand, ready to slap Fouzia, but stopped by the sound of his son crying. By introducing Ghaida as a perceived thread, the author creates an "imagined antagonist" for Fouzia, emphasising how even the mere possibility of a second wife can induce anxiety and insecurity in a woman's life within such a social structure. Fouzia's powerlessness and fear is turned into revenge through a feminist fantasy of witchcraft, when she seeks the help of the motherly character Fetha, believing that she could lure back her husband with the power of magic.

This novel's curious mixture of women, space and witchcraft raises an important question about the symbolic value of the 'witch' image. I argue that for these women, witchcraft is presented not only as a saviour but also as a feminist, empowering and solidarity tool. Precisely in the context of Saudi women's discourse of resistance, 'witchcraft' stands as a metaphor for 'power' sought by women who are locked into miserable situations and who, for a variety of different reasons, cannot walk away from their wretched lives. It is noteworthy that the character of Fetha is mysterious enough to fit the image of a feminist fantasy of a 'witch'. Laurel Zwissler makes a distinction between the historical, diabolic witch and the recent, feminist witch: 'The satanic witch as a criminal profile was both morally irredeemable and overwhelmingly gendered as female.'[57] Nevertheless, as Lyndal Roper articulates it, 'the witch is one of the only models of female power within [the] cultural context harboring deep discomfort with women'.[58] Zwissler explains further:

> You don't have to believe that accused witches were engaged in a rival religion or in magical practice to nonetheless believe that they were doing something interesting and threatening to powerful men. Some feminists wanted nothing to do with deities and rituals inspired by Wicca and women's magic movements, but identified with historically accused witches nonetheless. For these activists, witchcraft accusations were paranoid misogynist code for women's skilled abilities, such as healing, midwifery, agricultural knowledge, financial, social, and sexual independence. In this frame, it is irrelevant whether 'witches' were engaged in magic or ritual practice. Instead, 'witch' stands for a woman not properly subservient to patriarchy: a political rebel.[59]

It is not my intention to vindicate the practices of witches; what concerns me here is what they stand for and how the character of Fetha 'the witch' is humanized by the author. For instance, we learn that she is a victim of human trafficking, grabbed by strangers while playing in a field with her sister when she was only six years old. She was then sold to a rich woman, who in turn gave her to a private Syrian doctor; she lived with him and his wife, Lubna, for two years before she was sent to work for Lubna's mother in Jordan. There, she was treated like a maid and constantly made aware of her inferior status. On one of the family's visits to see the mother in Jordan, Fetha begged them to take her back. Reunited with the doctor's family, Fetha learned how to dress, how to make clothes, how to walk and how to style her hair. Flashbacks continue, and the reader learns that when she was 15 and had become a woman she was sold again to a family in the Arabian Peninsula, and worked as a carer for a young prince in one of the palaces. When the prince left for the United States, she escaped the ill-treatment of his mother and, miraculously, reached the house of a princess named Joud, who was famous for freeing victims of trafficking.

Hence, Fetha's identity is turned into a site of multiple oppression and multiple subject positions as, in Friedman's words, 'the intersection of different and competing cultural formations of work, race, ethnicity, class, sex, religion, and national origin'.[60] For instance, as a virtual slave moving from one place to another, empowering or limiting aspects of her identity shift according to her situation. She experiences class vulnerability when treated badly as a maid; conversely, when she moves back to the physician's house, different elements of her identity such as femininity and beauty are foregrounded. Fetha, being a victim of human trafficking and slavery of sorts, reclaims her agency, identity and her name – which was changed by the young prince to Fatin – and turns her oppression into strength. She does this by becoming the mother figure and the undisclosed sorceress who controls the community of women around her in the apartment building – the majority of whom, we learn, are also victims of gender oppression. Throughout *The Cloak*, she is portrayed as a strong character and a good listener to these women. She is attentive to their problems and offers them advice and, on many occasions, witchcraft that she claims to bring from a sorceress.

Interestingly, Ghaida, the single and beautiful neighbour living with her aging mother, is depicted as an independent woman who has never succumbed to Fetha's schemes. As the novel progresses, we learn that Ghaida has been subjected to nuisance pranks by an anonymous woman covered in a black *'abaya* (the 'cloak' of the book's title). The author complicates the relationship between Fouzia and Ghaida by endorsing the image of a playful Ghaida, foregrounding her gender identity in relation to her beauty and depicting her as something of a flirt while muting other axes of her identity such as her career as a nurse. It is only at the end of the novel that we are allowed to peek into her thoughts and acknowledge that she had her worries just like other women in the building:

> If I were from another background, if I had a bigger family, and a protective father, I wouldn't have gone through all this struggle alone, as if I am from a different planet, everyone is anticipating that I will make a small mistake, that I openly reject their old way of thinking, and their miserable life. How can they tolerate a lifeless life? Without comfort? This is a circle that is getting tighter, I am stifled, I don't know what I want and which way to go.[61]

Being beautiful, single and financially independent, however, sets her on a different path from other women.

Despite the novel's varied *dramatis personae*, it is actually Fetha who is the central character: the mother of Soha and the grandmother of the two girls, Nora and Mounira, she is presented as an extremely secretive, reticent and silent character. Her silence nonetheless engenders power, functioning in the context of her past oppression as an act of rebellion against the patriarchal discourse. Foucault comments on the ambiguity of such silence in relation to power:

> Discourses are not once and for all subservient to power or raised up against it, any more than silences are. Discourse transmits and produces power; it reinforces it, but also undermines and exposes it, renders it fragile and makes it possible to thwart it. In like manner, silence and secrecy are shelter for power, anchoring its prohibitions; but they also loosen its hold and provide for relatively obscure areas of tolerance.[62]

Fetha's silence is lessened by flashbacks and her stream-of-consciousness narrative, which fills in the story's gaps. On a similar note, her daughter Soha is given a significant textual space not only to express her trauma as a single mother battling breast cancer but also to denounce the male-dominant culture that allows polygamy. The author intentionally avows Soha's illness – describing how she lost agency over her body and collapsed in front of friends and how she, in an effort to reclaim this agency, communicates her excruciating pain, which she blames on the chemotherapy that she thinks has made her worse. She laments, ' "Do you see what happened to me, they removed my right breast?" As she reveals this, tears ran down her cheeks and her two daughters, who are sitting next to her, start crying too.'[63] The removal of her breast stands as a metaphor for her lost femininity; the narrator points the finger of blame at her husband for not being supportive of his severely ill spouse and, contrary to what most men would do, deciding to take another wife. Even when he is given a small narrative space, describing his visit to see his ailing wife and children, it is to accuse him of abandoning them and to instil antagonism between him and female members of his family – such as his daughters, Nora and Mounira. A tension – indeed, hostility – between the girls and their father is felt brewing in the background of the narrative – a hostility that is extended to almost all men and culminates in the two girls making sweeping generalizations about them: 'men are vague, fathers don't talk, they don't dream like children, they are scary, they are [only] good when it comes to paying family bills [...] men stink'.[64]

Rejection of female subjugation in the context of Arabia is registered through all of *The Cloak*'s female characters – including (unsurprisingly) Fetha, whose observations, monologues and silences in the first part of the book are in fact the author's way of deconstructing the notions of male supremacy and polygamy. For example, the reader is made aware that Fetha despises her son-in-law for abandoning her only daughter, Soha, and for taking another wife – something that she tries to resolve by using witchcraft. However, Soha's husband is not the only male marginalized or treated antagonistically in the novel. The caretaker Um Yousef's husband is disabled, while her son is a mini-patriarch who shouts at the neighbour's little girls when they step out of the building, and subjects Nora to harassment. Similarly, other muted male residents in the block are depicted negatively – like the father of Faṭma, another tenant, who dies later in the novel, leaving his small family to fend for themselves; and the block owner Um Nawaf's son, who is depicted as jobless and cruel to his mother, selfish and greedy. Stereotyping men as monsters is an attempt by the writer to create what Amy Millstone calls 'a climate of sympathy for the women victimized by such men'; Millstone adds (in the context of French feminist theatre), 'Thus the psychological motivation of women who revolt against abusive male authority appears not only understandable but imperative as well'.[65]

Unfortunately, although al-Jahni attempts to create a narrative that moves between two parallel worlds, the real and the magical, she fails to be equally convincing in both – especially when the all-seeing narrator maintains her own vision and perspective on the world. As a result, the interplay between the fantasy and the real in this novel is sustained with subplots that are somewhat confusing, particularly at the beginning, because they leave the reader baffled about the intended meaning – an effect that disrupts the narrative flow. For instance, these multiple subplots involve characters catching glimpses of a woman wearing an *'abaya* leaving unidentified items here and there in the building, and finding the mutilated and diseased body of a cat with a piece of amulet tied to his tail on the roof of the apartment block. This leaves Um Nawaf to conclude, 'Men are strong, they don't need voodoos, that's a woman's scheme.' Although these subplots add a layer of intrigue to the main plot, nonetheless they obstruct its narrative flow. It is only at the end of the novel that we learn about Fetha's sorcery and are able to tie it in with previous incidents that have taken place in the building.

The novel's climax sees the mystery of the *'abaya* resolved, when three of the women decide to keep a close watch on the building: the property owner, Um Nawaf, along with other female occupants of the block, Fouzia and Um Yousef. On hearing suspicious footsteps climbing the stairs one day, they follow the mysterious woman wearing the *'abaya* to the roof of the building, and there they see her casting spells, burning a piece of cloth soaked in old blood and murmuring ambiguous words. The three women are portrayed as standing behind her in disbelief, shocked to find that Fetha herself is the sorceress. Here, al-Jahni builds a powerful case for exposing people's selective adherence to ethics/religious texts that prohibit sorcery while they themselves persist in using it. The women's reactions capture how hypocritical they are on this issue – for example, Fouzia surprises everyone by saying 'yes, you did tell me [once] to bring an egg and rehearse [a] few verses and then break it at Ghaida's doorstep, so that she'll be driven away from our building, but I never thought that you are the one who casts spells, and on this roof!' Um Nawaf retorts, 'I need an explanation, Fetha, why do you practice witchcraft?' Fouzia then suggests that they call the police and have her punished. Fetha looks at them all and says, 'Now you're accusing me of wrongdoing? I am the one who supported you all, I am the one who listened to your problems and helped you deal with them, I am the one who knows all your mishaps and kept your damn secrets, am I wrong?'[66]

She moves closer to Um Nawaf and tells her, 'Do you remember when you came to me devastated over the scandal that could have happened in your old house, and I advised you to buy this building and stay away from that place?' She turns to Um Yousef: 'How many times did you ask me for help and money? How many times did you ask me for an amulet to get rid of your husband's moans? You accuse me of witchcraft now?' Um Yousef replies, 'I never thought you would do this, it is *kufur* – blasphemy!!' Um Nawaf settles the matter saying, 'Um Yousef, you didn't understand? We are all Fetha. This issue should stop here and never be reopened.'[67]

A slave in the past, Fetha has thus turned her multiple oppression into power, agency and individuality that manifest themselves in the other women's submission to her – a reminder that 'individuals are the vehicles of power',[68] as Foucault notes. The building is a female space after all, and Fetha is the true matriarch of that space. Her knowledge about life, about the secrets of these women and their innermost feelings enables her not only to dissuade them at the end from taking action against her but also to renew their sisterhood with the simple words, 'We are all Fetha'.

Notes

1 Elaine Showalter, 'Toward a Feminist Poetics', in Showalter (ed.), *The New Feminist Criticism: Essays on Women, Literature and Theory* (Virago Press Ltd: London, 1986), p. 135.
2 Omima al-Khamis is the daughter of Abdullah al-Khamis (a poet and founder of the daily newspaper *al-Jazirah*) and a Palestinian mother. Omima was born in 1966 and, in her own account, grew up surrounded by books, reflecting her parents' interest in literature and current affairs. She combined her own passion for literature with bringing up a family and a job as a director of educational media. Resigning from her job in 2010, she became a full-time writer. From al-Rasheed, *Most Masculine State*, p. 179.
3 Omima al-Khamis, *Baḥryāt* [Sea-wafted Women] (Dar Al-Mada: Damascus, 2006).
4 Al-Khamis, *Baḥryāt*, p. 8.
5 Linden Peach, in *Virginia Woolf: Critical Issues*, proposes that there are several dimensions to Derrida's concept – one being its applicability to the character of Septimus in Virginia Woolf's 1925 novel *Mrs Dalloway*, who, according to Peach, functions as a hinge via which the different threads of the texts are fused (Macmillan Press: New York, 2000), pp. 109–10.
6 Norma Alarcon, 'The Theoretical Subject(s) of This Bridge Called My Back and Anglo-American Feminism', in Héctor Calderón, José David Saldívar, Stanley Fish and Fredric Jameson (eds), *Criticism in the Borderlands: Studies in Chicano Literature, Culture, and Ideology* (Duke University Press: New York, 1991), pp. 28–40; Gloria Anzaldúa, *Making Face, Making Soul/Haciendo Caras: Creative and Critical Perspectives by Women of Color* (Duke University Press: New York, 1991), pp. 356–69.
7 Lamia Khalil Hammad, 'Border Identity Politics: The New Mestiza in *Borderlands*', *Rubkhatha Journal on Interdisciplinary Studies in Humanities*, Vol. 2, No. 3 (2010), pp. 303–8.
8 Cherrie Moraga and Gloria Anzaldúa (eds), *This Bridge Called My Back: Writings by Radical Women of Color* (Kitchen Table: New York, 1983), p. 290.
9 Stuart Hall, 'The Local and the Global: Globalization and Ethnicity', in Anne McClintock, Aamir Mufti and Ella Shohat (eds), *Dangerous Liaisons: Gender, Nation and Postcolonial Perspectives* (University of Minnesota Press: Minneapolis, 1997), p. 183.
10 Melissa Wallace, 'Writing the Wrongs of Literature: The Figure of the Feminist and Post-Colonialist Translator', *Journal of the Midwest Modern Language*, Vol. 35, No. 2 (Autumn 2002), p. 7.
11 Friedman, *Mappings*, p. 20.
12 Al-Khamis, *Baḥryāt*, p. 36.
13 Al-Khamis, p. 127.
14 Moraga and Anzaldúa, *This Bridge Called My Back*, p. 290.
15 Al-Khamis, *Baḥryāt*, p. 169.
16 Al-Khamis, p. 175.
17 Iris Marion Young, 'Five Faces of Oppression', *Philosophical Forum*, Vol. XIX, No. 4 (Summer 1988), pp. 37–60.
18 Al-Khamis, *Baḥryāt*, p. 14.
19 Judith Butler, *The Judith Butler Reader*, eds Sara Salih and Judith Butler (Blackwell Publishers: Victoria, Australia, 2004), p. 264.

20 Butler, *The Judith Butler Reader*, p. 266.
21 Al-Khamis, *Baḥryāt*, p. 15.
22 Michel Foucault cited in Judith Butler, *Subjects of Desire: Hegelian Reflections in Twentieth-Century France* (Colombia University Press: New York, 1999), p. 218.
23 Al-Khamis, *Baḥryāt*, p. 18.
24 Al-Khamis, p. 32.
25 Al-Khamis, p. 242.
26 Al-Khamis, p. 243.
27 Susan Friedman, *Mappings*, p. 23.
28 Al-Khamis, *Baḥryāt*, p. 117.
29 Hall, 'The Local and the Global', p. 183.
30 Qmasha al-Olayyan, *al-Zawjah al-'Athra'* [The Virgin Wife] (Dar Rashād Press: Beirut, 1993), p. 11.
31 Sean Homer, *Jacque Lacan*, 1st ed. (Taylor and Francis: Harvard, 2004).
32 Homer, *Jacque Lacan*, p. 243.
33 Homer, p. 153.
34 Friedman, *Mappings*, pp. 21–5.
35 Sandra M. Gilbert and Susan Gubar, *The Mad Woman in the Attic: The Woman Writer and the Nineteenth-Century Literary Imagination* (Yale University Press: New Haven, CT and London, 2000), p. 76.
36 Julian Henriques et al., *Changing the Subject: Psychology, Social Regulation and Subjectivity* (Methuen: London, 1984), 117.
37 Judith Butler, *Subjection, Resistance, Resignification* (Stanford University Press: Stanford, CA, 1997), p. 100.
38 Badriya al-Beshir, *Hend we al-'Askar* [Hend and the Soldiers] (University of Texas Center for Middle Eastern Studies: Austin, 2017), p. 13.
39 Badriya al-Beshir is a columnist on the daily *Hayat*. She was born in Riyadh in 1967 and married the famous actor Nasser al-Qasabi, whose popular satirical Ramadan show *Tash Ma Tash* ran from 1992 until 2011. She obtained a doctorate in sociology in Beirut in 2008.
40 In fact, her scheduled public lecture at Qatar University in May 2012 was cancelled at the last minute because of *Hend we al-'Askar*. Its challenging of issues of religious and social sensitivity has resulted in three allegations being levelled at the novel. The first allegation was of deviating from the teachings of Islam because the protagonist Hend reads a novel entitled *Christ Re-crucified*, whereas the Qur'an maintains that Jesus wasn't crucified in the first place. The second was that the author accused anyone who objected to her 'lecherous desires' of being joyless soldiers. Finally, it was claimed that al-Beshir offended the mother figure in the novel because her detractors looked on it purely as an autobiography and assumed the figure mentioned in the book was identical to al-Beshir's own mother.
41 Sunan an-Nasa'i 3104 In-book reference: Book 25, Hadith 20 English translation: Vol. 1, Book 25, Hadith 3106.
42 Al-Beshir, *Hend we al-'Askar*, p. 139.
43 Al-Beshir, p. 2.
44 Al-Beshir, p. 21.
45 An Arabic male garment.
46 Al-Beshir, *Hend we al-'Askar*, pp. 46–7.
47 Moneera al-Ghadeer, *Desert Voices: Bedouin Women's Poetry in Saudi Arabia* (London: I.B. Tauris, 2009), p. 50.

48 Al-Ghadeer, *Desert Voices*, p. 48.
49 Gary Alan Scott, 'Foucault's Analysis of Power's Methodologies', *Auslegung*, Vol. 21, No. 2 (1996), p. 128.
50 Scott, 'Foucault's Analysis of Power's Methodologies', p. 128.
51 Al-Beshir, *Hend we al-'Askar*, p. 74.
52 Butler, *The Psychic Life of Power*, p. 2.
53 Al-Beshir, *Hend we al-'Askar*, p. 69.
54 Virginia Woolf, *A Room of One's Own* (Harvest Books: New York, 1989), pp. 72–3.
55 A long, black garment worn by women, mainly in public.
56 Maha al-Jahni, '*Abaya* [The Cloak] (Almu'assasa al'arabyya Lilderāsāt Wa-alnashr: Beirut, 2008), p. 3.
57 Laurel Zwissler, '"I Am That Very Witch": On The Witch, Feminism, and Not Surviving Patriarchy', *Journal of Religion and Film*, Vol. 22, No. 3 (2018), p. 4.
58 Lyndal Roper quoted in Zwissler, '"I Am That Very Witch"', p. 4.
59 Zwissler, p. 16.
60 Friedman, *Mappings*, p. 21.
61 Al-Jahni, '*Abaya*, p. 175.
62 Michel Foucault, *The History of Sexuality, Volume 1: An Introduction*, trans. Robert Hurley (Vintage: New York, 1990), pp. 100–1.
63 Al-Jahni, '*Abaya*, p. 25.
64 Al-Jahni, p. 73.
65 Amy Millstone, 'French Feminist Theatre and the Subject of Prostitution, 1870–1914', in Pierre L. Horn and Mary Pringle (eds), *The Image of the Prostitute in Modern Literature* (Frederick Ungar Publishing Co.: New York, 1984), p. 23.
66 Al-Jahni, '*Abaya*, p. 186.
67 Al-Jahni, pp. 186–7.
68 Michel Foucault, *Power/Knowledge: Selected Interviews and Other Writings, 1972–1977*. (Random House USA Inc: USA, 1980) p. 95.

3
FEMINIZING HISTORY

The Female as a Repository of Memories

The Androgynous Subject: Raja Alem – *Khatem*: **'A Faulty Bride'**

Alem, in her 2001 novel *Khatem*, projects both male and female elements into the text through the androgynous Khatem, who is portrayed as a eunuch of sorts. Alem's choice to leave her protagonist gender-ambiguous and 'androgynous' – neither a boy nor a girl – arguably gives the writer the freedom not only to detach herself from the crippling strings of reality but also to rise above the restrictive life of women in the kingdom, as a subject. In an interview, Alem confesses,

> when I write I am free, like flying in my dreams, novels are extensions of myself. Through them, I enter into worlds that are both ancient and futuristic at once. I get joy out of overcoming restrictions and crossing the boundaries between the past, present and future, between the possible and the impossible, life and death.[1]

The events in *Khatem* take place in the early twentieth century, a time when the Ottoman Empire was declining. The father in the novel, Sheikh Naṣib, is a man of some social standing who has made his fortune from the empire's slave trade. His wife Sakinah has given birth to five sets of twins, each time a boy and a girl; however, the boys have been lost in wars and various epidemics that swept the area, so the couple are left only with girls. Sheikh Naṣib is depicted as desperate to have a son to honour his name, so he adopts Sanad, the son of a slave, and sets him free. It is around that time that Sakinah unexpectedly becomes pregnant again.

DOI: 10.4324/9781003539681-4

The most striking images in *Khatem* describe the birth of what turns out to be the much-awaited son into the novel's traditional Meccan family. The arrival of Khatem captures an emotionally charged moment for the parents, who are portrayed as tongue-tied, if not confused, at his birth – the moment that marks the beginning of the story. The narrator notes, 'when the newborn popped out everyone was silent including himself; he didn't cry even when he inhaled air into his lungs for the first time'. The author thus offers a space in which to engage the readers' imagination with open possibilities, yet hints at a secret unfolding right in front of their eyes.

The reader also learns that no one witnessed Khatem's birth except his father, because the mother refused to have a midwife to help her. This adds to the mystery surrounding his gender identity. No one knows for sure if Khatem is a boy or a girl – a confusion through which Alem intends to mock Arab and Muslim family traditions, which deem women a burden and the sole bearer of honour, by 'emasculating' Khatem. This type of mockery stands as a reminder of the philosopher Luce Irigary's technique that imitates 'man's woman' in her text, by turning it into 'a conscious mimicry or a goal-oriented interrogation of the idea and ideal of woman and man and their relation constituted by discourse, and also the conditions of philosophical discourse itself'.[2] Thus, the mystery of Khatem's birth serves as a reminder of Irigarayan parody, which 'however disruptive, does not displace the hegemonies it cracks open because the text's mimicry requires the reactivation of the cultural narratives it would expose'.[3]

The author thus opts to negotiate cultural narratives of gender bias by turning her protagonist's body into a site of contradiction – and by having the third-person narrative in the novel interfere with their flow. Such interference would usually compromise the credibility of the narrator and introduce a layer of uncertainty into the text; however, in this context it adds a layer of intrigue, surprise and an intoxicating quality. This is evident in the portrayal of Sheikh Naṣib's anticipation of a male heir, which stands in opposition to his gloom at the birth of Khatem. His reaction indicates that the newborn was not a boy, but the author leaves the reader guessing. Conversely, throughout the novel there is uncertainty on the part of the family – Khatem is treated by them as a girl when inside the house and a boy when he is outside – yet he is referred to by the narrator as a male (albeit a beautiful one). 'He' is pale-skinned with rosy cheeks, a beauty that stands out among the majority of darker-skinned Meccans. Gendered thus as neither male nor female, Khatem cannot be a man and so is depicted as wearing either male or female garments according to the event that he/she is attending. He is also portrayed throughout as a weak and effeminate character, wavering between the two worlds of male and female. Contradictions are, in fact, embedded in the very name Khatem – and this is no coincidence. It strongly resonates with a Muslim name for the Prophet Muhammad (the final Prophet) who is called in Arabic, *Khatem al-anbya'a* – which translates as the 'last prophet', conjuring up images of divinity and perfection, yet stands in total opposition to the behaviour of Alem's Khatem and his feminine qualities. It is through such contradictory geographies of identity that the author attempts to undermine the master narrative and criticize her lived reality, which until recently boasted unchallenged images of the male as universally masculine, fearless, strong, virile and so forth.

As Judith Butler says in *Bodies That Matter: On the Discursive Limits of Sex*,[4] a body that does not conform to heteropatriarchal norms is a subversive political body. The ambiguous and perhaps dark relationship between Khatem and the character Hilāl also subverts heteropatriarchal norms. As a child, Khatem was a friend of Hilāl, a black boy whose parents had been brought as slaves to Mecca. He would occasionally run from his home and secretly meet Khatem, but the two children were soon separated by the latter's parents. (The narrator hints, but never fully discloses, that the master's son/daughter should not play with the son of a slave.) The two become aware of their class difference, and Khatem becomes conscious of 'his' social boundaries while Hilāl grows bitter and a villain of sorts, knowing that he will never have a future with his love, Khatem. When they meet later as teenagers, Khatem is encouraged by Hilāl to explore the ghetto district of Mecca, known as Dehdairat Asas, a remote and deserted area that has only one house, which resembles a brothel. The madam of the brothel, Tuḥfah, sees them from her window and shouts to Hilāl, 'who's this attractive guy?'; Hilāl laughingly answers, 'This is a faulty bride, suitable for you and your brothel'. Tuḥfa, looking at Khatem again, says, 'Don't get me into trouble with daughters of high society, you devil, you brought me a girl disguis[ed] in a male garment?' Hilāl responds teasingly, 'This is a gift for you Shaikha Tuḥfa',[5] and then pushes Khatem inside the brothel.

This incident marks the beginning of Khatem's frequent trips from the affluent district in which 'his' family live to the underbelly of the city and the brothel. Alem's Sufi leanings emerge in the narrative, with Khatem depicted as moving freely between the usually rigidly segregated worlds of the male and the female; the upper world and the lower, debauched world; the affluent and the deprived – a reminder of Egyptian author Rasheed El-Enany's theme of exploring 'in symbolic terms the absolute in the life of both the individual and society'.[6] Khatem's 'journey' can be understood as a means of recovering a self that is under siege from social and political upheaval.[7] Thus, scenes describing Khatem's almost daily trips between 'his' house and the brothel are seen as comprising a spiritual and an identity journey of sorts, in which space has been created not only to speed up events in the novel but also to bring to 'his' attention issues of class difference and gender identity. It is a space of a kind that has been imbued with 'dynamic encounter', to quote Friedman – one that 'explores new possibilities and holds them open for the future [...] it also carves new spaces for action, invents new strategies for resistance, and weaves new discourses of identity'.[8]

Alem's protagonist also eventually discovers that 'his' father's wealth has come from selling slaves. 'He' witnesses how a man sells his four-year-old son into slavery because he cannot afford to feed him, and hears the weeping of his mother when the father takes the boy from her. Khatem is portrayed as clueless as to why the parents have dressed the boy in his best outfit. Hilāl then sarcastically tells 'him', 'This is one of hell's gates filled with demons, this is a place forbidden to the children of notable families, who live in paradise, on the other side of the mountain.'[9] The image of the gate as 'filled with demons', with functions such as separating the two worlds of masters and slaves, is repeated throughout the novel, serving as a reminder of the human trafficking that was widespread in many parts of the world including Arabia. The metaphor of the gate stands for the master-and-slave relationship and the ugliness of life that can only be seen when the gates are opened. This master-and-slave relationship is reinforced by the binaries inherent in many spatial imageries, including the two sides of the city of Mecca separated by the mountain, hell/paradise, poor/affluent, and demons/notable families.

Similarly, Khatem's sexual confusion reaches a peak when Hilāl attempts to brutally rape 'him' on 'his' way home – an event that forces into Khatem an awareness of 'his' confused gender identity when 'he' is portrayed as desperately trying to process and filter the rape. The portrayal of this incident constitutes a deviation from the universal heterosexual ideology of patriarchal culture. The ugliness of the incident makes Khatem run to the nearest mosque in an attempt to reclaim 'his' soul and probably find a cure for the dual gender identity of which 'he' is suddenly made aware.

By reconstructing the rape, the author fleshes out time in space through what Russian philosopher Mikhail Bakhtin defines as a chronotope[10] of the actual streets and the mythological spaces through which Khatem is chased by Hilāl in a scene that enables the reader to feel the pain, fear, hurt and insecurity building up in the youth. Such acts of harassment/rape force Khatem to acknowledge 'his' identity as a subordinate – or, to quote Hilāl, 'a faulty bride' – and they constitute 'one of the most traumatic forms of "gender trouble" where the female body is enforced into a certain category of gender that emanates from inequalities of sex'.[11]

The Androgynous Subject: Raja Alem – *Khatem*: History, Myth and Feminism

History and myth – one narrating facts, the other fiction – are, argues Friedman, both inseparable from narrative – and, specifically, the kind of narrative associated with the epic tradition.[12] Raja Alem's *Khatem* has a strong narrative drive, in both its subplots and overarching storyline: a drive that claims feminist, historical, mythic and religious discourses, and that is overdetermined by the author's exclusion as a woman from such discourses. It also constitutes an attempt to retrieve history from a purely male perspective in the sense that Alem attempts to claim her own Hejazi identity through time and space, with certain themes filtering through her novel.[13] These include the hammam and the Ottoman concept of the harem quarters, which traditionally housed women who had mostly been kidnapped from various parts of the empire, treated as prostitutes and made to act as mistresses to rich men. Alem employs a feminist critique that intersects with race, class, and various forms of identity, allowing her storytelling to illuminate the layered and complex challenges faced by women across time. By retelling history through this lens, Alem's narratives become powerful tools for revealing the compounded struggles often obscured by traditional male narratives.

In claiming these discourses, Alem sets in motion a series of cultural narratives through which she intends to both expose and mock – raising questions of whether pre-existing, anti-patriarchal attitudes are reinforced or removed in her readers' minds. This partly explains why I have elected to study a second aspect of this particular novel here: I find Alem's engagement with feminist ideas in *Khatem* to be a little challenging. This is not only because her writing is too subtle to be labelled simply 'feminist' but also because her choice of an androgynous character suggests a spurning of male/female dichotomies. This choice also raises questions as to whether it is an attempt by the author to emasculate and oppress the male in her novelistic world as a means of compensating for women's oppression in the real world. Or could the duality in Khatem's identity be simply an outlet for exploring the outside world from within a repressive society?

Whatever the reason, it is very hard to dismiss the fact that Alem is a feminist at heart who is trying to rise above the anger, frustration and political activism that are usually associated with feminism. One would therefore assume that if her writing is not the product of a pure feminist perspective it is surely a projection of the writer's personal experience, which testifies to a considerable amount of mature anger. By focusing, in *Khatem*, on the human experience rather than on a female experience, Alem probably intended to avoid the usual clichés associated with the discussion of women's issues in Saudi Arabia. In an interview, Marilyn Powell, a Canadian Broadcasting Corporation presenter and writer, asked Alem, 'What is it like to be a woman living in this ancient atmosphere [Saudi Arabia in the 1990s]?' to which she simply replied, 'You yearn to rise above the female form that's been smothering you for decades; you want to find a way to crack the crippling veneer, the taboos, the restrictions.'[14] Thus, Alem's writing is probably a reflection of the oppressive and sexist world around her, which finds its way into her text through themes of androgyny, helping her 'to choke and repress her anger and ambition'.[15] This is not surprising, for in most of her works Alem offers a subversive rewriting of familiar myths and stories that tend mostly to undermine patriarchal power and offer a rereading of the male-dominated literature that has for many years relegated women to the peripheries of their texts.

This subtle feminist leaning in Alem's work stems from the fact that she was raised unconventionally at home. Her father instilled in her a respect for women's emancipation and inviolability, and encouraged her to dabble in diverse schools of thought – something that emerges in the Sufi and feminist elements in her works. One cannot, however, mention Raja without her sister Shadia, the renowned artist, because art and literature manifest a level of perpetual engagement in the duality of male and female energies that shroud both their works not only with mysticism but also with an androgyny of sorts, which is at the heart of Sufism.[16] Ali al-Shadawi, a Saudi novelist and critic, said of one of Alem's earlier works that

> Raja in most of her novels collaborates with her sister Shadia – whom she has a strong spiritual and artistic bond with – and the result is outstanding because both the visual art and literature convey sexless creatures, that are neither male or female, and surely [have] no identity or a comprehensible form.[17]

Although this appraisal is commendable for its recognition of her Sufi leanings – evident in the use of sexless creatures and the duality of male and female experiences – it does run the risk of denying Alem her unique feminist approach to such issues.

It is remarkable to note how women writers like Alem have developed a feminist discourse of their own by using the female body as a canvas on which to scrutinize futile social, cultural and political discourses. Here, Alem questions discriminatory laws against women by showcasing female characters as at least submissive, if not mute. The five daughters of Sheikh Naṣib are silent throughout *Khatem*, in a way echoing both women's marginality in Arabia's society and its model of propriety that equates their desirability and beauty with silence, virtue and charm during that period. The narrative silence of sheikh Naṣib's daughters thus becomes a mirror to how social constructs of the time rendered women voiceless, presenting them as objects of desire whose worth was tied to their adherence to these ideals. The daughters' silent presence emphasises themes of gendered expectations and the subtle yet significant power of social customs in shaping identity and agency. In an interview with Mary-Lou Zeitoun,[18] Alem recalled how, like most girls of her generation, she was marked by this culture. When she published her first article at the age of 17, readers thought she was a boy because of her gender-neutral name. Then, when they were told that she was a girl, they said, 'She must be ugly.' In this interview, Alem referred to this idealization of the silent and ethereal woman – a topic that is given a 'sidelong glance' in this novel.

Ridding Khatem of the female form is meant to empower not only the sisters but also the entire family in the face of a purely patriarchal culture. Hostility to the female and to the culture of silence that has come to define women's lives is debated, if not challenged outright, by Alem, as well as other Saudi writers such as Saba al-Herz in her book *Al-Akrūn* (The Others – see Chapter 6), by intentionally creating androgynous characters who acquire a false sense of freedom and power among their female peers in this strong patriarchal society by wiping out the protagonist's femininity through simply abandoning the soft voice and female dress. Indeed, such characters exist in today's Arabia, but Alem here sheds light on the root cause of this phenomenon and blames a sexist society that favours boys over girls for creating intersexual characters. In this novel, her feminism surfaces when she questions Khatem's gender identity – and, in doing so, she is undoubtedly undermining patriarchy and the 'house of men', so to speak.

Alem succeeds, however, in blending history and mythology. For example, Khatem's ability to trade 'his' sexual identity and persona depending on the occasion enables 'him' to travel between the upper world of 'his' family and the debauched world of the brothel without fear. This is especially so towards the middle and end of the novel when Khatem's feminine and artistic energies are depicted as being harmoniously in tune with 'his' surroundings, signifying a profound yearning to have a taste of the outer world and to break free from both stifling social mores and his gender-related anxieties. Alem adamantly denies any feminist leaning by stressing in another interview, with author James Strecker, 'From where I see our society, I look at both males and females as dominated. But writing was the one domain I moved in freely because, when I write, I am attached to some energy above physical forms and thus I am no more a female nor a male.'[19] However, no matter how Alem tries to tone down her frustration about the male-dominated culture of Arabia, the mutilated sexual identity that is polarized in and projected onto the protagonist Khatem is unmissable – pointing to Alem's frustration with Arabia's male-dominated social order. In an early interview with Saddeka Arebi in *Women and Words in Saudi Arabia*, she states,

> When I portray deformed characters, I in fact signify a deformed reality. I have come to realize that people do not want to see themselves as deformed, they are afraid that if they look harder they will recognize themselves in my characters.[20]

From the very start of the novel, the narrator draws the reader's attention to Khatem's humane side and innate musical quality, which sets 'him' apart from other characters, portraying 'him' as imbued with a mystical and divine aura. Alem shapes Khatem's unique character through the use of multiple voices as she negotiates and creates 'his' polyphonic space. For example, the narrator affirms that everyone thought that Khatem was a *ghawyah*, or possessed by music spirits – including Tuḥfah, the madam of the brothel. Also, Sakinah, 'his' mother, recalls how when she was giving birth to Khatem she heard thumping sounds reverberating over her head, sounds that she had never heard before in her life. A supernatural element is thus introduced from the beginning by the different voices in the novel, including the omniscient narrator who confirms that the same sounds continued to echo in Khatem's ears – more so in the evenings. Sakinah envisioned what the future held for the child:

> Khatem's movement made him look like he was under a magic spell [...] the household waited for him to reach puberty and menstruation, except Sakinah who believed that Khatem would grow with the flow of the music of the *oud* [Eastern music instrument] and not the flow of blood.[21]

In this scene, Sakinah's belief that Khatem would grow with the flow of music rather than the flow of blood suggests a deep symbolic interpretation of Khatem's identity and destiny. One has, however, to give Alem credit for her beautiful portrayal of Khatem as a child running this way and that, which is enchanting at the very least and cunningly draws the reader's attention to the musical ear and talent that 'he' has possessed from a very young age. When, as a little 'boy', Khatem was listening to soft music coming from a distance, 'he' would carelessly follow wherever it went. It is in this passion for music, in fact, that Khatem's femininity and masculinity are in tune. Later on, this fervour is directed to the lute, and especially around a female singer called Zeryab – named after the most famous male Arab vocalist of the Umayyad period (he died in the year 852), a point that causes some confusion for the resourceful reader about what exactly Alem is alluding to by giving a female character a male name. One would assume, however, that the author has thereby probably transcended the physical world of male/female. This transcendence of the male/female duality marks a shift in Saudi women's literature, forming a continuum in which gender identity, patriarchal culture and social issues are linked and treated head-on.

A vague friendship develops between Khatem and Zeryab, which, according to the narrator, is competitive on many levels – such as beauty and their common passion for the lute. The narrator points out,

> A strange relationship between Khatem and Zeryab began and it revolved around the lute; Zeryab's immersion in the lute made Khatem feel eliminated and excluded. He felt jealous. And when Khatem played the lute, Zeryab felt that the tunes came from a remote part of Khatem's soul; a place unknown to her.[22]

Khatem is depicted as transcending the male/female dichotomy when 'he' is with Zeryab; 'he' is portrayed as losing 'himself' to the lute and forgetting about 'his' confused identity – emphasizing a magical and supernatural element emanating from Khatem, and a dark secret within 'him'. This secret can be identified through the psychoanalytic model of the unconscious that sees a relationship between music and myth: a form of language that tries to break down the various data, dichotomies and dualities that are integrated within us. Claude Lévi-Strauss claims that myth and music are in fact one and the same: they merge and reunite in their very structure when 'there are myths, or groups of myths, which are constructed like a sonata, or a symphony [...] or any of all the musical forms which music did not really invent but borrowed unconsciously from the structure of the myth'.[23]

Frequenting female spaces like the brothel and the hammam, playing his lute while watching women's naked bodies, allows Khatem to revisit 'his' 'gender trouble'. Looking at 'his' naked body in the mirror, the youth contemplates the idea of ridding 'himself' of maleness yet the idea of the 'door' closing and 'him' being locked in the private sphere stops 'him'. The symbol of the door fits perfectly with the theme of androgyny, notes Amira El-Zein: 'without this door standing between two worlds, there would be no story to tell'.[24] Indeed, the door serves as a symbol of separation, segregation and of gender roles; without it, there would be no 'gender trouble' and no feminism.

> [Khatem] would stay up all night ordering her body to hold on to her femaleness and tearing off the memory of her maleness. She would contemplate this idea, then she would panic at the thought of not being able to be a male again; there won't be a door open for her to explore the roads and their surprises. Her panic would turn into a nightmare over losing the power that comes with wearing the male's garment that would set her like a peacock on a mountain; wearing that garment gives her a power that cannot be underestimated, a power that allows her to open and close as many doors as she wants to. It is a power that she became addicted to; tearing it off is going to be like permanently castrating her ability to be free.[25]

The delayed disclosure of Khatem's male identity underscores the thematic significance of gender in the novel. By keeping the protagonist's identity ambiguous until the climatic conflict, the author invites readers to reflect on how gender roles shape both perception and fate. The revelation during a moment of violence, where men are targeted but women are spared due to cultural codes, highlights the stark realities of life dictated by gender.[26]

Jeddah, a Metaphor for a Subjugated Woman: Laila al-Juhani – *Barren Paradise*

Born in Tabouk (in northwest Saudi Arabia) in 1969, educator and author Laila al-Juhani won the Sharjah Award for Arab Creativity for the short novel *Al-Ferdūs al-Yabāb* (Barren Paradise) in 1999. She has written three other novels: the outstanding *Jahiliyyah* (The Days of Ignorance) in 2007, which was translated into English in 2014; *Da'iman Sayabqa al-Hubb* (Love Will Always Remain) in 1995; and *40 Fi Ma'na an Akbar* (40 The Meaning of Getting Older) in 2009. Translations of the title *Al-Ferdūs al-Yabāb* were not consistent: there is *The Waste Paradise*, by Shereen Abouelnaga; *The Desolate Paradise*, by Mandy McClur; and *Barren Paradise* by Salma Jayyusi. I find that the last translation captures the spirit of the original title.

The novel courageously offers a fictional glimpse at the underbelly of otherwise scenic Jeddah, unpacking the enigma of forbidden love and pregnancy out of wedlock in a city that prides itself on receiving millions of pilgrims on their way to the nearby sacred centre of Mecca. We are told about the tragedy of al-Juhani's heroine, Saba: how 'Amer, whom she had loved and given herself to, had jilted her in order to marry her best friend Khalda after learning about her (Saba's) pregnancy. In this novel, intertextuality is used abundantly and plays a significant role in shaping the narrative and enriching the reader's experience. By embedding references, quotations, and allusions to other literary works, the author creates a layered text that invites readers to engage with the story on multiple levels. The intertextual elements can serve various purposes, such as providing explanation, drawing parallels, or contrasting different ideas and characters, thereby adding nuance and depth to the novel's overall message. More specifically, I look at the intersection of history, religion, literature and folklore, enabled through the literary device of intertextuality – including allusions and quotations that were used to express the author's critique of stale traditions. I find that Julia Kristeva's contribution to the previous post-structuralist theories of Bakhtine, Ferdinand de Saussure and Barthes, among others, is particularly helpful in reading this novel. In *The Kristeva Reader*, she argues that the notion of intertextuality replaces that of intersubjectivity when we realize that meaning is not transferred directly from writer to reader but instead is 'mediated through, or filtered by, "codes" imparted to the writer and reader by other texts', and that this occurs 'through deliberate compositional strategies such as quotation, allusion, calque, plagiarism, translation, pastiche or parody'.[27]

For instance, the novel opens with Saba in deep shock at seeing the treacherous 'Amer with her best friend Khalda; she wishes to warn Khalda but cannot. Haunted by remorse, Saba is portrayed as 'powerless' and 'silent' in the face of societal prejudice. This portrayal can be a powerful commentary on the need for societal change, as it sheds light on the injustices faced by exploited women. The author gives Saba a textual space to articulate her innermost worries in a double discourse, to create a layered narrative that deepens the reader's engagement with Saba. This double discourse allows Saba to reveal her secrets and agony, offering a multifaceted view of her tragedy and emotions. Hence, Saba's thoughts and feelings are shared directly with the reader, often in the form of internal monologue that is permeated with allusions and intertextuality. For instance, Saba's 'And

Michael blows the trumpet, and the details of my slaughtered love are laid bare and are resurrected naked', a sentence that resonates with verses from the Qur'an: 'the trumpet will be sounded and behold! They will rush out to their lord from their graves.'[28] Embedded in the verse is a distinctive audio and mental imagery that holds Saba accountable for what she did (or failed to do). The image of the prophet 'Michael blow[ing] the trumpet' captures the idea of sin and punishment at the heart of Islam, whereas the image of the dead rushing out from their graves symbolizes the end of life for Saba: a barren paradise. In another episode, the author reveals the depth of Saba's sorrow through religious connotations:

> Oh dear Khalda, don't open the door to agony with your own hands. I on the other hand, deserve to go to the hole of hell for seventy autumns. For, I have tricked the guards and slipped into paradise before God allowed anyone to. I deserve to go to hell, once for my sin, another time for standing there in front of you powerless to shriek 'don't Khalda', powerless to cry or even hum.[29]

This passage resonates with a hadith from the Prophet Muhammad: 'Indeed a man may utter a statement that he does not see any harm in, but for which he will fall seventy autumns in the fire.'[30] It calls to mind a historical period of deep religiosity, serving as an ideological backdrop to Saba's dilemma. This approach is deeply embedded in the novel through words such as 'guards', 'paradise' and 'hell', staging Saba as the very model of a sinner who has tricked the guardians of virtue and religion and slipped into an illicit relationship – echoing society's judgement of her. These religious connotations reveal Saba as living in a constant field of struggle between love and socio-religious restrictions, which culminate in her question: 'Isn't it an agony to be a woman?'[31]

The first part of this short novel is thus told by Saba herself, who is facing pregnancy outside marriage alone. Imagining the public scandal that would inevitably erupt should she choose to have the child prompts her to procure an illegal abortion. She decides to undergo this prohibited procedure on her own in an abysmal backstreet establishment. The physical setting of the clinic that Saba goes to, in a remote part of Jeddah, increases her anxiety. The pain that she experiences captures the shocking dilemma that comes from the collision between women's bodies and social norms, exposing the true level of female status in the Arab world.

This pain and anxiety are conveyed to the reader by the narrator's aiming the antagonism of the situation at the nurse who performs the abortion on Saba – from the first moment, in fact, that she appears in the story. She is called 'that woman', described judgementally as 'a forty something' and further demonized by phrases such as 'her features give off the feeling of harshness' and 'her face is like a stone'.³² 'That woman' inserts a pair of scissors in Saba's womb, cuts off some of her flesh and finishes the abortion by placing a tube in her womb, which the latter later pulls out in an attempt to rescue her child. Complications occur and she bleeds, but does not seek help, indicating her inner desire for suicide – especially when the narrator tells us that she is 'lying on her bed as if waiting for death'. This painful and ghastly abortion scene has been intentionally devised to internalize the idea of women's suffering in a society that condones men's mistakes but not those of women. The reader is forced to leave the relative comfort of the narrator's viewpoint and to follow the perspective of Saba herself, who goes through a delirium of sorts that allows us to glimpse her anguished unconscious, reminiscing over the good old days and tirelessly trying to fill in gaps of who is to blame for her dilemma. Has society conditioned 'Amer to be the oppressor and the coward that he is? These monologues, which constitute the bulk of the novel, make the narrative read like a huge secret being disclosed to the reader – both before and after the protagonist's death. They also bring to the forefront the link between the 'I' of the woman and the 'they' of society, which should be in line with both the ideals and cultural values of Islam. In other words, Saba's anguish and delirium allow the reader to closely observe the association between gender and family codes of honour and male oppression.

Although the intertextuality adopted in this novel tends to be cumbersome at times, it nonetheless represents a social, traditional and ideological backdrop for the character. In other words, parody and historical and literary intertextuality build up a dialogic relationship between the author, the reader and the text. In the fourth chapter of the novel, titled 'The Fall of the Rose', which alludes to Saba and her final fall, al-Juhani draws on historical discourse. She compares Saba's tragedy with the fall of Andalusia and Jerusalem: 'Please help me, another Granada will fall, another Jerusalem will be taken, please look at me, help me, don't lose me.'³³ Saba imagines what other people might say: 'leave her, she is cursed, compares herself to Andalusia and Jerusalem'.³⁴

The narrator herself intervenes in the flow of the narrative to express her feminist grievance, mainly by discarding layers of hypocrisy and the lure of imagined masculinity. This becomes evident in a comparison between love and a dunghill: 'didn't I say to you, Saba, love is a dung, and I am its cock that crows?' – an echo of Ernest Hemingway's *The Snows of Kilimanjaro*, in which the character of Harry makes a similar comparison: 'love is dunghill', and 'I'm the cock that gets on it to crow.'³⁵ Al-Juhani's narrator notes that "Amer is a garbage rooster' whom she brands as extremely devious: a man who admonishes Saba with total vulgarity, 'the love between us is finished [...] go look for the father of this baby elsewhere'.³⁶ He taunts her further, saying, 'go and tell others that I made you pregnant if you can. I dare you, do you hear me, I dare you Saba.'³⁷ This incident marks out 'Amer as a true misogynist, whose actions are symbolic of stale traditions that use a code of honour to silence women and excuse men's wrongdoing.

This approach also draws on Mikhail Bakhtine's notion that any text is constructed as a mosaic of quotations; any text is the absorption and transformation of another. Roland Barthes makes an analogy between text and textiles, declaring that a text is 'a tissue [or fabric] of quotations drawn from the innumerable centers of culture', emphasizing the 'fluid[ity]' of the text, with its many levels of meaning. For instance, parody and imitation in this novel transmit what others might say about Saba: all the gossip, rumours and opinions that shape her existence and her choices in life, compelling her to get rid of the baby and lose her life in the course of such a perilous undertaking. She is destined to be socially stigmatized just as her son, if he were allowed to live, would always be treated as a criminal. Saba perceives how people would react to her pregnancy and how they would spread rumours about her. She even imagines the whispers of people who would say she had slept with many men, that she was a whore and so on. These polyphonic voices act as a reminder of society's dominant power over women, as seen in

> [t]he influence, by which I mean the consciousness of other groups impinging upon ourselves; public opinion; what other people say and think; all those magnets which attract us this way to be like that.³⁸

In a similar vein, al-Juhani anticipates not only the alienation of a fatherless child in a society like hers but also his/her daily suffering from that society's immeasurable prejudice and discrimination. Saba laments, 'Getting rid of you is a crime, I know, but keeping you is even more abhorrent. No one would ever forgive me, not even you. Do you understand what I am saying baby, whom I will never see?' She adds,

> I would love to touch you, put my hand deep in and pat on the featureless piece of flesh, nip it and tweak it in there [...] kiss it before passing it to death. Kiss the blood and heart that is beating so hard, and cry. Would a fetus have eyes? I don't want you to have eyes so that you don't look at me when I dare to cast you out; I will not tolerate the innocence of your accusation and the question in everyone's eyes, why?³⁹

The eyes are said to be windows of the soul; they symbolize the higher self, knowledge, power and spirituality. Saba's unborn child, on the other hand, stands as a symbol of possibilities, emergence, liminality and transformation – all qualities that are annulled by the act of abortion. This incident is further confirmed through literary phrases and titles in order to link events in the novel with literary discourses. For instance, Saba remembers her college years when she studied the great works of English writers, such as *Jacob's Room* by Virginia Woolf. She recalls the first time she read the novel, and how she mused that very night on the image of the crab that was left in the room persistently trying to escape the container he was put in but falling back into the bottom of it – 'just like me now', she opines. The 'container' or 'vessel' in most cultures symbolizes the womb; the crab in this context is suggestive of Saba's own struggle – torn between her loving desire to keep her baby and the need to get rid of it. The link that the author draws between Saba, her foetus and Woolf's crab is unequivocal, signifying her level of despair – specifically, her own end: 'everything finished and vanished in the abysmal depths even the Paradise Lost'.[40]

The images invoked by Saba in her hallucinations are saturated with the binary thinking of old and new Jeddah, suggestive of the massive chaos that has taken place within her – her serenity having been traded for the anarchy of pregnancy out of wedlock. Through Saba's eyes, the novel attempts to signal a transformation in people and places, shedding light on the secrets behind the harshly gender-defined spaces of Jeddah through her somewhat anarchic recollections of her rendezvous with 'Amer and her feelings about this love. In fact, Saba's body acts as a metaphor for the 'subjugated land' and as a medium to signify the social status of women, whose problems lie in the selective systems of privileges that men enjoy over them. At one point, she notes, 'Jeddah is a woman like me, but she never hands in her key to anyone.'[41] The city is thus portrayed as a flirtatious woman, flaunting her attractive body to people but never gullible (as Saba regards herself as having been).

Khalda takes over the narration of the shorter second part of the novel, offering the reader another point of view and discourse – one of sisterhood and respect among women against the dominant male discourse. On hearing the tragic details of Saba's death, for instance, Khalda becomes aggressively resentful of 'Amer, her fiancé and cousin. Via a lengthy monologue, she claims that Saba is more precious to her than he is: 'I knocked on his door and said, Saba is dead, I won't forgive you, I won't forgive you [...] I spat out on him.'[42] Khalda further blames her aunt for having such a corrupt son: 'Recklessly I started spitting out on him, before turning to my aunt and hysterically shouting at her: you too, damn you, you're the one who was pregnant with his bad seed, you should have died before conceiving him.'[43] Through such passages, al-Juhani clearly debunks stereotypes of the diffident and silent woman. This is further emphasized by Khalda's narration, in the course of which she also admits, 'I watched him in his previous relationships and I knew that he would come back to me, not because he loved me but because he will never trust anyone but me.'[44]

Linda McDowell contends that place is a sort of spatial text that can be interpreted differently according to gender, class, ethnicity, age and life experience.[45] For al-Juhani, place, as exemplified by the city of Jeddah, is a text of rich cultural and historical meaning. The final chapter of *Barren Paradise*, entitled 'The Stenography of the Soul', shows Khalda reassessing the history of Jeddah in order to understand women's place in the wider universe. The city is known locally as 'Jaddah', a name that literally translates from Arabic as 'grandmother': in Eastern folktales, it is regarded as the burial place of the grandmother of humanity, a figure who is interred there in a structure bearing the name 'the Tomb of Eve'.[46] This historical intertextuality is meant to create multiple layers of meaning in the reader's mind and to identify common themes between Eve and the protagonist Saba – such as love, suffering and expulsion from paradise. It is presented through a parallel narrative – that is, the love between Eve and Adam, a story through which Khalda vindicates Saba for having loved the wrong man:

> When Moses, peace be upon him, called out, the sea parted and each parting wave was like a mighty mountain. And now here you are before the sea, longing to make a sign to the waves and cry out: 'Open up, Abu Khalid!' You'd see the damp sand, the seaweed whitened by the ebb, the fish leaping, the lobster and tiny sea creatures that leave their frail prints on the sands. You've moved your fingers over these prints, and they'd fade and vanish. That would make you feel sad. What you were going to leave behind you was, you'd reflect, a mere flimsy mark to be erased by the waves and the footsteps hurrying along the sand. It would all be so swift that no one would be aware of you, lying as an illegible line amid all this clamour.
> 'Open up Abu Khalid!'
> Not to flee the Pharaohs of today, but to cling to the sand, indeed to write about the sand; about Jeddah, sunk beneath the sea. About Eve's footsteps, which she left on these sands so many ages ago as she walked towards Adam who longed to see her. Almighty God had her walk to him from Jeddah, and they met on Arafat.

This extract shows Khalda recalling the love story of Adam and Eve, and engaging in the dualities of Jeddah past and present – thoughts of good and evil, innocence and adultery, and life and death in the land of Jeddah. This passage ties in with the philosophical dialectic of life and death deeply entrenched in the novel's narrative structure. It also runs parallel to other abstract dualities such as modernity and tradition, chaos and harmony, good and evil, and happiness and misery. This life/death duality forms a concrete beginning and end, and also indicates the life or death of a community – a point bolstered by the idea that there is eternity and oneness after death, a place where al-Juhani's heroine may be united with her baby. It is a place where all dualities will end and the enigmas of the world will be resolved.

On the surface, Saba's narrative of despair and victimization may seem to endorse reductive views of women defined purely by biological difference: how, under certain ideological and cultural circumstances, women's bodies pay a high price. However, as Khaled Rabi has pointed out,

> [t]his theme of despair and escape which the author chose as an end for the novel, is in fact a way of giving women back some of their rights that seem to have vanished from society's consciousness with the advent of cultural materialism.[47]

Thus, choosing suicide for Saba is symptomatic of the author's feminist tendency to call attention to the societal disparities affecting women. From this, I argue that Saba is Khalda's 'mad' double, constantly pinpointing the loopholes of her culture by acting as mediator (from beyond the grave) for her friend, who represents the average woman in Arabia. This allegory is rooted in their names, Saba signifying 'youth' and Khalda 'eternity', which simultaneously highlight the former's tendency to follow her heart and, along the way, her failure to foresee the perils of love. Al-Juhani even proposes an urban-based comparison between her two main female characters, defining through them the two cultures within Jeddah: the visible and conservative one, and the subculture of the 'deviants', who probably dream of another, more hedonistic, reality.

Critics have suggested that the device of the mad double connotes the power of resistance and carries signs of repression. Hélène Cixous, using Freud's idea of hysterical history, sees the power of the repressed working in the same way that 'anachronism has a specific power, one of shifting, disturbance, and change, limited to imaginary displacement [...] That is how the hysteric, reputed to be incurable, sometimes took the role of a resistant heroine'.[48] The delirium experienced by Saba, culminating in what appears as self-destructive acts like bleeding or suicide, echoes Freud's interpretation of hysteria as a potent, albeit indirect form of rebellion. What's powerful here is that this form of rebellion, although seemingly passive or self-destructive, often leads to real shifts in their circumstances or perceptions. its not resistance in the usual sense but an embodied challenge that, in breaking down the self, also breaks down the rigid confines of their reality.'[49]

'The Old Is Dying and the New Cannot Be Born': Nora al-Ghamdi – *Compass Direction*

Nora al-Ghamdi's[50] 2002 debut novel, *Wejhat al-Bouṣlah* (Compass Direction), captures a rupture in the fabric of nomadic tribal culture through the stories of two women in southern Arabia and their struggle against the tyranny of the head of their tribe, the elder Aboud al-Sabti, and his sons. The narrative space of the novel is exceptionally wide and open, with accounts of fields full of lush trees and female characters depicted as having more freedom than the average urban woman. Hence, they are portrayed as hopping between their large house, the valley, the fields and the clinic. This choice of setting and cultural narrative sets the scene for the author to portray rural society in action, documenting the interactions that these women have within the tribal and patriarchal social order of Arabia.

As with Raja Alem and other Sufi writers in Arabia, feminizing history is a component of al-Ghamdi's Sufi writing. This explains the latter's recollection of Arabia's history from a woman's point of view, through a narrative discourse that adopts what Abdullah al-Ghothami dubs 'feminizing the groundwork'. In his 1996 book *Women and Language*, al-Ghothami illuminates this idea:

> it is an alternative to a confrontational discourse. It's a tactic through which women writers attempt to read the past from a woman's point of view, that is, by probing women's memory, so that she can be the hero and doer. In doing so, the author sets [the] ground for the woman memory project, by which to regain the cultural balance that relies on both sexes.[51]

Unlike other Saudi novels of its generation, *Compass Direction* capitalizes on the historical 'punctum' of slavery in the Arabian Peninsula and, to a lesser extent, the Palestinian cause and the Gulf War of 1990 by turning them into markers of social memory – a shared temporal past that takes on a new meaning through its two female protagonists, Fetha and Nariman. By the transmission of spatial and temporal memories, the author subtly problematizes three bygone social issues – that of forced marriages, violence and slavery – with an examination of their historical context and impact, through cultural narratives that 'encode and encrypt [...] norms, values, and ideologies of the social order'.[52] These issues are contested through the three generations of black women who occupy the world of the novel: Fetha, the grandmother; Baraka, the daughter; and the granddaughter, also called Fetha.

In spite of the fact that slavery is prohibited in Islam and was officially abolished in Saudi Arabia with the kingdom's ratification of the UN Slavery Convention in 1962, Al-Ghamdi in this novel aims to problematize the struggle for gender equality in contexts with a history of slavery. Since the protagonist Fetha is black, in this novel al-Ghamdi builds a strong major plotline encompassing slavery and colour bias in rural Arabia, fusing it with mystery and elements of a spiritual–spatial 'fourth' dimension. This blend not only highlights historical and societal issues but also adds a layer of metaphysical intrigue, inviting readers to explore complex dimensions of reality.

The history of human trafficking on the Arabian Peninsula is evoked in this novel through its narrative space, or what Mikhail Bakhtin defines (as we saw in the introduction to this chapter) as the 'chronotope' – a merging of space and time presented in the language and discourse of a novel – wherein, in this case, the open realm of the desert serves as the spatial chronotope of the poignant overland trek on which thousands of captured slaves were dragged. A re-enactment of the history of displacement and slavery is discernible in the detailed, physical and psychological abuses that are captured in this novel. In it, the story of a black former slave woman is spiritually resurrected, helping to break the long silence of other ex-slaves and to speak, perhaps for the first time in Saudi women's novels, about the history of slavery in pre- unification Saudi Arabia. This technique helps readers to understand how the grandmother was a Yemeni princess and how she ended up as a slave in the Southern Valley, revealing the ways in which 'characters who move through narrative space and time occupy multiple and shifting positions in relation to each other and to different systems of power relations'.[53] The cultural narrative of *Compass Direction* is tied in with a brutal description of the savageness with which the elder Fetha was captured and the horrific experience that she went through, which transformed her life dramatically from a sumptuous existence as a princess in her prime to a slave wearing tattered clothes and sleeping in a filthy room surrounded by insects, rats and other animals. The narrator explains,

> Fetha is that slave woman who got used to imprisonment and lost all hope of going back to her land [...] she [was] released from her prison after seven months when al Sabti [her abductor] decided to chain her by [her] feet to allow her to move around.[54]

Oppression and silence overcome the elder Fetha (then still a young woman) to the point that she makes a desperate and moving attempt to take her own life by tying her long tresses around her neck several times. Because of this incident, Aboud al-Sabti decides to chop her hair off. The narrator intervenes at this point in order to describe how this newly captured slave had no choice but to succumb to her misfortune and start seducing her captor – however, her identity as a princess is muted while her femininity is foregrounded; she survives her captivity by using her body as though she is seeking to nullify her slavery and the graphic brutality of her imprisoner. This explains the vengeance nurtured by Fetha – the grandmother – and her hatred for the al-Sabti patriarchs, which is passed on to her offspring and is especially felt by her granddaughter, who bears the same name. Al-Sabti himself, the narrative suggests, is a scoundrel of almost Dickensian proportions: a slave trader in pre-Saudi Arabia, who caught Fetha like an animal one moonlit night in the desert, raped her many times and then tried to sell her in the slaves' market – failing to do so, however, because her traumatized physical condition made her unappealing to buyers. Stuck with the beautiful yet damaged slave, he pursues her even further, crawling into her bed each night and raping his powerless captive multiple times until she bears him a son, Yousef, and then a daughter, Baraka. The narrator notes,

> That slave woman who was capable of seducing her kidnapper, tamed him with her incessant chattering – something that men in that village were not familiar with. In the middle of the night, one would hear her cheerful laughter with al Sabti and the sounds of commotion that only settled down in her bed.[55]

In spite of their different skin colour, Fetha and her children eventually become part of the al-Sabti clan – especially after the death of Aboud al-Sabti, her master and the father of her two children. Through Fetha's female offspring, the author succeeds in offering a space for the reader to ponder racial issues in Arabia by analysing the challenging family dynamics and the discourse of multiple oppressions within such dynamics. For instance, Baraka – the elder Fetha's daughter – is a woman who suffers her fate in silence; she is depicted as locked into a slave-like servitude and as constantly occupying the kitchen space, cooking for and serving the rest of the clan. Her subjugation serves the reader as a reminder of the character of 'Anab's mother, Zaitounah, in Badriya al-Beshir's *Al Erjouḥah* (The Swing – discussed in Chapter 4). In a similar vein, a non-discursive narrative of power and powerlessness is carefully woven into the text, with women depicted as inhabiting the private and marginal space while men occupy the public and central space. In particular, the novel's *Eid* scene (concerning a Muslim religious festival) shows precisely how the Sabti women carefully move between segregated male and female spaces. When Aboud al-Sabti enters the harem space to pass on his good wishes to female members of his family, his presence, the author notes, brings sublime joy and happiness to the women, who are portrayed as dashing to the door to see him. Thus, unequal gender hierarchies are textualized by the author to further indict traditions that permit the likes of al-Sabti to wield unchecked power over the female members of his family.

These stories create a new geographics of identity that emphasizes the fluid interaction of race, class and gender. They do so by moving beyond white/black binaries and looking at relations between two or more marginalized groups – in this case, black women versus women of colour, servants versus masters, and women and foreign men (the characters of Thamer and Jaber) versus the al-Sabti menfolk. As we have seen previously, the multiplication of oppression 'creates its antithesis, a multiple richness and power'.[56]

Through the two cousins, Nariman and Fetha – the daughters of foreign and cast-out mothers, abandoned by one of their parents and left alone in the big al-Sabti household – the reader is made aware of women's struggles for love and freedom within a large and old-fashioned tribe. Fetha is portrayed as the antithesis of Nariman in attitude and physique: she is naturally strong, stubborn, beautiful and full of life, while Nariman is plain and weak. The latter confesses her utter lack of cleverness as well as her naivety, saying, 'Stupidity is part of one's life [...] Fetha, on her wedding day, accidently burns the border of her bridal veil, so I jump to her rescue and extinguish it with my hand.'[57]

The narrator's identity is never fully disclosed but is suggested to be Nariman. She is portrayed as trying to come to terms with what happened following the shocking death of her cousin and childhood companion, the younger Fetha. This enveloping, angelic character, who contrasts her own passivity with the more subversive character of the now-dead Fetha, assumes a totally different persona as the story unfolds. Her longing for a companion who acted as a role model for her, and at times even caught her in silent fits of jealousy because of the love between Fetha and Thamer, is replaced by shock and brooding over the mysterious disappearance of her beloved cousin Fetha's body.

It is not surprising, then, that the opening chapter sees the narrator (Nariman) in a constant state of struggle, which she tries to overcome by the act of remembering and analysing her past with the help of Alameh – who features as an imagined lover and interlocutor, acting as a substitute for her lost cousin Fetha. This explains the significant narrative space given to Alameh, whose presence contributes to Nariman's new sense of subjectivity; the narrator observes, 'in the absence of Fetha, he is the impossible dream man', he represents 'a question and exclamation mark in Nariman's confused memories' in conversation with her higher self, symbolically alluded to as Alameh, which literally translates as 'knowledgeable' and is described as a 'throat [that] flutters in my chest'. The throat in this context stands as a metaphor for the narrator's higher self, which is seeking justification for Fetha's shocking death in order to extinguish what she describes as 'a massacre' inside her. The narrator further confirms a connection between her soul and memory when she refers to the 'ear', as in 'my ears laugh at me, my earloop, a pocket of hidden dust from the recent past'. Such lines show an example of the significant feminist discourse that Saudi women writers employ to describe the division between self and society, and their grievance against social retribution for women who dare to transgress the latter's code of honour. In fact, if we read the text more carefully, we realize the unfolding space of separation between the narrator and Fetha. It is imperative to ask: Why does the author employ this elusive gesture? What does her sarcasm suggest? Is she trying to cancel out a fact, or reality, from her memory? It seems important that we neither reduce the meaning of the opening few lines nor ignore the fact that the 'ear' corresponds to the reflexive act of 'laughing' aimed at the narrator. The 'ear', as a site of hearing, turns inwards into the conscience, metaphorically alluded to as 'throat' while the 'ear' signifies all the rumours that circulated in the al-Sabti village following the death of the younger Fetha and the disappearance of her body. This beginning sets the tone of the novel, apparently recounted by Nariman, and fixes the various 'voices' of Fetha, al-Sabti, Thamer, Jaber, Ḥomoud, Jamila and Baraka in what seems like an autobiographical memoir that reveals the intersection of culture and identity. Curiously, the narrator attempts to distance herself from the younger Fetha, as if withholding what she is trying to let go of: the feelings that might blind her from seeing the truth – that is, Fetha's cheating on her husband and her pregnancy by Thamer. A judging voice, coming from the higher self, interrupts her memories in what amounts to a collision between the internal and external domains that reflects a division between the psychic self and society.

The most striking image of Fetha comes when she is described as dying while the baby inside her is stuck between her legs. It is an emotionally charged scene in the narrative; a temporal threshold that marks the onset of delirium in the narrator and a rupture in the narrative space between now and then, past and present. Just like Laila al-Juhani's protagonist in *Barren Paradise*, discussed above, Saudi women writers occasionally revert to terminated pregnancies, mostly out of wedlock, which calls into question the significance of pregnancies, birth and dead babies as narrative devices. I argue that in Saudi women's fiction of resistance, failed pregnancies and unborn babies stand as a metaphor for subjugated women and an interregnum of sorts, echoing Antonio Gramsci's famous lines 'the old world is dying, and the new world struggles to be born: now is the time of monsters'[58] – in this context, the "monsters" are precisely the entrenched customs that oppress women, personified by figures like Al-Sabti and his son Homud.

Although the author hints at a secret relationship between Fetha and Thamer – one that goes beyond courtly love – it is never openly disclosed. While such subtexts might have helped in the build-up to the shocking death of Fetha and the disappearance of her body, the author fails to provide a comprehensible explanation – and both readers and critics are left pondering her fate. Her death is shrouded in obscurity and secrecy, especially when Thamer is described as stuffing a cloth-like dummy that resembles her body and spraying it with Fetha's perfume, which makes it reek, adding another repulsive dimension to this tragic event. The al-Sabti family is portrayed as being vaguely worried about the eruption of scandal in their small town of Sail Valley. There is, however, a 'gothic' element to the disappearance of Fetha's body that evokes a mythological image of a return to life reminiscent of Western Victorian-era novels. The stuffed dummy buried in Fetha's grave and the stench that recalls demons and witchcraft are totemic of community sin and its hand in the irrevocable damage to her in life, whereas her missing body indicates a return to the much-coveted state of freedom after death.

Significantly, al-Ghamdi also carefully documents colour bias and the terrains between power and powerlessness within the female members of the al-Sabti family. For this purpose, discourses of positionality as theorized by Friedman foster an interactional analysis of identity – specifically, one of contradictions and relationality – whereby one axis of identity, such as gender, should be understood in relation to others, such as sexuality and race. The discourses succeed in fostering this identity through the character of the younger Fetha, whose identity sits at the crossroads of various formations of power and powerlessness – of being extremely dependent on a point of reference (that is, her proximity to the power of the al-Sabti patriarchs), and of the powerlessness arising from her blackness and gender.

This concept is highly dialogized through the depiction of Fetha's wedding night and the struggle within her over having Ḥomoud as a husband as she recalls her mother, Baraka's, words: 'Listen my girl, we're a stigma to the family and of a different colour too; thus, we can only survive by being cunning and sly, otherwise we'll diminish if we're passive.'[59] This comes as a warning to Fetha who, according to her mother, should be cunning enough to possess Ḥomoud's 'seed' and win him over to her side – thus placing even more pressure on the bride-to-be, who knows that her prospective husband still prefers his first wife, her cousin Athba, to her. Baraka's words explain Fetha's keenness to have a child with Ḥomoud; she reflects, 'who can stop me? I've made up my mind.'[60] Although Ḥomoud is depicted as still being in love with Athba, he is encouraged by the male-dominated society to marry as many women as he wants to – or as his father dictates for him. Nevertheless, when his father tells him to marry Fetha, he declines at first, saying, 'I love my wife.'[61] Ultimately, however, marriage obviously has no real value for polygamous men, and this is perhaps what the author wants to bring to the forefront through her deployment of such characters. In the event, Ḥomoud unintentionally awakens the muted scars of colour discrimination lying within young Fetha's psyche:

> For a year and a half now I've been watching him sneak out of my bed to Athba's and come in the weaning hours of morning with his body covered with a towel [...] I look at him with my weary eyes and open them widely when he pinches my cheeks and says 'good morning beauty'. I remembered the first night of marriage and all the pain I felt when we consummated marriage. I felt his body and was scared by the voice of a small woman that resembled me and came from somewhere close, I panicked and froze and I saw the face of Baraka and the old Fetha shouting at me 'steal him before he steals you'. Steal him, he's yours, give birth to a third Fetha, I became a thousand body in one, I twirled like a poisonous snake. I twirled and stretched my body until he came under my control in spite of his big body. I remembered the faces of Sabti and Jamila so I strengthened my fist around him.[62]

While such scenes of intimacy may be criticized for excessive flagrance, nonetheless these details not only reveal the sadistic side of the younger Fetha, who seems to take revenge on behalf of her mother and grandmother and their hatred of the al-Sabti men, but also provide another discourse on colour bias and forced marriages, which are rife in the rural parts of the kingdom. For example, Baraka constantly reminds Fetha of the old days when she used to ask her own beloved grandmother, 'Grand Mum why are you dark and my family is white?'[63] This is a very difficult question indeed, and one that reflects Fetha's feeling of inferiority and difference from the rest of the al-Sabti clan – including her husband and his favourite wife, Athba. Fetha's jealousy is provoked every time Ḥomoud sneaks off to Athba at night, leaving her envious of her light-skinned rival. Such questions constitute subtexts that help readers to understand the complexity of Fetha's situation. Her insecurity triggers an urge in her to have a child with Ḥomoud, 'strengthening her fist around him' in an attempt to reclaim her body and the identity that has been marred by what she perceives as the black blood on her side of the family. Through Fetha, we learn the meaning of being half-black in a society that pays much attention to ancestral roots, which, the writer hints, have minimized her chances of marriage – a point that prompted al-Sabti to pressure her into marrying his son Ḥomoud in the first place when he got wind of a sign that she might be in love with the Egyptian Thamer and was meeting him illicitly:

> Women saw Fetha sneak to the phone, Athba caught her in the middle of the night standing almost naked in the kitchen, they swore but I couldn't believe them. [...] Jamila says that she saw white spots on her new clothes and a smash on the edge of the window glass that overlooks the lemon trees.[64]

Fetha, the granddaughter, contemplates how she tried to compensate for her feelings of inferiority by seducing Ḥomoud:

> I stopped caring about him once I was sure of his subjugation to me. I allowed my exhausted body to drown in Ḥomoud's body heat and my ear to listen to the different insect buzz and some graceful footsteps that reminded me of Thamer; who came between me and Ḥomoud in the middle of the night, reminding me of old miserable days when al Sabti caught me sneaking in an attempt to avoid him when he reprimanded me 'stop', 'if your father was here we wouldn't have needed to ask you'. It didn't occur to me back then that I would grow up and it was time for me to sign a paper assigning al Sabti as my male guardian, a paper that allowed him to marry me off to anyone he consented to; it dawned on me then that I wouldn't stray from the road aunt Baraka walked along.[65]

To recollect another man while she is in bed with her husband transmits a great many untold stories that al-Ghamdi intentionally avoids openly disclosing to the reader. The omnipresent author is assuredly in control of the text because she hints at events and ideas in this way but never directly broaches them, which makes it hard to decipher at times. When she is with Thamer, Fetha feels like an equal – not of a different colour but, rather, simply a beautiful woman; additionally, with her he is not a foreigner or a womanizer but a lover. By signing the guardianship paper, she has given up her dream of having a new life that would be different from those of her mother and grandmother, who were treated not as wives or ladies but more like slaves and domestic workers as they toiled day and night for the al-Sabtis.

Notes

1 Interview with Saudi Arabian writer Raja Alem: 'When I write I am free, like flying in my dreams', 2014. Available at https://qantara.de/en/article/interview-saudi-arabian-writer-raja-alem-elegy-lost-era
2 Virpi Lehtinen, *Luce Irigaray's Phenomenology of Feminine Being* (State University of New York Press: Albany, 2014), p. 43.
3 Luce Irigary cited in Susan Stanford Friedman, ' "Beyond" Gynocriticism and Gynesis: The Geographies of Identity and the Future of Feminist Criticism', *Tulsa Studies in Women's Literature*, Vol. 15, No. 1 (Spring 1996), pp. 13–40.
4 Judith Butler, *Bodies That Matter: On the Discursive Limits of Sex* (Routledge: London; New York, 1993).
5 Raja Alem, *Khatem* (al-Markaz al-Thagāfii al-Arabi: Beirut, 2001), p. 82.
6 Ziad Elmarsafy, *Sufism in the Contemporary Arabic Novel* (Edinburgh University Press: Edinburgh, 2012), p. 156.
7 Elmarsafy, *Sufism in the Contemporary Arabic Novel*, pp. 24–5.
8 Friedman, *Mappings*, p. 19.
9 Alem, *Khatem*, pp. 87–8.
10 A configuration of time and space represented in language and discourse.
11 Shereen Abouelnaga, *Women in Revolutionary Egypt: Gender and the New Geographies of Identity* (American University in Cairo Press: Cairo, 2016), p. 124.
12 Friedman, *Mappings*, p. 236.
13 The narrative 'time-space' of the book occurs when the entire region of Hejaz (western Saudi Arabia) was a province of the Ottoman Empire, a period lasting from 1517 to 1918.
14 *Writing Arabian Style*, 2002. Marilyn Powell talks to Raja Alem. Available CBC IDEAS Sales Catalog (A-Z listing by episode title). www.cbc.ca/ideas/IDEAS-Catalog.pdf
15 Elaine Showalter quoted in Toril Moi, *Sexual/Textual Politics: Feminist Literary Theory* (Routledge: Abingdon and New York, 1985), p. 77.
16 Camille Adams Helminski, *Women of Sufism: A Hidden Treasure* (Shambhala: London, 2013).
17 Ali al-Shadawi, quoted in Hasan Namy (ed.), *Multaqa Jama'at Ḥewār* [The Forum of Ḥewār Group] (Jeddah Literary Club: Jeddah, 2006), p. 330.

18 Mary-Lou Zeitoun, 'Lipstick and a Veil: Saucy Saudi Scribe Needs Brother's Ok to Date', *NOW* magazine, Vol. 22, No. 10 (7–14 November 2002). https://nowtoronto.com/news/lipstick-and-a-veil (accessed 20 July 2022).
19 *James Strecker Reviews the Art*, 2 May 2013. Available at http://jamesstrecker.com/words/?p=583 (accessed 3 May 2022).
20 Arebi, *Women and Words*, p. 113.
21 Alem, *Khatem*, p. 247.
22 Alem, p. 139.
23 Claude Lévi-Strauss, *Myth and Meaning: Cracking the Code of Culture* (Schocken Books: New York, 1979), pp. 50–1.
24 Amira El-Zein, *Transgender, Culture, and Social Class in Early Twentieth Century's Mecca: Raja Alem's Khatam* (Georgetown University School of Foreign Service in Qatar: Doha, 2016), p. 14. Available at www.researchgate.net/publication/308274208_Transgender_Culture_and_Social_Class_in_Early_Twentieth_Century's_Mecca_Raja_Alem's_Khatam (accessed 3 May 2022).
25 Alem, *Khatem*, p. 176.
26 Alem, pp. 249–50.
27 Julia Kristeva, in Toril Moi (ed.), *The Kristeva Reader* (Blackwell Publishers: Oxford, 1991), p. 30.
28 The Qur'an, 36: 51.
29 Laila al-Juhani, *Al-Ferdūs al-Yabāb* [Barren Paradise] (Al-Kamel: Germany, 1999), p. 6.
30 Jami` at-Tirmidhi 2314, Book 10, Hadith 2314 Vol. 4.
31 Al-Juhani, *al-Ferdūs al-Yabāb*, p. 8.
32 Al-Juhani, p. 19.
33 Al-Juhani, p. 33.
34 Al-Juhani, p. 33.
35 Ernest Hemingway, *The Snows of Kilimanjaro, and Other Stories* (New York: Charles Scribner, 1970), p. 8.
36 Al-Juhani, *al-Ferdūs al-Yabāb*, p. 7.
37 Al-Juhani, p.7.
38 Virginia Woolf, 'A Sketch of the Past', in Jeanne Schulkind (ed.), *Moments of Being: A Collection of Autobiographical Writing* (Harcourt: London, 1985), p. 80.
39 Al-Juhani, *al-Ferdūs al-Yabāb*, p. 13.
40 Al-Juhani, p. 35.
41 Al-Juhani, p. 23.
42 Al-Juhani, p. 70.
43 Al-Juhani, p. 73.
44 Al-Juhani, p. 68.
45 Linda McDowell, *Gender, Identity, and Place: Understanding Feminist Geographers* (Minneapolis: University of Minnesota Press, 1999).
46 Rym Ghazal, *In Unmarked Saudi Tomb Lies 'Grandmother of Everyone'*, 25 September 2008. Available at www.thenationalnews.com/world/mena/in-unmarked-saudi-tomb-lies-grandmother-of-everyone-1.507432
47 Khaled Rabi quoted in Hasan Namy (ed.), *al-Riwayya al-Nesā'yya al-Saudyya: Khetāb al-Sard* [The Saudi Women Novel: Discourse of Narration] (The Cultural Club: Jeddah, 2006), p. 454.
48 Hélène Cixous, in Cixous and Clément, *The Newly Born Woman*, p. 9.
49 Cixous.

50 Al-Ghamdi had previously published only two collections of short stories, '*Afwan la Zeltu Aḥlam* and *Tahwa*, in 1996. Nevertheless, she is considered a prominent writer whose few works reveal high artistic skills and boldness in defying restrictions, and recall the writings of Syrian author Ghada al-Samman.
51 Abdullah al-Ghothami, *Women and Language* (Center of Arab Culture: Beirut, 1996), p. 206.
52 Friedman, *Mappings*, pp. 8–9.
53 Friedman, p. 28.
54 Nora al-Ghamdi, *Wejhat al-Bouṣlah* [Compass Direction] (Almu'assasa al'arabyya Lilderāsāt Wa-alnashr: Beirut, 2002), p. 159.
55 Al-Ghamdi, *Wejhat al-Bouṣlah*, p. 162.
56 Friedman, *Mappings*, p. 20.
57 Al-Ghamdi, *Wejhat al-Bouṣlah*, p. 85.
58 Antonio Gramsci, English translation quoted from *Selections from the Prison Notebooks of Antonio Gramsci*. Translated by Quintin Hoare and Geoffrey Nowell-Smith (eds) (Lawrence and Wishart: London, 1971).
59 Al-Ghamdi, *Wejhat al-Bouṣlah*, p. 154.
60 Al-Ghamdi, p. 99.
61 Al-Ghamdi, p. 175.
62 Al-Ghamdi, p. 176.
63 Al-Ghamdi, p. 154.
64 Al-Ghamdi, p. 113.
65 Al-Ghamdi, p. 177.

4
NARRATIVES OF VIOLENCE
Communicating Corporeal Anxieties

Physical violence against women has always occupied a central space in contemporary Saudi women's fiction – but particularly so from the mid-1980s onwards. The women writers documented throughout this chapter boldly incorporate the female body and voice into their texts, assigning a symbolic meaning that reveals a deeper social and ideological malaise. By doing so, they establish a new feminist discourse that serves as a counter memory to male literary traditions, which have historically marginalized women's suffering. This particularly literary strand bears witness to the imbalanced gender power relations resulting from deeply entrenched traditions. The writers collectively critique the mental and emotional cultural conditioning of women, which perpetuates their oppression. The narratives discussed in this chapter highlight a chicken-and-egg dilemma, illustrating how women's silence in the face of male tyranny perpetuates further violence. Drawing on Friedman's *Mappings* and Foucault's concept of 'power/knowledge',[1] we can see how both discursive and non-discursive practices of oppression and violence inherently generate their antithesis: power. Foucault's theory posits that power and knowledge are intertwined, such that the exercise of power always creates new forms of knowledge and vice versa. This relationship means that oppressive practices – whether through language (discursive) or actions (non- discursive) – inevitably create spaces for resistance and empowerment.

Female writers, by textualizing and archiving moments of violence against women, are subverting the dominant patriarchal male discourse. This subversion occurs through the creation of counter memories and alternative narratives that challenge and disrupt the hegemonic stories perpetuated by male literature. By documenting and exposing the realities of women's

DOI: 10.4324/9781003539681-5

experience, these writers reclaim the power that patriarchal structures seek to suppress.

These works present a counter-narrative to the hegemonic discourses that have dominated Saudi male literature for almost 30 years, discourses that Derrida might identify as 'hors-textes' – texts that marginalize and silence women. By focusing on the medium of struggle and resistance, these female writers locate sites of potential hope and emancipation. They illuminate the ways in which entrenched structures of discrimination can be challenged and ultimately transformed. Thus, the act of writing itself becomes a form of resistance, a means of reclaiming agency and rewriting the social and ideological scripts that have long oppressed women in the kingdom.

The stories that Saudi women writers tell, by naming and exposing the abusers, play a crucial role in highlighting areas where protections for women are insufficient. This act of storytelling itself contributes to reducing the threat of violence against women and bolstering the growing calls for legal redress. As Lila Abu-Lughod notes, the simple act of 'naming and criminalizing forms of violence can have positive effects. Such narratives can encourage legal reform and the education of judges, helping governments and communities to appreciate the seriousness of violence against women'.[2] By bringing these issues to light, women writers not only raise awareness but also promote a cultural shift towards greater accountability and protection of women.

Contemplating Sacred Values: Laila al-Juhani – *The Days of Ignorance*

Laila al-Juhani – author of *Barren Paradise*, discussed in Chapter 3 – takes the issue of racism and prejudice to a different level in her 2007 novel *Jahiliyyah* (The Days of Ignorance), through a forbidden-love story between the white Līn and black Malek. *The Days of Ignorance* is set in the holy city of Medina, in the western province of Saudi Arabia, historically famed for having given refuge to the Prophet Muhammad after he migrated from Mecca. Both cities are known as places of movement and trade – hubs of diversity, multiculturalism and Islamic cosmopolitanism, with millions of pilgrims arriving for the *hajj* or the lesser pilgrimage, the *umrah*, all year round.

In this novel, the author offers a critique of the continuity of *jahiliyyah* (ignorance) or pre-Islamic social norms that have persisted to date. It particularly focuses on the perceived impossibility of interracial marriages in Medina between those of Arab origin and those of African descent, or *takruni*,[3] despite Qur'anic verses and Islamic teachings that preach Islamic fraternity and equality. Hence, the cultural narrative that the author attempts to expose in this work – namely, the continuity of the painful racial divide and gender discrimination that go against the core values of Islam such as social justice and the equality of all humans before God. For this purpose, the narrative structure of *The Days of Ignorance* is aligned with two temporal frames – one of them taken from the pre-Islamic lunar calendar, incorporating names of days and months that are difficult to understand for the average Arab reader. For example, *Munis*the 15th of Wail* is juxtaposed with another, fictional, date – the *Twelfth year after desert storm 3 a.m.* – although *desert storm* is treated by the author as a 'punctum' and a turning point that signals a transformation in the collective consciousness of a people after which, nonetheless, stale traditions persisted.

Another temporal frame transpires through titles and synopses of news updates on the war on Iraq as reported by the main media channels at the time – producing a text suffused with hypotext, and political and historical intertextuality. The titles of the chapters are deliberately vague: 'Falling Sky'; 'He Has Not Yet Seen the Angels'; 'What's Beneath the Color?'; 'The Smell of Sorrow'; and the final one, 'Google Hallucinates'. These hypotexts provide a layered interpretation of events, through which al-Juhani seeks to raise questions about the continuity of the discourse of ignorance, racism and ethnic discrimination that was rife in the pre-Islamic period, or *jahili* times, in Mecca. Moneera al-Ghadeer observes that this is 'meant to present the crisis in a society that dabbles with social media while subscribing to traditions that serve its interest'.[4]

As in her previous work, al-Juhani captures the reader's attention in the opening lines of the novel – this time, with a bloodied body and a worried perpetrator asking, 'is he dead?' The all-seeing narrator, who is in full control of the narrative, leaves the reader pondering the fate of the unknown victim because, until the end of the novel, Malek is in a coma. Ensnaring the reader further, Malek even remains nameless in the first part of the novel, with the character Hashem referring to him as an animal, 'a stinking animal' who is worthy of torture, and the narrator tells us 'as for Hashem, he was waiting to get his hands on the animal' and 'to put the animal-at-large in his proper place'.[5] Spoiled with money and cars, Hashem has grown up to be a failure. A womanizer with no education, employment or prospects, he envies his sister Līn for having a life that has meaning; the narrator notes, 'that serenity of hers killed him'.[6] To display his manhood, Hashem strikes a patriarchal stance towards his sister, and constantly watches her until he discovers her relationship with Malek. Shocked by what he sees, Hashem channels his anger and violence towards Malek rather than Līn, because 'killing her would bring her relief, and he didn't want her to have any relief. He wanted her to suffer for a good long time'.[7] The novel's torture scene is recounted by several voices – the omniscient narrator, the violator and an accomplice:

> He [Hashem] heard the cracking of bones, and suddenly realized that he didn't want him to die. He pushed [another friend] Ayman away from him, saying, 'that's enough! If you keep on this way, he's going to die!'

Ayman extricated himself from his grip, saying, 'So let the dog die, then.' He pushed him farther away this time and grabbed the stick out of his hand, screaming, 'Enough! Enough!'

The heavy stone became hot, and heavier than before. All his strength left him, giving way to fear. He knew now what awaited him. He knew Musa's fate wasn't far from him. Why had he assumed that he was immune to such fate?

He didn't want to turn to see the beaten body again. But he did turn. When he took a good look at Malek's body for the first time, he discovered to his pained surprise that there was nothing wrong with him. He wished he'd discovered some defect in him – any defect. But all he saw was a humble aspiration being buried without a shroud. Everything seemed still as death as the cool, pallid evening glow enveloped everything in sight. With difficulty he shuffled over to the body and stood near its head. He bent down, placing his hands under the body's armpits, began pulling it away from the sidewalk towards the entrance of the building.[8]

Remembering Musa – a black 'pervert' at Hashem's school who ended up in prison – right after the assault is significant, not least because Musa was black but also because both Hashem and Musa are rendered equals in the face of the law. Reversing the discourse of racism by staging Hashem as a criminal is evident in the author's attempt to 'turn the tables' in the same way that she has Līn do to her brother in the novel, when she demands to know about the 'murderers'. In contrast, the assault on the victim (Malek) strips him of his agency; he is rendered powerless in the face of a violator like Hashem. This is a force that generates a narrative meaning – a subtext of powerlessness and victimization, a struggle between good and evil – in which Hashem is demonized and turned into a 'murderer'. Scenes of violence in literature are often important for what they represent: ideology; culture; and, above all, the ugliness that many people try to avoid looking at. Such scenes thus engender a shift in the reader's perspective and attitude towards the oppression and cruelty that they are witnessing – a reminder of Laura Tanner's words: 'violence is a form of resistance when it is exposed before the eyes of the reader'.[9]

The second chapter begins from the victim's perspective: 'he wished he would die'. As Līn is portrayed as being interested in 'what's beneath the color', she remains by the bedside of her dying beloved. Via alternating points of view, al-Juhani complicates the subject of interracial marriage, registering a feminist grievance against tribal laws that continue to apply to minorities. Unlike her mother, who is appalled and angry with her, Līn's father is caught in a dilemma, fearing that his daughter will be ostracized by society or even destroyed: 'God, what would people do to his daughter if he said yes to Malek?'[10] The crossing of racial boundaries and the expression of desire and love for an unapproved suitor contest both the 'piousness' of people and the marriage options set for women in that society. It is through such stories of forbidden love that a contact zone – as a site of repeated confrontations – is erected, and racial boundaries are sustained and intensified, generating violence and resentment towards both Līn and Malek. Hence, this novel forces the reader to confront the plight of women as they struggle for freedom from the twin yokes of patriarchal and familial oppression on the one hand and a paternal judicial system on the other: a system that, at the time, would not consent to the marriage of a woman without the blessing of her male guardian – be it a father, brother or uncle.[11] (As of August 2019, women in the kingdom were granted the right to register for divorce, marriage and apply for official documents without their guardian's permission.)

In the discourse of Saudi women's fiction of resistance, relationality, as suggested by Friedman, has been helpful in analysing the epistemological standpoint of identity and the dynamic of relationships among characters. It has also assisted in moving beyond the binaries of black and white, which Homi Bhabha describes as 'an important feature of colonial discourse' and 'its dependence on the concept of "fixity" in the ideological construction of otherness'.[12] This is because 'within a relational framework, identities shift with a changing context, dependent always upon the point of reference'.[13] Identities also change with historical, political and social circumstances. In sum, the discourse of relationality forms a link between gender and other axes of identity, with different aspects of identity functioning relationally as sites of inclusion or exclusion. For example, in contrast to her brother, Līn is made aware of her position as an inferior despite being a good, educated woman with a stable career. She is also treated badly by her own mother – a situation that reaches a tipping point when she announces her decision to marry Malek.

In *Gender Trouble: Feminism and the Subversion of Identity*, Judith Butler disputes Simone de Beauvoir's famous statement,[14] saying, how can one become a woman if one wasn't a woman all along? And who is this 'one' who does all the becoming? Is there some human who becomes its gender at some point in time? Butler then poses the most important questions: What is the moment or mechanism of gender construction? And when does this mechanism arrive on the cultural scene to transform the human subject into a gendered subject?[15] Butler deconstructs de Beauvoir's binary pairing of sex/gender with her 'performative theory of gender' – and by deconstruct, I mean that Butler read de Beauvoir not to renounce her theory but to go beyond the limiting binaries offered by the French thinker, by shifting the issues on to performativity and gender as a social construction of women's identity using Foucault's theories from *Discipline and Punish* and *Power and Knowledge*. Bearing in mind Butler's 'performative theory of gender', and her illuminating question 'what is the mechanism of gender construction?', we can see how al-Juhani exposes the repressive social and familial mechanisms that turned Līn into 'the black sheep of the family'. One of these mechanisms is the way in which society has shaped the family's expectation of their daughter's marriage. Performed through the abusive brother, who watches over his sister with no sense of remorse, and the mother who acts as a guardian of futile traditions, this is evident in the author's description of her in the passage below. The all-knowing narrator clarifies,

> It was the rage of a ten-year-old girl who'd come to an early awareness that she wasn't wanted but didn't understand why, the isolation that had confined her spirit, the loneliness that had sapped her, the neglect, the disregard, and the belittlement of everything she'd ever accomplished in her life. For more than twenty years, she hadn't meant a thing to her mother.[16]

In fact, Līn recalls how miserable her mother was about not having a son; she remembers her trying so hard to conceive in the hope of becoming the mother to a boy, going to doctors and trying various medicines and amulets until she had Hashem. In contrast to Hashem, Līn is described as a 30-year-old unmarried woman, calm and loving; she is focused on her medical studies and her work at a hospital. After graduating from King Abdulaziz University in Jeddah, Līn finds employment at a home for the underprivileged where she is loved and appreciated for her work; the narrator comments, 'she had something to do, something to look forward to, something to dream of'.[17]

Perhaps the most important contribution of *The Days of Ignorance* is its ability to debate racism in Arabia, through a contradictory discourse of sorts. The narrative contests negative images and stereotypes of Afro-descendants by juxtaposing the debauchery of the fair-skinned Hashem with the goodness of Malek – reversing the discourses that criminalize black men collectively and subverting issues of racism and negative representations of them generally. The different voices in the novel voluntarily reprise the cultural stereotype attached to Afro-descendants, illustrating a complex interplay of internalized bias, societal expectations, and resistance. Thus, cultural signifiers denoting racial bias, such as 'criminals' and the subaltern professions of the bourgeois family – 'football players' or 'singers' – are used to accentuate difference and prejudice. In this contradictory discourse, the identity of Malek in terms of his race and colour is foregrounded throughout the novel, whereas his good character and handsomeness is muted. This is most noticeable in the incident in which 'a traffic policeman checked his identification at a traffic light [...] even disapproved of his wearing traditional garb. After looking at his license, he said, "Well, well, well!! You've even got yourself looking just like one of us! Let me see your residence card." '[18] Malek is therefore rendered a symbol for those who are denied integration into society because of their 'knotty circumstances'.[19]

Subverting Silence: Badriya al-Beshir – *The Swing*

> Descending into earth is our inheritance from our grandmothers; from Eve to my mother Nora. Our fate is to ride the swing before we are forced to get off; we go to paradise only to be expelled from it.[20]

The Arabic title *Al Erjouḥah* has within it an image of movement, fluctuation and change that metaphorically alludes to women's unpredictable status. It locates the novel's three female characters at a pivotal juncture where 'travel' becomes a journey of adventure, highlighting their personal growth, the challenges they face and the transformative experiences they encounter. In the Swiss city of Geneva, these single, thirty-something, attractive women are in a place in which to enjoy all that a consumer economy has to offer. In this sense, the novel becomes an intervention in the public sphere – merging the private and the public with the personal and the cultural – in which these three 'musketeers' are depicted as transgressing all boundaries and being lured into a world of inappropriateness, crazy clubbing, drinking and dating. This offers a 'female counter memory' that challenges predominant identities – mainly, the *saḥwa*-constructed images of mythological figures: woman as the 'queen of her home', the 'princess bride', the 'pearl in a shell' – simply by recalling women's stories.

The novel gains momentum when the three characters accidently bump into each other on arrival from Riyadh at Geneva Airport after a several-year hiatus. Their union activates 'cultural memory' – more precisely, Paul Connerton's notion of the 'act of transfer': 'an act in the present by which individuals and groups constitute their identities by recalling a shared past on the basis of common, and therefore often contested, norms, conventions and practices'.[21] The trio are set on subverting the logic of the patriarchy, through rebellion, negotiations or even mocking society's laws – thereby shocking the reader.

Drawing on Butler's aforementioned theory of gender as 'performative' – that is, produced by the reiterative power of discourse to construct and constrain that which it names (which is particularly helpful in making sense of subtle gendered performances and power relations that transpire in the issues debated in this novel) – I contend that, in Saudi women's fiction of resistance, engaging with taboo issues allows stories to be communicated in both individual and collective knowledge. Most importantly, in writing about the three 'musketeers', the author succeeds in broaching taboo topics. Breaking the silence surrounding issues that are often left unspoken is crucial for social change and for opening a dialogue that can help challenge and dismantle harmful norms.

The novel examines the social order that recognizes the female as a marker of family and community honour – deviations from its prescribed norms can lead to severe social consequences, including shame, ostracism and violence. This has created gender hierarchies and exclusions, resulting in limitations placed on women, and what Khaled Abou El Fadl identifies as 'social death'.[22] For this, I look into the social and psychological processes that facilitate violence against the female characters using the concept of contradictory subject positions that branched out, in the 1990s, from the idea of multiple oppressions – one of the six discourses of identity delineated in Friedman's *Mappings* (as discussed in the Introduction). This concept focuses on the phenomenon of contradiction as 'fundamental to the structure of subjectivity and the phenomenological experience of identity'.[23]

The Swing benefits from its rotating viewpoints, allowing the author to dive into the heads of the three protagonists – Salwa, 'Anab and Maryam – and enabling the reader to see, through them, racial, gender and sectarian prejudices. For instance, the novel opens with the all-seeing narrator giving a bleak appraisal of Maryam and her perspective on Riyadh. The author links the collapse of her marriage to Meshari with the occasion on which she and her husband were having dinner at a pizza restaurant with another couple. The religious police dragged the four of them off; both men and women were humiliated and later ordered to sign a consent paper not to go out with another couple in public again. This incident leaves deep scars on Maryam and her husband, whose self-esteem is shattered as he feels powerless to protect his wife.

Maryam leaves for Geneva to search for Meshari, who fled to an unknown destination following an incident with the religious police which left him struggling with a sort of trauma-induced depression. Using the third-person point of view, the narrator comments, 'Maryam left Riyadh, as in the summer months, pale and sore, like a pregnant woman, but with dust'[24] rather than with child. Here, the Saudi capital is turned into a psychological and discursive tool, metaphorically alluding to women's subjugation and the couple's personal traumatic confrontation with the religious police. This correlation is further validated when Maryam looks down from the departing plane and sees Riyadh as 'a tranquil cemetery of sand'. The narrator adds, 'Maryam did not know that there were others who referred to their home country as "cemetery", until she read about an Italian woman who said the same thing about her town Venice; a piece of paradise.' In this passage, the author vindicates Maryam's negative view of Riyadh by relating it to her traumatic experience that took place in Riyadh – thus justifying the significant chunk of narrative space that is given over to Maryam's and Meshari's confrontation with the guardians of morality in the first chapter.

The same idea is further endorsed by the narrator who poses the question, and I quote, 'why are women dominated by traditions more than men? Why is culture so skilful in producing iron cages, shrouds and ropes for women only, while men fly far away from their domineering culture?'[25] In this sense, culture has contoured women's geographics of identity, curbing aspects of identity in which the subject normally exercises agency. Hence, family, traditions, class, education, religion, location, the past, the present, knowledge and gender all inform Saudi women's choices in life.

The main protagonist, Salwa, is given a large textual space in the narrative, and her experience, challenges and evolution are thoroughly portrayed. For example, her first marriage offers a discourse of violence that is compounded by the capitalist economy, consumerism, low self-esteem and an abusive husband – all of which are divulged through flashbacks and a third-person narrative. Her first husband, the rich Abdulrahman, sensing her dislike, beats her regularly, inflicting serious injuries. Each time she is struck, Abdulrahman showers her with jewellery the next day – a reminder of Laura Tanner's view on the power of money, rooted in the capitalist economy, in which 'wounds of the body can be erased by waving a check'.[26] In fact, this violence begins during their ten-day honeymoon, a point that makes Salwa realize that it was not a good idea to travel with him alone; since then, every time she is beaten she turns to the support of her family members, who come to her rescue. The narrator explains,

> Salwa says that Abdulrahman is a good man who does not hit her on purpose. Everything that happens is because of bad luck that stands in their way, like, he would be nervous that night or she would offend him somehow. And mostly, she's the one to blame.[27]

This passage suggests that Salwa has been bullied by her husband into believing that she is the provoker of his violence. Al-Beshir here stages the silence of Salwa, her family and friends in order to reproach social traditions – asserting how, under certain ideological and cultural circumstances, women's bodies pay a high price for their perpetuation. Talking about her distress to family and close friends on the phone actually makes it feel less traumatic – young and lacking in experience, Salwa thus starts to believe that being beaten by her husband is the norm and that most marriages are like hers. Her gullible approach to married life raises questions in the reader's mind of whether it is her low self-esteem that is keeping her with her abuser or the male-dominant social order that has shaped her identity or restricted her actions? Every time she is brutally beaten by her husband and her face is bruised, her mother Nora, a divorcee herself, advises her to abandon him, telling her, 'sooner or later you're going to leave him'. It is only when Salwa actually fears for her life that she is forced to seek a divorce. The character is portrayed as having no interest in pursuing her education or a career, lost among her 20 siblings and in need of social recognition. The narrator explains, 'girls have no ambition but to get married and have children, the ones who get to spend their life with a husband without him taking another wife are absolutely lucky'. Salwa's choices in life echo Françoise d'Eaubonne's words:

> Women were trained to view marriage as the only career to which an 'honest' woman could aspire: the education of a well-heeled young woman tends to turn [her] into a luxurious parasite; she is duped, she is amused with frills, playthings and madrigals; she is permitted the arts of refinement, as are the geisha or the hetaerae [an ancient Greek courtesan], but she is denied serious study and culture [...] those few signs which would open the mind.[28]

On returning to her family home as a young divorcee with no career and no intention of developing herself as an individual, Salwa secretly remarries – the heartthrob, prince-like character Sultan – entering into a form of 'secret marriage' on the strength of his promise that their union would be made public sometime in the future. In this marriage, the female body is turned into a commodity for the powerful husband to manipulate through acts of dominance, transforming her in the process into a mere object of desire – redeemable via the ready availability of money. Not surprisingly, her new husband's promise is eventually broken and she becomes a two-time divorcee. She subsequently begins fooling around with Sultan, the ex-husband whom she still loves, in the hope that his money will erase the feelings of humiliation.

With her being treated like a mistress, Salwa's marriage is anything but dignified or normal – a point that enrages her younger brother on seeing Sultan's driver waiting for his sister in the pre-dawn hours, minutes before the call for *Fajr* prayer. Salwa's secret marriage turns her body into the means by which gender becomes 'performative'; the act of smuggling her in and out like a call girl is a traumatic form of 'gender trouble' wherein the female body is forced into acts of prostitution. This causes shame for her brother, who bursts into tears and tells her, 'Do you think you are cheap, that you make yourself available for night pickups? [...] Do you think it is proper to go out in front of all our neighbors at that hour?' His anger allows the reader to grasp the social stigma attached to secret marriages. Under the pressure of male members of Salwa's family, Sultan eventually divorces her – but she still loves him and spends time with him in Europe. Salwa's disappointment with her two marriages drives her to self-destructive bouts of alcohol, drugs and adultery. At the end of her trip to Geneva, she is depicted as penniless and in need of money; on her insistence, Sultan meets her in a remote hotel in the city's suburbs, and they consummate their love out of wedlock – not even in a secret marriage.

Alongside Maryam's and Salwa's stories, *The Swing* also describes the life of 'Anab, Salwa's long-time friend, a black-skinned girl who is brought up in the palace where her parents work. Through this character, we are allowed a glimpse into the status of ex-slaves and their offspring in contemporary Arabia – and how, despite the law reinstating their full rights (a long time ago), some remained locked in servitude (by choice and feelings of loyalty to their masters) and went on to have and raise their children in the same palaces and quarters. The author points out, 'they did not see a big difference between being slaves or servants, because they were grateful to have food and shelter, better than the poor who stood every day on the doorstep of their master'.[29] The dark-skinned, young girl 'Anab is portrayed as enjoying a carefree life compared with that of the lighter-skinned girls who are protected and sheltered from the preying eyes of the palace's males. For instance, 'Anab is allowed to wander the corridors of the palace in the *haramlek*-like quarters (women-only accommodation), even during the hours of the siesta, oblivious to her sensuality and the risk of harassment or even the unthinkable: rape.

This all ends one day when, during her daily patrols, playing with her pink crayons, she is snatched and raped in the palace, in broad daylight, by an unidentified white man. Raped, 'Anab is reduced to a passive signifier, with her body turned into a mere object of desire. Al-Beshir goes even further, to link rape with colour bias – especially when 'Anab is depicted as innocently trying to wipe out the ugliness of what has happened to her by desperately rubbing her black skin. It is a moment that captures 'Anab's realization of her difference from other, lighter-skinned girls in the palace who are protected against such assaults because of their title and complexion. This incident archives and textualizes a moment of great violence, wherein gender and race are foregrounded while other constituents of the victim's identity – of her being an innocent, ten-year-old girl, for instance – are muted. By categorizing the man as white, the author asserts the dominance of one group over the other. Her narrator comments,

> When she walked into daylight again, she saw her red blood covering her black skin. She walked crying in pain, deep inside, she felt that she was damned, yet she couldn't curse the white hands, nor be angry at them, hold them liable or incriminate them. Contrariwise, she damned her black skin and the pink crayons.[30]

In *The Swing*, al-Beshir succeeds in breaking the prevailing silence on violence by depicting the petrifying psychological processes and consequences of rape. 'Anab's mother, Zaitounah, adds insult to injury as, fearing a scandal and the possibility of her daughter's pregnancy, she marries her off almost immediately to a member of the palace staff, who is depicted as chewing *gat*[31] all day long. The marriage is a kind of hell, and when it finally ends it has totally transformed 'Anab into a careless and loose woman, lacking self-esteem, the painful and humiliating memories of both rape and marriage having caused a rupture in her conscience whereby the psychological assault on her from within carries a long-term force that brings about her self-destruction.

As mentioned earlier, the discourses of contradiction and positionality are more informative than the old dichotomies of male and female that are embedded in gynocriticism because they scrutinize the various layers of a narrative and disseminate knowledge about the social order itself. For instance, examining 'Anab's dilemma in relation to the privileged situation of the lighter-skinned girls living in the same palace allows the reader to appreciate other axes of the protagonist's identity. We learn that women may be united by gender but are nonetheless divided by their race and class. Likewise, 'Anab's blackness is blamed for her rape – a point that is later forced into her consciousness when a friend and travel companion (Maryam, in fact), upon hearing how she and Salwa spent the night clubbing and smoking hashish in one of Geneva's nightclubs, asks, 'Aren't you embarrassed of what you're doing? Aren't you afraid that people might see you?' The narrator answers Maryam, saying that 'Anab 'was numbed to feelings of shame and [the] fear of crossing social boundaries because her black colour, of which she was made conscious when she was raped at a young age, set her free from any alignments of shame and propriety'.[32]

It is no surprise that violence and abuse transform these silent and pretty girls into defiant women. Their unpleasant experiences with men stand as a testament to the patriarchal culture that allows men to abuse women without being held accountable. The misfortunes of 'Anab and Salwa, in particular, bring with them a sense of liberation from the heavy shackles of conformity; they are depicted as enjoying a wild and hedonistic lifestyle after their supposed falls from grace. Hence, violence in this context is evoked as having a symbolic meaning for the patriarchal tyranny, and it acts as a fuelling agent and an active force in the creation of a narrative that shatters the silence of women – defying, as it does so, Arabia's silent model of propriety.

Discipline and Punishment: Hana Hejazi – *Two Women*

Hana Hejazi's *Emra'tān* (Two Women) incorporates themes of gender-charged violence. It presents a story, many aspects of which might seem all too predictable: forbidden love between a man and a woman, the wrath of the young woman's father and her resulting physical abuse and incarceration. Yet the text treats such themes of discipline and punishment in an unfamiliar way by turning the female body into a site of social, political, economic and religious conflicts. I find that parallels exist between Hejazi's novel, and the ideas and imagery of the prison that she creates, and Foucault's writings on the disciplining of the female body and the 'Birth of the Prison'. The strength of this concept lies in its ability to mediate on discipline, power, gender and subjectivity – all of which are especially relevant to feminist analysis.

For this purpose, I examine the physical and psychological experience that Hejazi's protagonist undergoes as 'sustain(ing) a particular view of society' because, as Mary Douglas notes,

> The social body constrains the way that the physical body is perceived. The physical experience of the body, always modified by the social categories through which it is known, sustains a particular view of society. There is a continual exchange of meanings between the two kinds of bodily experience so that each reinforces the categories of [the] others.[33]

This exchange exposes a bias in cultural practices and the dominant discourse, which has engendered in women's fiction an 'imagery of prison'[34] – in both the metaphorical and actual senses of the word – which seeks to challenge gender-based violence through stories.

Two Women investigates familial and cultural codes of behaviour through the protagonist Laila and her friend Marām, each representing a 'slice' of human experience and a piece of the cultural diversity seen in Arabia. For instance, the two women, as the cover illustration of the book suggests, come from different backgrounds: the modern Marām represents the other side of the coin to the traditional Laila. This dichotomy of modern/traditional, good/bad, strong/weak and patriarchal/matriarchal is embedded in the two women's familial and social relationships, pulling the narrative in opposite directions. Although gender is the central constituent of their identity, the geographics of identity that this 'new text' emphasizes comprises a fluid interaction of class and national origin along with gender – a combination that straight binaries usually fail to notice.

The novel's alternating character viewpoints, in addition to that of the narrator, help the reader to understand the struggle of women in a closed society who, like people elsewhere in their twenties, strive to fall in love and lead an exciting life. For instance, Marām is portrayed as a strong woman blessed with parents who have given her the confidence to live her life without the fear of being interrogated by her brother or society, whether about her intentions or her whereabouts. In fact, Marām remembers the influence of her father's words on her life, as he admonished her brother whenever he caught him questioning his sister's behaviour. He told his son, 'Do not act like a macho man' – and the word macho is repeated by the mother even after the father's death, whenever her brother tries to play the role of a male guardian. Laila's family stands in stark opposition to that of Marām, with the former's father depicted as crude and abusive of her mother. The novel attempts to examine the difference in attitude between the two girls, and comes to the conclusion that Marām's father loved her unconditionally and gave her the confidence to enjoy life to the full whereas Laila's bigoted father fostered fear and diffidence in her.

A strong friendship develops between the two girls after they meet at work. Laila notes,

> Me and Marām, we became two tresses on a head, two knots on a thread, or two sleeves on a shirt, I don't really know how we became best friends. What does she see in me, to be my friend, could it be people's rejection of her, could it be my traditional character? And why was I attracted to her, her laughter, her openness to the world, her love for life?[35]

Indeed, this friendship empowers Laila to the extent that she starts to rebel against her family's strict rules and the oppressive reality of her mother's life. She no longer responds to her brother's never-ending commands, so her elder sister does things on her behalf and her mother curses her for not being obedient while the father turns a blind eye because all he cares about is the monthly salary that he has thus far taken from both her and her sister.

Marām, on the other hand, is portrayed as acknowledging the social stigma attached to single women living on their own, yet she cannot be bothered to waste her life worrying about the social codes of behaviour and the segregation laws that would stop her from seeing her male friends. However, her unfolding monologues and introspections not only give voice to the muted female perspective but also help to peel off layers of ambiguity and vagueness surrounding this character, who is depicted as a relaxed person right from the beginning in the sense that she has had extramarital relationships with men – including with the character Sami. In fact, it is through Marām that Laila meets Ahmad in one of the cafés in Jeddah and falls in love with him. However, when they decide to marry, her father is infuriated because of the so-called 'social and class divide', an intertextual similarity with al-Juhani's *The Days of Ignorance*, discussed earlier, which also grappled with society's class divisions.

Two Women, then, addresses the issues of class divide, forced marriage and patriarchal tyranny head-on through the plot device of a father who tortures his daughter on a daily basis and locks her up in a room in the hope that she will return to her senses and be deterred from marrying Ahmad. Laila's bodily confinement is meant not only to rehabilitate her to fit back into prevailing moral codes of behaviour but also to discipline her and teach her to be submissive to her father and the wider patriarchal society. This tackling of the issue of violence against women comes from Hejazi's experience as a medical practitioner and a writer who contributes to several newspapers and magazines – a factor that lends credibility to her portrayal of the victims of gender-based violence. When Laila decides to marry Ahmad in court, without the blessing of her family, the judge deceives her by contacting her father, who comes rushing to seize his daughter and take her back home – leaving a perplexed Ahmad waiting for her outside the courtroom. Her father is helped to escape from the back door of the courthouse by the judge. Laila later recalls the incident:

> I made a mistake, for a moment I thought this judge can be my guardian, and I was wrong to have told him that the one I love is waiting outside to marry me. The judge looked at me in scrutiny and said you are the daughter of Muhammad bin Saleh, and I held my breath, and nodded. He whispered something to his assistant, who left the room and came back with a mobile phone, the judge took the mobile and left the room. I felt something bad was going to happen, I shivered, and I felt cold, I asked the assistant where the judge had gone? He put his finger on his mouth to shut me up, I was scared. The judge came back and started probing me about my brothers, I was more scared, I couldn't answer. He then asked me if I have brought Ahmad with me to court, it was then that I started doubting his words. I wondered how it was going to end, if they were going to put me in jail with accusations over ethics. If I can call Ahmad for help, he was out waiting for me, but no, I didn't want them to find him.
>
> The judge started preaching to me about women in this day and age, about being a good daughter, he told me that women will be the fuel of the hell-fire, he's sure that I would be one, unless I repent. I tried to leave but I couldn't, he shouted at me to sit. Then he looked at the policeman who suddenly appeared. I was sure there and then that they were going to put me in jail [...] I was waiting for my destiny [...] when I saw my father and brother, I collapsed on the chair, the judge then shook hands with them and took them outside the room. They returned after a little while, my brother furious and wanting to hit me but my father yelled at him.
>
> My father held me from the back of my neck, and dragged me saying cruelly 'walk in front of me, damn you bitch.'[36]

The omniscient narrator, who is in charge of the novel, describes how Ahmad was subsequently driven to insanity by what had happened: he recalls Marām saying of Laila, in answer to his questions, that 'she disappeared'. Subsequently, her friend tries to call Laila but her mobile phone is switched off. Her absence from work escalates Marām's fears, so she tries to call her at home and, after a long wait, the bone-chilling voice of Laila's father answers, saying that she is visiting her aunt in Deera[37] before he hangs up.

Finally, Laila's own account fills in the gaps of what has happened: how the judge conspired with her father and how she was smuggled out through a back door, forced into the car and locked up in her room once they got home – her father and brother taking turns to torture her that day until she became unconscious. 'I woke up the next day, I tried to open my eye, I found out that one of my eyes was completely closed. Did they extract my eye? I was able to open my other eye.'[38] Laila's imprisonment is taken to another level when, two weeks later, she is transferred to a deserted room on the roof of the house; a prison-like space that keeps her away from the family. She is left in that room to rot, and the reader accompanies her as she contemplates how her life has turned out after all that she has suffered.

Drawing on Foucault's *Discipline and Punish*, the chapter 'Solitary Confinement' turns Laila's body into a 'means of discipline and punishment that is bound to produce "subjected and practiced bodies, docile bodies"'.[39] In this section of the book, Laila's tortured body is discursively transformed into a site for a narrative of discipline and punishment, and a tool for the assertion of patriarchal tyranny: the protagonist is regularly tortured in order to force her to comply with society's laws of behaviour. Hejazi succeeds in politicizing the female body throughout the novel, in fact. Laila's imprisonment is highly dialogized – especially when, as she is covered in the darkness of her *'abaya* and thrown into that rooftop room, she thinks, 'Is he going to throw me in this room, full of rats and evil spirits?' When she opens her eyes, she is shocked to find that her father has reorganized it especially for her detention. Left like a pariah, little more than an animal, Laila is portrayed as too depressed to pay attention to her appearance. When one day her mother opens the door, Laila sees the look in her eyes and realizes how frightening she must appear. She instinctively tries to comb through her hair with her fingers, but she then wonders, 'I am the prisoner, why do I feel guilty for looking horrible?' To her surprise, she notices that her mother has also visibly aged in the intervening few weeks. The bathing scene that follows is highly problematized, with the mother portrayed as lovingly giving Laila a bath, rubbing her hair and scrubbing her body of the dirt that has accumulated on her over time. Laila starts to develop warm feelings towards her mother, only to find out that her family has conspired to marry her off to the 60-year-old Saleh, who already has two wives.

Two Women's unfolding monologues reveal not only its protagonist's physical discomfort but also another pain beyond that of the physical body: the demands and pressures of the social body. Its soliloquies turn the novel into a sort of prison memoir, which interrogates patterns of oppression and gender discrimination that contribute to women's incarceration. Breea Willingham, writing in the context of female black inmates in the US penal system, suggests that such 'writing allows imprisoned women to create their own discourse within an oppressive system and in an oppressive space. Though their writing[s] may not dismantle the system, they create a space where the women find their voice and educate themselves' – and although 'writing in prison may not be behaviour that is always seen as explicitly political, it can become important to the resistance to structures of privilege, exploitation, and power'.⁴⁰ Thus, the novel gives the reader an insight into its protagonist's physical and psychological decline, which is located in the humiliation that she feels the minute her father 'dragged her [off] like a sheep' on that doomed day on which she went to court to marry the one she loved.

Laila's countless introspections offer the reader an answer as to the root cause of the disastrous family dynamics depicted, which lies in the protagonist's rejection of her father's tyranny and her mother's powerlessness, and her fear of becoming like her mother – a passive victim of violence, who is also beaten day and night by the father. But, unlike Laila's father, the author allows some textual space for the mother to speak for herself, in a chapter entitled 'Mothers'. Here, Laila's mother is partly vindicated and given a voice to explain herself, saying, 'It wasn't easy for me to be beaten up during the day, and sleep with him at night.' She then goes on to recall how her husband was violent from day one, and how she tried to escape from his sadistic attacks a few times but was returned to him every time she would seek help from her own mother – who, like most traditional mothers, acted as a guardian of the patriarchy, encouraging her daughter to perform the traditional gender role of submissive wife and mother regardless of her husband's tyranny. We are told that all mothers play the same roles with their daughters. If Laila's mother is portrayed as complicit in her daughter's imprisonment, it is because she was herself a victim of the patriarchal culture.

Although Marām is depicted as a strong woman who is not affected by the gossip of neighbours about her, the reader senses the growing social pressure impinging on her soul – especially after the death of her mother, when her spontaneity is eventually replaced by scheming as social and familial pressure force her to become more calculating. The novel's rhythm accelerates towards the end, when Marām attempts to physically rescue Laila from her forced marriage. She wraps her friend in an *'abaya* that she brings with her to the salon where she is being groomed for her union with the multiply married and elderly Saleh. Having disguised the bride, they sprint into a car that has been waiting for them. Both women are depicted as clueless as to where to go, however, so they silently head towards the sea and start putting stones in their *'abayas* with the intention of committing suicide. Time and again, Saudi women writers offer death as the only solution to their protagonists' dilemmas. Although the narrative of *Emra'tān* attempts to transform the bodies of the two women into emblems of women's struggle, the suicide scene itself feels somewhat forced – not least because Marām does not have enough reason to desire her own suicide but also because, having come this far, Laila could have eloped with Ahmad instead of drowning herself. The final scene presents the two women more as sacrificial lambs than as achieving the intended goal of the book – that of depicting a deep social and ideological malaise.

Notes

1 In this neologism (in the original French, *savoir-pouvoir*), coined by Foucault, the most important part is the hyphen: this links the two aspects of the integrated concept together.
2 Lila Abu-Lughod, *Do Muslim Women Need Saving?* (Harvard University Press: Cambridge, MA, 2013), p. 115.
3 For further reading on the subject, see Ronald Jackson, *Scripting the Black Masculine Body: Identity, Discourse, and Racial Politics in Popular Media* (SUNY Series Negotiating Identity: Discourses, Politics, Processes, and Praxes) (SUNY Press: Albany, NY, 2006), in which he argues that the social assignment of black people to an underclass has multiple origins, two of which are the institutions of slavery and the mass media.
4 Moneera al-Ghadeer, 'Layla al-Juhani, *Jahiliyyah*', *Journal of Arabic Literature*, Vol. 2, No. 2/3 (2011), pp. 269–71.
5 Laila al-Juhani, *Jahiliyyah* [The Days of Ignorance] (Bloomsbury: London, 2015), p. 33.
6 Al-Juhani, *Jahiliyyah*, p. 11.
7 Al-Juhani.
8 Al-Juhani, p. 35.
9 Laura E. Tanner, *Intimate Violence: Reading Rape and Torture in Twentieth-Century Fiction* (Indiana University Press: Bloomington, 1984), p. 15.
10 Al-Juhani, *Jahiliyyah*, p. 110.
11 For further reading on the subject, see Yamani's 'Some Observations', p. 274. Yamani gives a detailed description of Saudi women's marriage tradition: marriage, a social and religious contract, is threatened by the possibility of separation or polygamy. These practices are perceived differently in different parts of Saudi Arabia. The country is vast and culturally heterogeneous, with customs prevailing among its tribal inhabitants that differ from those of urban dwellers, and which even differ within the same region in accordance with the socio-economic position of the family.
12 Homi K. Bhabha, 'The Other Questions: Stereotype and Colonial Discourse', *Screen*, Vol. 24, No. 6 (1 November 1983), pp. 18–36. Available at https://doi.org/10.1093/screen/24.6.18 (accessed 4 May 2022).
13 Friedman, *Mappings*, p. 47.
14 'One is not born, but rather becomes, a woman' is the opening line of Book II of de Beauvoir's *The Second Sex*; it is widely regarded as her best-known statement.
15 Judith Butler, 'Monique Wittig: Bodily Disintegration and Fictive Sex', in Judith Butler, *Gender Trouble: Feminism and the Subversion of Identity* (Routledge: London, 1990), pp. 151–3.
16 Al-Juhani, *Jahiliyyah*, p. 61.
17 Al-Juhani, p. 29.
18 Al-Juhani.
19 Al-Juhani, p. 123.
20 Badriya al-Beshir, *Al Erjouḥah* [The Swing] (al Saqi Books: London, 2010), p. 89.
21 Paul Connerton, *How Societies Remember* (Cambridge University Press: New York, 1989).
22 Khaled Abou El Fadl, *The Great Theft: Wrestling Islam from the Extremists* (Harper Collins: New York, 2007), p. 254.

23 Friedman, *Mappings*, p. 21.
24 Al-Beshir, *Al Erjouḥah*, p. 8.
25 Al-Beshir, p. 154.
26 Tanner, *Intimate Violence*, p. 97.
27 Al-Beshir, *Al Erjouḥah*, p. 74.
28 Françoise d'Eaubonne quoted in Horn and Pringle (eds), *The Image of the Prostitute*, p. 22.
29 Al-Beshir, *al Erjouḥah*, p. 121.
30 Al-Beshir, p. 124.
31 A Yemeni type of hashish.
32 Al-Beshir, *Al Erjouḥah*, p. 120.
33 Mary Douglas, *Purity and Danger: An Analysis of Concepts of Pollution and Taboo* (Routledge: London, 1996), p. 68.
34 Angela King, 'The Prisoner of Gender: Foucault and the Disciplining of the Female Body', *Journal of International Women's Studies*, Vol. 5, No. 2 (2004), pp. 29–39.
35 Hana Hejazi, *Emra'tān* [Two Women] (Dar al Saqi: Beirut, 2015), p. 12.
36 Hejazi, *Emra'tān*, pp. 95–6.
37 An old town near the capital, Riyadh.
38 Hejazi, *Emra'tān*, p. 105.
39 Foucault, *Discipline and Punish*, p. 138.
40 Breea C. Willingham, 'Black Women's Prison Narratives and the Intersection of Race, Gender, and Sexuality in US Prisons', *Critical Survey*, Vol. 23, No. 3, Reading and Writing in Prison (2011), p. 57.

5
TRAVEL, WOMEN AND THE CITY
The Literature of Encounter

Focusing on the city is essential because, as Henri Lefebvre explains, it serves as a space of urban encounters that produce new experiences, and establish complex and transparent relationships with the world.[1] Examining the issue of cultural encounters with a focus on the impact of the city in Saudi women's fiction means breaking away from previously held stereotypes of Saudi women, who are perceived as consistently occupying the private space. It also means challenging the predictable polarization of private and public spaces by focusing on a feminist trajectory within the intersection of gender, identity and globalization. In this trajectory, the city is seen as a space of 'rich interdisciplinary symbolic geography capable of telling stories'[2] – stories that would never have been told without exposure to the urban realm. When Saudi women write about the city as locals or tourists, interdisciplinary layers of anthropology, psychology, political science and sociology come into play. They offer women writers who choose to explore themes of the city and globalization a space to negotiate identity, agency and social change. This negotiation often contests the traditional map of home, ideologies and beliefs. It is important to assess these cultural differences and understand how global interaction aids the spread of women's rights and feminism, which Susan Friedman defines as the production of 'local agencies'.[3] The city, thus, becomes a dynamic backdrop where Saudi women can assert their identities and explore the transformation potential of urban environments in the context of globalized cultural exchange.

Mapping these spatial and temporal encounters is crucial for the creative growth of locational feminism, as Friedman notes.[4] She raises important

DOI: 10.4324/9781003539681-6

questions in relation to those intercultural narratives 'of how does each space reflect the cultural production of spatialized meaning? Or, determine the nature of or change in character? Or, provide the conditions within which the agency of the characters must maneuver?'[5] Therefore, examining these narratives closely offers insights into how protagonists navigate conflicts and excitements during their travels. Their awareness of existing between two different societies enables them to navigate between their new reality and old traditions more effectively. Such encounters generate a multiplicity of stories that interest me particularly because they offer solutions beyond androcentric frameworks, fostering agency in the characters as the narrative unfolds. Edward Said's concept of 'Travelling Theory' further illuminates this process:

> Like people and schools of criticism, ideas and theories travel – from person to person, from situation to situation, from one period to another. Cultural and intellectual life are usually nourished and often sustained by this circulation of ideas, and whether it takes the form of acknowledged or unconscious influence, creative borrowing, or wholesale appropriation, the movement of ideas and theories from one place to another is both a fact of life and a usefully enabling condition of intellectual activity.[6]

Said emphasizes how ideas are transmitted, adapted and transformed across different contexts. This theoretical framework helps us understand how intercultural narratives reflect and shape the experiences of Arabia's women as they navigate between traditions and globalized worlds.

Analysis of Saudi women's literature reveals the fact that cosmopolitan hubs have become alternative geographies of freedom and love in the collective memory of people. Cities like London, Paris and Toronto have accumulated metaphors of personal freedom in Saudi and Arabic literature to varying extents. The writers examined in this chapter, whether intentionally or not, create a new text of comparisons between 'home' and 'abroad'. Such comparisons accelerate cultural flow and encourage intercultural contact. This contact, argues Friedman, challenges the concept of home, denaturalizing the domestic space and exposing it as anything but 'stable'. Instead, it often serves as 'a site of intense alterity, oppression, marginalization and resistance for women'.[7] These debates about home and abroad began on a micro level in the 1960s–1970s with the first generation of Arabia's women fiction writers, who engaged in comparisons of 'here' and 'there', often with intertwined cultural and identity axes. This trend continued and flourished with the second generation, and is particularly prominent among millennial writers who view the world as borderless.

SECOND GENERATION VOICES

From Riyadh to Toronto – Transcending the Limitations of Cultural Definitions: Omima al-Khamis – *The Leafy Tree*

In *al-Warefa* (The Leafy Tree, 2008),[8] Omima al-Khamis explores love and beauty within the context of Saudi women's culture and its interplay with such ideals. The book's central character, al-Jawhara, a medical doctor and a new divorcee, is marked right from the beginning as a skinny and unattractive woman. This issue had been dealt with previously by Qmasha al-Olayyan, in her collection of short stories *al-Zawjah al-'Athra'* (The Virgin Wife – see Chapter 2), in the sense that al-Olayyan broaches the issue of female ugliness as a marker of social and familial failure. Al-Khamis, by contrast, focuses here on the protagonist's life outside traditional feminine gender roles of marriage and motherhood, and succeeds in turning her protagonist's lack of beauty into a vehicle for change and, to borrow Monica Carol Miller's words, 'social rebellion'[9] – of pushing social boundaries whenever the opportunity presents itself.

Al-Jawhara, who comes from a traditional background, interacts with a globalized reality: a hospital in Riyadh with its foreign staff and, later on, with Canadian society when she is offered a scholarship in Toronto. Al-Khamis draws on elements of feminism in her protagonist's determination to swim against the current and pursue her dreams. Through her journey to Canada, the protagonist challenges traditional roles and stereotypes. I find that Susan Friedman's concept of the 'contact zone' and 'hybrid identity' is instrumental in understanding the protagonist's identity formation as she navigates and integrates multiple cultural situations, which inherently questions and disrupts oppressive norms of her original and adopted cultures. In the process, *The Leafy Tree* and other, similar, works borrow tropes from an older tradition of European travel literature, of '[r]eversing the gaze at the Other by offering an aspect onto "home" societies that often distinguishes the narrator's now "enlightened" understanding from those societies as a product of their intellectual and physical journey Westward'.[10]

The all-seeing narrator also informs the reader how it was another globalized reality that played a part in al-Jawhara's divorce: globalized images of beauty raised the expectations of her bridegroom, who was then disappointed by her looks. '[H]er ex-husband the "fat" Ṭalāl caused her so much pain and depression, because she didn't resemble the image he had in mind'. The added twist of the 'fat' husband highlights a discriminating culture that judges women on their appearance but not men.

The Leafy Tree thus sheds light on the importance attached – by both the marriage 'market' and its menfolk, generally – to physical beauty over female intelligence, and how global images of the ideal body have institutionalized alienation by intervening in people's fantasies. Undergoing self-doubt and a search for identity, al-Jawhara tries to comprehend what occurred in her marriage to cause it to fail: Could it be that she was too thin for his taste? Too dark-skinned perhaps? Working in a government hospital in Riyadh allows her to problematize this 'beauty myth' through her *burqa* and the narrow lens of physical appearance. Her preoccupations with beauty resonate with the old notion 'a woman's face is her fortune', and reflect an obsession with beauty as the main determinant for the success of a marriage. This idea is critically explored by Naomi Wolf's book *The Beauty Myth*, which examines how beauty standards are used as a means of social control.[11] Wolf offers a feminist critique that a woman's value is tied to her looks, advocating recognition of women's talents, intelligence, achievements and contribution to society. Certainly, an alignment can be drawn between Wolf and al-Jawhara, in the sense that Wolf's critique targets the traditional roles and stereotypes imposed on women, mainly the idea that a woman's value is tied to her appearance. Both the protagonist's journey and Wolf's critique seek to dismantle limiting and harmful societal expectations.

The narrator points out that 'Dr al-Jawhara started observing the bodies of other women – the way they move and their curves – after her first marriage in which her husband was obsessed with the female body.'[12] At work, she contemplates the figure of Adrienne, a physiotherapist from New Zealand, and she wonders if Adrienne's husband is happy about her thin lips. Al-Jawhara concludes that the difference between herself and the physiotherapist lies in the confidence that is born of having 'proud fathers' who are attentive to what their little daughters say. This can be surmised from the way in which Adrienne interacts with others, the way she exchanges small talk with her colleagues: women like her, al-Jawhara reflects, don't look at people's eyes begging for acceptance or an encouraging remark from time to time – a weakness born of self-doubt. Insecurity, al-Jawhara concludes, has kept her in a loveless marriage for a year, or what she calls being trapped in the 'grey area' – that is, being married yet rarely seeing her husband. This point is confirmed by remarks that she overhears later on, that on the first day of their marriage 'the "fat" Ṭalāl threw himself at his mum's lap and cried that he [didn't] want her'. The mother admonishes her son, and tells him to 'stay in that marriage so that the bride's reputation is not ruined'. This portrait of the man is a necessarily emasculating and humiliating one: in matters of romance, he is a mere boy and does his mother's bidding.

Although she tries to maintain her identity as a Muslim woman in Toronto, unfavourable comparisons between Riyadh and the Canadian city surface in the novel. In Toronto, the protagonist ditches the *neqab* (full-face veil) because, like the *burqa*, 'it is a boundary where cross-cultural translation is always fraught with difficulty'.[13] After much deliberation on what to wear and how others will perceive her – and just before she dons the headscarf, as she weighs the pros and cons of wearing the *neqab* – a dialectic rendering of Edward Said's seminal work *Orientalism*[14] is detectable in her conscious and unconscious self-identification with constructed Orientalist images: 'I will look like the animated character Batman', 'but I have to cover my hair to look prim', 'maybe I should wear a woollen hat, but it's not cold outside'. This self-talk shows how pervasive negative stereotypes can lead to internalized self-doubt and self-reproach among Muslim women. Often resulting in a conflicted sense of self, a pertinent case in point is al-Jawhara's quest for identity amidst her feelings of dislocation and her mediation of the two cultures: her Islamic beliefs on the one hand and the desire to fit into a Western culture on the other. She goes through what Said defines as Hegelian dialectic, where identity formation involves a process of thesis (orientalist stereotypes), antithesis (resistance and counter-narratives) and synthesis (a more complex and integrated self-identity). Al-Jawhara is portrayed as navigating the two cultural contexts with difficulty; negotiating the requisites of Islamic practices and Western culture. Her internalization of Western social norms brings about a change of heart in towards men, as well as a clash between her Islamic beliefs and the new identity that she is trying to embrace. Accordingly, she decides to go out on a date with her male colleague, Bernard, only to find out that he is Jewish: 'the word Jew rang in her head', 'when she felt that she needed to breathe, she excused herself to go to the toilet', mocking and muttering to herself in the mirror, 'ya salam, ya Jahair, hooking up with a Jew and talking to him in a sassy way'.

This encounter shows the new geographics of identity in a way that articulates not its organic unfolding but rather the mapping of territories and boundaries, the dialectic terrains of inside/outside or centre/margin, the axial interaction of positionalities, and the spaces of dynamic encounter – 'the contact zone', the 'middle ground', the borderlands, *la frontera*.[15] Thus, the contradiction of al-Jawhara's identity within conflicting systems of class, gender and religion prompts her to reject the conventional roles of a miserable wife or a divorcee in Arabia, and choose instead to mix in a global world that nurtures different axes of her identity, that is, intelligence, education and, most importantly, finding fulfilment in professional pursuits.

On a deeper level, this encounter offers what Said defines as a counter-narrative, which presents the protagonist as trying to integrate into Western culture; her social/dating decisions however involve navigating a complicated cultural terrain. Al-Jawhara chooses to resist the external pressures of both her original and the new culture in Canada. She negotiates her identity on her own terms, balancing and blending elements from both worlds. Accordingly, she takes a long breath and returns to the table, trying hard to stay calm so that she can continue her training in Bernard's department. This encounter shows the protagonist as exercising agency, and a pragmatism that conflicts with local attitudes back home. Her decision to stay calm signifies a pivotal moment of identity transformation. These moments illustrate how the protagonist has moved beyond the limitations of her local culture, embracing personal growth and change.

This transformation can be understood in the context of Edward Said's *Orientalism*, whereby the protagonist's journey to Canada culminates in acquisition of a hybrid identity, which reflects a synthesis of cultures and identities. This process is emblematic of the dialectical interaction between East and West. Thus, when al-Khamis' protagonist mixes with male colleagues, and even goes out with some of them to a film and a café, there is no explanation by the writer as to why the character is no longer maintaining the traditions of her country of origin at that point; simply, the *neqab* that once protected her from social contempt is unnecessary in Toronto and she has transcended the limitations of cultural definitions of a 'good woman'.

Paris – A Sliding Door Moment: Zaineb Hefny – *Women on the Equator*

Zaineb Hefny in the epigraph of her (1996) collection of short stories, *Nesā' 'End Khaṭ al-'Estewā'* (Women on the Equator), declares,

> To Eve ...

The only one accused of Adam's exile from paradise,
to her ...
I contribute those revolutionary words, hoping they provide her some relief.[16]
Despite the author's bold declaration, readers were still offended by the perceived transgression and obscenity in this work. Their reaction was largely influenced by the timing. The collection was published in the 1990s, a period when women's visibility and voice were being fiercely contested by the *saḥwa*. The fact that Hefny released this work under her real name exacerbated the situation, as radicals ensured she faced penalties for challenging the prevailing conservative culture. In a phone interview I conducted with Zaineb in 2018, it was evident that anger and bitterness still lingered. Her resentment was directed not only at the religious clerics that had punished her but also at ordinary members of the public who had bombarded her with malicious prank calls at the time. This has left her with bitter memories and an even stronger sense of feminism. In a paper presented at the American University in Cairo in 2011, she admitted,

> When I write I unveil, and when I am totally infused with my creative writing, I play and dance with the heroines of my novels, I practice sadism and masochism on them every now and then. And I also, stick my tongue

out at social traditions and say, 'look I've created women who are able to defy you without the fear of being stopped by police or intimidated by fear of having my reputation tarnished.'[17]

In a lecture delivered earlier in 2007, Hefny publicly demanded women's rights, stating,

> I came here with the intention to shout, shout and shout. So everybody can hear my voice, and understand that the social whirl of luxury and oil fields that had a role in our upbringing; the severity of our traditions, that makes sure women stay permanently under house arrest, will not stop us from demanding our rights.[18]

Her choice of wording is remarkable because it reflects the author's mounting frustration – her desire to shout and speak up in a time that valued women's silence. This feminist side of her is discernible not only in the stories she writes but also in their memorable titles – for instance, *Nesā' 'End Khaṭ al-'Estewā'*, with its steamy equatorial connotations, is highly suggestive, symbolizing the anger of women reaching a boiling point. Hefny cautions throughout this collection that women might explode and deviate from the right path if not given enough space, mobility and freedom to express themselves in society.

Hefny in this short story challenges restrictive social norms by adopting 'travel' as a mobilizing metaphor that cuts against the mobility norms of the society in question. This metaphor is frequently used by Saudi women writers who resist the social division of space. The first story, titled 'Forbidden Womanly Rhythm', investigates the interrelationship between self and otherness, focusing on the protagonist's development of personal identity, through the perennial themes of femininity and extramarital relationships. The protagonist Safa is granted a spatial and interactive 'freedom' through 'travel', which facilitates a romantic encounter with a stranger in Paris. Safa is portrayed as wandering the streets; walking by the River Seine; shopping; and meeting this stranger, with whom she ends up spending the night in his hotel room.

By recalling what happened that night in that room, the author shows control over temporal metaphors, the use of flashbacks and stream of consciousness, which allows the character to broaden her recollection in order to make sense of what had occurred. This is, in fact, evident right at the opening of the novel, with the protagonist remembering, 'I woke up early feeling the heat of his body that was glued to mine' and 'I gently lifted his arm that was clinging to my waist'. When this stranger woke up, however, he took money from a bag next to the bed and placed it near her. She felt ashamed, and asked him what it was. He answered, half asleep, 'Take it, it's your right' – acknowledging her as a prostitute, and offering money as compensation. This made her feel disgusted, and, needing to cry, she threw down the money and hurried out of the hotel. Safa's experience in the story offers a "sliding door moment", as it shifts her trajectory by confronting her with an unexpected, even jarring perspective. This encounter functions as a wake-up call, forcing her to confront assumptions, biases, and questions about identity and self-worth. The interaction depicted here between the two characters gains the symbolic meaning of exchange values, whereby the money in this incident is representative of male economic power and chauvinist behaviour, reducing her to a mere object of desire and degradation. This incident highlights, complex questions about freedom, space, and agency for women within restrictive society. this moment, where Safa is misjudged as a prostitute, seems pivotal, it exposes underlying assumptions that constrain women's identities and independence, especially in foreign or supposedly "free" spaces.

Hefny seems to suggest that true freedom or agency for women can't be fully realized when societal norms-whether at home or abroad- continue to limit how women are perceived. Safa's experience reflect that even in a setting like Paris, traditionally seen as a symbol of liberation, women from certain backgrounds or with or with particular identities are still subjected to stereotyping and constrained by others' expectations. The incident in Paris seems to question whether escaping a physically restrictive environment is enough, or if deeper ideological shifts are necessary to enable genuine freedom and agency for women.

Far from being unusual, the episode reminds Safa of other dehumanizing experiences, when she was recognized only as an object of desire, reflecting the shameful dynamics within the Saudi hierarchy of gender identity. One such incident occurred when her mother spotted her on the balcony in a clinging dress. She had been much younger then, but that had not stopped her mother from beating her hard and warning her that she would harm her if she ever dressed that way again. Although standing on a balcony is not typical in Saudi culture, its inclusion here highlights the influence of Egyptian literature on the author (the influence of Egyptian literature on Saudi writers is discussed earlier, in Chapter 1). The depiction of the mother as a guardian of patriarchy, punishing and disciplining her daughter to preserve her purity, exemplifies the concept of Arab family honour. The second incident occurred while Safa was with her first husband. She gave in to his temptation, and slept with him before their official marriage, an act she has regretted ever since because it led to a lack of trust from him. Their relationship was marked by constant arguments, ultimately resulting in a marriage that lasted for only two months.

In this short-story collection, Hefny daringly exposes the hypocrisy in society that condemns women for expressing their desires while glorifying men for the same behaviour. Safa's quest for personal freedom is continually thwarted by societal forces – her mother, her first husband, and finally the man she encounters in Paris. Hefny provides Safa with a narrative space of freedom that contrasts sharply with the constraints of her life back home. Safa's journey could be seen as both literal and metaphorical, as she moves between spaces of limitation and liberation, forcing the reader to question the boundaries placed on her. Her time abroad, reveal the complexities of seeking freedom and individuality within the pressures of a conservative society.

London – An Alternative Home: Zaineb Hefny – *Twisted Legs*

If London is a temporary destination for many travellers, it is an alternative homeland for the dual-national Saudi/British Sara and her family, around whom Zaineb Hefny explores hybridity in her 2008 book *Siqan Multawiah* (Twisted Legs). This novel builds on what Gloria Anzaldúa defines as 'invisible borders'[19] – spaces in which, in this novel, Saudi/English identities encounter each other. This encounter involves contradictions and oscillation between two or more cultures, resulting in Hefny's novel in a clash between the eldest daughter, Sara, and her parents. Sara becomes part of the Saudi-diaspora 'site' for investigating familial, global, political and cultural processes, in which context she constantly struggles with her inherited patriarchal and tribal culture.

The book opens with Musa'ad, her father, heading to the police station to report Sara's disappearance from their London family home near Regent's Park. This tense beginning sets the stage for a narrative deeply rooted in the themes of diaspora and the axial contradictory positionality of identity, that is, the central and defining role that the protagonist's negative perception of her homeland plays in shaping her identity and her life choices. As the story unfolds, it becomes clear that Sara's disappearance is not just a physical absence but also a symbolic exploration of her struggle with her diasporic identity. For this, a significant textual space is given for the protagonist to vindicate her disappearance. This space is reflective of the author's feminist approach as it emphasizes the importance of women's experience, and seeks to understand how power dynamics operate on a global scale, recognizing the importance of local contexts while advocating for women's solidarity and rights. So when Sara narrates her side of the story, telling how she was brought up in London, of attending mixed schools and comparing her life in the British capital with her impressions of life in Arabia – impressions formed during their annual summer vacations there – a parallel embedded narrative is presented to the reader, replete with notions of home and abroad, reflecting the complex dynamics of identity and belonging in a global context. Hence, Sara's relationships with the diasporic community in London and her circle of English friends are depicted as flourishing, with shared common interests and values, highlighting the strength and resilience of diasporic networks. More precisely, Sara is portrayed as an intellectually engaged woman, her beliefs and discussions forming the backbone of her relationships. For example, the internal monologues and the intimate dialogues that are recounted between Sara and her many interlocutors – such as her first love, the Iraqi Adel, later killed in a bomb attack in Baghdad; her group of English friends; her second love, the Palestinian Zyad; and her female cousins back home – shape her consciousness and allow her to undergo tremendous personal changes. Such conversations reveal how her personal life is marked by a struggle to find a sense of belonging and freedom. Adel once asks her if she ever feels homesick like he does; she replies, 'To the contrary, I feel that I am tied with heavy shackles, every time I step into my country, I feel that there are mutilated creatures stalking me wherever I go. Each road junction makes me feel that I am a concubine; a slave concubine.'[20] At this point, the protagonist is portrayed as unable to reconcile her local roots with global connection.

The novel's narrative technique relies on building plots and subplots that not only signify the tension mounting within her towards the patriarchal culture and tradition 'back home' but also incriminate the male-dominant society. For example, Sara's English girlfriend Rebecca – who could easily be mistaken for a Middle Eastern girl with her dark hair and olive skin – was eager to introduce her Arabic boyfriend to her parents. Rebecca's mother, Merriam, reacted with visible discomfort. The omniscient narrator reveals Merriam's internal struggle, a mix of anxiety and cultural prejudice, as she nervously rejected the idea. Merriam, fearing that her daughter might repeat her mistake, confesses to Sara that Rebecca's real father is a Saudi man, who promised to marry her but then abandoned her.

The narrator further explores Sara's alienation by recounting how, every year, Sara and her two sisters are reminded of their strict, conservative tradition – from the national dress, the *'abaya*, which they put on as soon as they step out of the plane, to the fear of the religious police when they are in public places; and, last but not least, her cousin Haya's tragic story. As a new divorcee at the age of 30, Haya tries to escape her oppressive family by accepting a friend's request to see one of her cousins who is searching for a bride like her. The man suggests that they meet up in a public place before officially proposing to her family. The minute they sit down in the café and before they can exchange a word, the religious police, who roam public spaces and streets, attack them and put them in prison. The reaction of Haya's father is tyrannical: he pulls her hair and screams, 'You ruined my reputation, I never laid foot at a *hai'a* [religious police] center. From now on, you're not allowed to go out of the house.'[21] Shattered by what has happened to her, Haya decides to take her own life by swallowing sleeping pills – she does so, and never wakes up. Sara is appalled and shaken by what happens to her cousin; she feels alienated from her family and starts growing closer to the hybrid identity of the diaspora community exemplified by Zyad.

In documenting the struggle building within Sara, the author succeeds in depicting her as someone with a hybrid identity. Questions running through her mind of 'here' and 'there' are examined through many binary oppositions and weighing things up – a process of which Theodor Adorno rightly says, '[d]istance is not a safety zone but a field of tension [...] a terrain that houses new subjects of criticism'.[22] This tension here culminates in the subplot comprising Haya's tragic story, which propels Sara into taking her fateful decision to elope with Zyad. This decision resonates in turn with

James Clifford's essay 'Notes on Theory and Travel', which problematizes the difference between émigré and diasporic experiences and in which he notes, '[d]iasporic populations regularly "lose" members to the dominant culture'.[23] Losing Sara to the dominant culture – that is, the Westernized culture of London – is the only answer given by the author, who makes it clear through her protagonist's journey from doubt to certainty that she, unlike other émigrés who can exist between two societies, could not develop any sense of belonging or allegiance to her homeland.

The Millennial Revolutionary Writers: Third-Generation Voices

Most third-generation voices were born in the 1970s–1980s and began writing in their twenties and thirties – for example, Raja al-Sanea, who published *Banat al-Riyadh* (Girls of Riyadh) when she was only 24. Their works reflect all the thematic concerns of the 'chick-lit' genre, focusing on two major issues: consumerism, with its emphasis on shopping, travel and fashion; and female identity, highlighting love, marriage and career issues. More specifically, their fiction is replete with global images and protagonists who internalize the 'other', modern, Western culture – mostly depicted as immersed in mall culture, meeting up at cafés and restaurants, sipping cappuccinos and indulging in shopping sprees. And unlike the average Saudi woman, including those novel characters thus far described, these heroines are depicted as globetrotters who can pack their bags whenever they want and escape an unwanted social or familial situation. Undoubtedly, globalization, marketing and consumerism have amplified the emergence of authors who are totally absorbed by the cosmopolitan dream – or what scholar Marilyn Booth dubs, with reference to Raja al-Sanea, 'global celebrities'.[24] In an email interview that I conducted in the early stages of writing this book, I asked Saudi critic Muhammad al-Abbas about the influence of globalization on millennial authors. His reply was,

> Globalization is an infinite change factor on humanity in general. We have a globalized literature and prospects of universal people who are rebelling against tribal, ethnic, social group or class definitions. Also, marketing plays an important role in the politics of translation, as well as networking inside and outside their borders. Also, when the 'other' decides to translate a novel, he/she chooses a work that consolidates his/her Orientalist perceptions and prejudiced stereotyping. What has been translated so far does not mirror the real literature of either men's or women's fiction in any way. The West is not concerned about foregrounding the positive aspects of our societies; to the contrary, it is obsessed with issues of women's oppression, extremism and some aspects of social contradictions.[25]

I argue that these authors introduce a Saudi version of the 'chick-lit' narrative as a new trend in writing, along with common threads that link their political involvement to 'lipstick' or 'third-wave feminism'. Instead of elaborating on the 'chick-lit' thematic engagement, I will focus rather on their gender politics and the feminist aspects of their works that have been overlooked by both reviewers and translators – as noted by Booth herself in her paper, '"The Muslim Woman" as Celebrity Author and the Politics of Translating Arabic: Girls of Riyadh Go on the Road'. I argue that *Girls of Riyadh*, among other works examined in this chapter, is a fully fledged feminist text that attests to the rise of a new, revolutionary generation who are flagging up the need for a reinterpretation of religious texts and a revision of futile cultural laws. The chatty tone of this writing invites us to rethink not only the role of social media in fast-tracking new patterns of thought and behaviour in women but also the role of globalization as a figurative, almost colonial force in shaping processes of cultural exchange. Such a rethink offers us a lens through which to examine the experiences of a young, highly digitized, hybridized elite of mostly third generation authors who are turning to fiction writing in order to vent their frustration and undermine the dominant-male discourse. Most importantly, the uproar caused by the publication of almost all the later works under discussion in this chapter has prompted me to comment on how these texts function as a counter memory comprising unevenly distributed multitudes of points that correspond to the ideas of 'power' and 'defiance', which prompt a debate about the rights of women within Islam. I believe that overlooking the involvement of these authors in the double struggle of Muslim women – that is, between futile traditions and religion – is simply unproductive for the purpose of this study. Instead, I raise the questions of what their narratives convey in terms of feminism, how globalization is transforming Arabia's youth culture and how it is fast-tracking the ways in which Arab women respond to social and religious control.

As I have indicated earlier, in the Introduction's section 'Transversality in Women's "New Texts"', this genre shows the emergence of a 'new text', fully independent of the dominant discourse, which is oppositional and challenging to existing conditions – one that is capable of establishing a relationship with the sociopolitical realm. Hence, these texts can be seen as a source for 'reading' the changes that have occurred over the last two decades, marking a new women's geographies of identity in which female literary protests and demands have been 'documented' and 'archived'. For instance, the authors' recurrent harsh critique of the religious police and the futile cultural laws that they flag up in their works is nothing but a reminder of founding Islamic feminist texts, through which their authors attempt to 'push the limits of the earlier discourse in thinking out-of-the-box but not out of an Islamic context', as Margo Badran notes.[26] Thus, hostile encounters between women and agents of the religious police heighten Arabia's female authors' expression in terms of the language and the issues over which they choose to voice their frustration, if not outright revolt. This 'new text' strongly criticizes the role played by religious institutions in perpetuating women's poor status against the backdrop of the master narrative, or, as Anne McClintock puts it, 'the discourse of a patriarchal culture, [which] disseminated and propagated a fixed image of gender that considered women to be the markers of identity of the nation'.[27]

Apart from the works included in this chapter, new texts written by this generation persist in relating events to the temporal–historical 'punctum' of *sahwa*. For instance, Munira al-Subai, in her 2007 novel *Bait al-Ṭa'ah* (The House of Obedience),[28] gives a sidelong glance at the protagonist, Nora, who is affronted when her best friend Azizah discloses to her that she has been to a restaurant to finally meet the man with whom she's been having a courtly love affair for over a year. Nora admonishes her: 'Are you crazy, you met him in a public place? What if the religious police had caught you?' Likewise, Sara Maṭar, in her 2008 novel *Qabīlah Ismha Sara* (A Tribe Called Sara), alludes to Saudi women's fear of the religious police when her narrator discloses to the reader,

> I confess that I have met Ma'ath in my town twice or more; we used to go to one of the beautiful cafés, but we decided against it after I had recurrent tummy aches [...] I started to sweat every time someone walked into the place. So we both thought of meeting across the border in Bahrain.[29]

For reasons such as this, it is not surprising to see that the Riyadh of (male author) Turki al-Hamad is at odds with that of, say, Raja al-Sanea; although their protagonists are both university students, they nevertheless explore life differently. Unlike her male contemporary, al-Sanea merges the private and public in her work – helping, in the process, to dispel some of the mystery surrounding the life of the Saudi woman in what Madawi al-Rasheed calls (in a phrase that she also uses as the title of her 2013 book) *A Most Masculine State*, whereby the spatial segregation of false barriers and processes are deeply ingrained in Arabia's cultural dynamic. Al-Sanea's *Girls of Riyadh*[30] invokes images of harem women suddenly exposed to the eyes of strangers. The author describes the Saudi capital not as a city as such but more as a series of feminine, segregated, enclosed spaces of 'women only' universities and 'girls' nights in' behind closed doors with metaphors of, discrimination and marginalization. In stark contrast, the Riyadh of al-Hamad defies the three taboos of religion, politics and sex through his male protagonist Hisham al-'Āber, who explores an extramarital relationship in broad daylight, drinks alcohol and becomes politically active in the city. Al-Hamad's work lends the highways and outskirts of this most conservative capital a different meaning – one that invokes metaphors of the open road, freedom and movement. It is this difference between men's and women's writing that encouraged me to further examine how women have explored the city; how they have metaphorically inscribed meaning to it; and, most importantly, how a globalized culture and its universal ideals has helped them to construct, negotiate and contest boundaries.

From Alisha Campus to London – 'Lipstick' Feminism: Raja al-Sanea – *Girls of Riyadh*

The title of this novel, whether in Arabic or English, contains within it a form of creative ambiguity: Is this a story about girls *in* the city of Riyadh? Or is it a tale that has a girl *from* Riyadh as its narrator (who exposes, through scandalous emails, the hidden and forbidden at a time in history when women were excluded from the public scene, given that the timeframe of its publication was 2005)? Is it, alternatively, a story that maintains the author's privileged view *of* Riyadh, excluding and including items in the narrative that fit her own social class, or is it reflective of women's general view in Arabia?

In fact, Raja al-Sanea chooses to combine all these possibilities, thereby providing us with a fictional account of Arabia's society at a time of heightened religiosity and setting a new literary trend for women's writing that has structural resonance with key staples of the 'chick-lit' genre such as Candace Bushnell's *Sex and the City* and Helen Fielding's 1996 *Bridget Jones's Diary* in the sense that they all use emails as a narrative device. This allows the use of a dominant, first-person, confessional voice that is in total control of the narrative. Al-Sanea's narrator, for instance, presents herself to her readers as '*moi*', a feminist who takes them on a cultural tour of sorts – a 'tour' that angered the religious establishment and the conservative audience in the kingdom, not necessarily because of its explicit scenes or profanity but simply for portraying the lives of four girlfriends embroiled with seduction, desire and platonic love stories, and for swimming against all the currents of a highly religious milieu that had, for almost three decades, upheld women's concealment from the public eye.

The extreme reaction to this novel was reflected in the introduction on the author's webpage. It states, 'a Muslim writer from Saudi who became famous through her bestselling novel [...] the author received death threats for bringing her nation's women into disrepute'.[31] The novel also encompassed 'the attractive dimensions that fascinate and enchant those who seek the secrets of Arabia "behind the veil" ',[32] which al-Rasheed extensively broached in her book *A Most Masculine State*. The webpage presented the author as a Muslim woman who was resisting, if not directly challenging, the dominant patriarchal discourse by symbolically wearing the wrath of the religious sect as a badge of honour – marking a new geographics of identity for women in Arabia, evident in the combination of being a Muslim woman and of being politically involved (with death threats and lawsuits filed against the author following her novel's publication). This activism is further emphasized through the author's identification with third-wave (so-called 'lipstick') feminism, and her willingness to confront a fiercely patriarchal culture while maintaining her femininity. This is symbolically alluded to in the narrator's announcement in the epigraphs to some chapters, which mention her applying her 'signature bright red lipstick' and brushing on her 'bright red rouge' before engaging with the subject matter. This act of putting on lipstick before addressing social traditions and constraints aligns with the global consumer culture to which the narrator of *Girls of Riyadh* and her friends belong. It reflects a feminist stance that embraces traditional femininity as a form of empowerment and self-expression while challenging and critiquing the societal norms that constrain women.

Through a Yahoo! account, the narrator communicates messages between the four friends, disclosing their emotional and familial challenges in the secluded society of Riyadh. The chapters open with an email heading 'seerawenfadha7et', which literary translates to a 'story exposed', that resonates with the popular Lebanese talk show 'seerawenfata7t'. This instantly recognizable headline draws the reader into a narrative of endless, gossip-like chatter that fits the genre of 'chick lit' and true-to-life thematic concerns – all permeated by hybridity, the privileged lifestyle enjoyed by its four participants and the English language that has crept into its text. All of this contributed to the unprecedented popularity of *Girls of Riyadh*, which according to a major Arabic online bookstore has topped its bestseller list for many years, bringing this novel into its seventh edition. In the first chapter, the author quotes lines from the famous Syrian poet Nizar Qabbani's collection, *Journal of an Indifferent Woman*:

> I shall write of my girlfriends,
> For in each one's tale
> I see my story and self prevail,
> A tragedy my own life speaks,
> I shall write of my girlfriends,
> Of inmates' lives sucked dry by jail,
> And magazine pages that consume women's time,
> And of the doors that fail to open,
> Of desires slain in their cradles I'll write,
> Of the vast great cell,
> Black walls of travail,
> Of thousands, thousands of martyrs, all female,
> Buried stripped of their names
> In the graveyard of traditions.
> My female friends,
> dolls swathed in gauze in a museum they lock;

coins in History's mint, never given, never spent;
fish swarming and chocking in every basin and tank,
while in crystal vessels, dying butterflies flock.
Without fear
I shall write of my friends,
of the chains twisted bloody around the ankles of beauties,
of delirium and nausea, and the nighttime that entreaty rends,
and desires buried in pillows, in silence.[33]

Known for its direct poetry, Qabbani's was one of the few voices that addressed gender-related taboos – from the predicament of the sultanate daughter to the women locked in unhappy marriages. Qabbani was, and is still, considered an indispensable feminist voice; al-Sanea's choice of this particular poem signifies an affinity with his criticism of the region's culture. Its wording strikes a chord with that of *Girls of Riyadh*'s female characters, who are portrayed as struggling with social constraints just like Qabbani's female subjects, depicted as chained, jailed, silenced, 'martyrs [i]n the graveyard of traditions'.

Reminiscent of one of Qabbani's female subjects, Gamra's lavish wedding to Rashed is not what it seems; rather than a love story ending in a happily-ever-after marriage it is, on the contrary, a tale of misery. The character of Rashed is portrayed as having been in love with a Japanese woman prior to his wedding, and having married Gamra only to appease his family. The couple travels to the United States, where Gamra is depicted as lonely and struggling to stay in a miserable union. The narrator mocks stale and discriminatory traditions by disclosing to the reader the fact that Gamra was warned by her mother not to consummate her marriage on her wedding night so that she wouldn't be judged as 'easy'.

In contrast, the character of Sadeem sleeps with Waleed after their marriage contract, a few days before the official wedding night, but is divorced the following day because she's too bold and 'easy' for Waleed's liking. Sadeem, shocked at receiving what she calls a 'no-fault divorce' right before her wedding – and being motherless – cannot find a shoulder to cry on, nor confess to her father what happened that night when she and the 'beast [...]' Waleed were alone together. She decides to go to London to escape the painful memory, and 'her fancy wedding dress and gorgeous wedding veil (which had been shipped, custom-made, from Paris) [which] were still lurking in her wardrobe in Riyadh, sticking out their tongues at her in derision every time she opened the closet door'.[34] Choosing to cancel the ceremony and to flee Riyadh, Sadeem partly escapes the social stigma of being jilted shortly before her wedding day.

Interestingly, patriarchal power is mitigated in this novel as its father figures are either eliminated or depicted as pro-women – a coincidence perhaps, but an important factor in the eponymous girls' autonomy: they are free to travel back and forth between Riyadh and the West. Sadeem's father, in support of his traumatized daughter, arranges a summer internship for her in one of London's banks, an arrangement that gives her a sense of independence and excitement. From then on, the city of London gains the metaphorical significance of a 'surrogate mother' to motherless Sadeem and a place that heals and empower her, filling a maternal role that guides her toward growth and self-acceptance in the face of loss. London therefore, provides Sadeem with a sense of stability, familiarity, and safety-qualities traditionally associated with a maternal figure. Wandering the streets and parks of the British capital therefore functions as a negotiator and mediator to help Sadeem come to terms with what has happened and to digest and process her dilemma. Her alienation is lessened through flashbacks and her stream-of-consciousness narrative – which fills in the story's gaps, allowing her to broaden her memory to make sense of what has happened to her. Sadeem's escape to London also gives the author a wider fictional space in which to analyse the contradictions that arise from the meeting of two cultures, with the social constraints brought from 'back home' by Sadeem being juxtaposed with the freedom of the modern world. She is constantly depicted as wandering the open spaces of London and assessing her inherited beliefs – a process of scrutinizing and perhaps adjusting her own ideological lens, unconsciously searching for similarities and differences between her ethnic identity and the hosting country, challenging in the process her core beliefs through the chaos of displacement.[35]

Al-Sanea pays special attention to cultural formations in the character of Sadeem.[36] Comparisons between home and abroad are evident in the narrator's observation, 'Sadeem packed away her wound along with her clothes and carried it all from the Dust Capital of the World to the Fog Capital of the world'. London in this novel resonates with the London of Samar al-Megrin's *Women of Vice* (discussed below) because it serves as a mediator between the protagonist and her home culture: a place in which to process what has happened and to reorganize and prioritize the heroine's life choices away from the shackles of her home society. Sadeem is portrayed as crying, reading, walking the parks and roads of London 'alone, estranged, radically displaced and melancholic' in a manner reminiscent of Malcom Cowley's definition of the term 'displaced' whether as a result of exile or tourism.[37] Interestingly, while in London she also begins reading the novels of Ghazi al-Gosaibi and Turki al-Hamad, male Saudi Arabian writers of an earlier generation. The political content of their works raises questions in the protagonist's mind about her own family's indifference to public affairs. The all-knowing narrator of *Girls of Riyadh* observes,

> Why had none of her relatives, male or female, got involved in a political cause, supporting it with their very souls as had been the case when Ghazi and Turki were young? Why was it that young people these days had no

interest in foreign politics unless it was the scandalous behaviour of Bill Clinton and Monica Lewinsky? Or, in domestic politics only the flagrant corruption of the Saudi telecom company? It wasn't just her, Sadeem – all of her classmates and everyone at their age were on the margins when it came to political life. They had no role, no importance.[38]

This passage signifies a new geographics of identity, one in which 'contact zones' change Sadeem's analysis of home – helping her, in Friedman's words, 'to break logjams of thought by casting the conditions of home in a new light and by illuminating the structures interlocking home and elsewhere'.[39] Sadeem, in this work, acts as an oppositional text that engenders a new narrative of change and reform; she is depicted as exercising agency and enjoying a relatively privileged life and freedom that is not available to the average woman 'back home'. She ventures outdoors, reads books and enjoys the freedom of doing things on her own. No longer oblivious to global issues or isolated from the world, Sadeem is depicted as having had her awareness of politics raised by her sojourn in London.

And just like culture, feminism travels to remote places via local agents who have become global citizens. Cities like London can act as liberating experiences for women, as well as spaces in which to negotiate identity and agency while igniting revolt against their cultures. And it is precisely this discourse of situational positionality as a marker of identity that I find most interesting – not only because it shifts characters' identities from powerlessness to power but also because of its ability to textualize women's growing feminism.

An Orientalist discourse of sorts transpires in the narrative when the author describes King Saud University, Alisha Campus, and the female students who are aware of Arwa, the *boyat* (see Chapter 6's 'Hell Is Other People'), who dresses differently. The girls gossip about the white *sarwal* (baggy trousers) that she wears under her skirt. David Glover and Cora Kaplan contend that women who adopt a masculine dress code and manner of behaviour are in a way evading the heavy social and psychological burdens of femininity.[40] Such women's choice of masculine dress is an attempt to negotiate their spaces and identity because they seek to eradicate the female body, which is deemed to be causing *fitna* and chaos for unrelated men. Thus, the rebellion of these *boyat* can be understood as a protest against both the strict laws to which they are subjected on a day-to-day basis and the feminine bodies in which they feel trapped.

Unlike the *boyat* of Alisha Campus, Michelle – the Westernized nickname for Misha'el, another of the four girlfriends in *Girls of Riyadh* – dresses as a man simply because she wants to enjoy cruising around Riyadh with her friends. Portrayed as a free soul and in love with Faisal, we learn that her hope of marriage to Faisal has crashed due to his mother's objection to their union because of Michelle's family lineage. It is within this storyline that this character is caught oscillating between the two cultures – Saudi and American – feeling the tension arising between the two and producing a discourse of contradiction that is more informative than the old dichotomies of 'here' and 'there', 'us' and 'them', which scrutinize the various cultural layers, while disseminating knowledge about the social order itself.

The author effectively creates images of Michelle that highlight her 'hyphenated' identity, that raise questions about her sense of belonging. Michelle's struggle to blend in with her surroundings is depicted through her actions, such as carrying her puppy around to visit friends and primarily speaking English, which further underscore her identity as an Americanized 'yuppie', raised in the United States. The narrator explains that Michelle's father's relocation to Riyadh during her teenage years was a pivotal moment, marking her character with Western attributes that seem out of place compared to the novel's more traditional characters. Michelle's inability to integrate into Riyadh's social circles reflects her struggle to reconcile her American upbringing with her Saudi heritage. As she navigates two distinct cultural landscapes, she constantly feels caught between worlds, neither fully belonging to one nor able to abandon the other. This duality creates an enduring tension, where her sense of self is challenged by the expectations and values of each identity. Making her experience deeply complex and, at times, isolating.

From London to Riyadh – Paradigm Shift: Samar al-Megrin – *Women of Vice*

The *uber*-metropolitan discourse pervading Samar al-Megrin's 2008 novel *Nesā' al-Munkar* (Women of Vice) should be read within the spectrum of cultural exchange and activism. Its narrative invokes metaphors of cultural pressure similar to those in Raja al-Sanea's work, with the difference being that *Women of Vice* reads more like an anthropological study than a novel *per se*. Thus, the significance of space as a situational marker of identity underlies the narrative structure of the book, in which the protagonist Sarah moves from Riyadh to London then back to Riyadh, then to prison and ends up back at her 'home' with limited options in life (of remarrying and finding a suitable job). Each of these sites foregrounds a different aspect of the protagonist's identity, 'empowering or constraining her in ways that shift according to her location'. Through a first-person narrative, Sarah reflects on London as a pivotal site where East and West intersect, emphasizing how each space she inhabits shapes her experiences and sense of self:

> The last time I went to Hyde Park was when I was six years old, the images of lovers have since then been associated with it. At the time, when my father asked us where do you want to go, I would raise my voice and say, 'Hyde Park', my father's laugh was harmonious with my voice, 'Sarah wants to go to the lake and feed the ducks [...] I secretly wanted to see lovers, how they kissed, how they stared into each other's eyes, I saw in their eyes something that I missed as a Saudi little girl. My mother would

say [about them] 'infidels,' although I was young, I didn't agree with my mother's rejection of their behavior. I had to pretend sometimes that I was disgusted by their behavior, so that she wouldn't notice my contemplations, especially after that day, when I was almost caught, as I was extending my hand for the duck on the lake, even after it was empty, my eyes were on some lovers, as I was thinking of how miserable our life is, my father shouted at me, be careful the duck will eat your empty hand.[41]

By staging the protagonist's inward and outward gazes, the author registers a fascination with the West. This fascination, however, collides with the mother's reaction and the Occidental discourse that she embodies, characterized by terms like 'disgust' and 'infidels'. Sarah's contemplation and acceptance of the West echo Edward Said's stages of how new ideas travel. According to Said, there is first an origin, where an idea is born; second, a distance traversed, where the idea moves through various contexts; third, a set of conditions for acceptance or resistance; and fourth, a transformed idea occupying a new position in a different time and place.[42] In the novel, the final stage is exemplified by Sarah walking in Hyde Park as a divorced woman in love with Raif, realizing her childhood dream. This scene illustrates how Sarah and Raif, by pursuing their desires in defiance of cultural norms, exemplify the transformed and incorporated idea of Western influences within their new context.

The strength of this narrative lies in its ability to capitalize on the historical punctum/impact of the *saḥwa*, transforming it into a marker of political memory and a shared past with new significance. Drawing on Clifford's suggestion in his aforementioned essay, which links location with political activism, London is depicted as having significantly raised Sarah's level of political awareness and empowered her sense of agency. On her return to Arabia, she is shown challenging the religious police,[43] demonstrating how London has served not only as a refuge from the constraints of Arabia's society but also as a space for introspection and activism.

In this context, London functions as both a window of freedom and an instrument for Sarah's self-examination, fostering a dialogue that leads to protest, activism and locational transnational feminism. This form of activism, referred to by Friedman as locational feminism, promotes local agencies within a global feminist framework. This theme, discussed by Clifford in 'Notes on Theory and Travel', underscores how Sarah's experience in London catalyses her activism and contributes to a broader discourse on feminism and social change.

> 'Location' here, is not a matter of finding a stable 'home' or of discovering a common experience. Rather it is a matter of being aware of the difference that makes a difference in concrete situations, of recognizing the various inscriptions, 'places,' or 'histories' that both empower and inhibit the construction of theoretical categories like 'Woman,' 'Patriarchy,' or

'colonization,' categories essential to political action as well as to serious comparative knowledge.[44]

Back in Riyadh, Sarah is portrayed as blinded by what she perceives to be love and the desire to reunite with her lover, Raif, after their return from London. She arranges to meet him at a restaurant in Riyadh, seemingly unaware that the restaurant is under surveillance by agents of the religious police. In a swift turn of events, the couple is apprehended and dragged off to prison. In prison, Sarah faces abuse and is sentenced to three years of imprisonment, a punishment exacerbated by her gender, and her status as a member of an underprivileged family, reflecting Helena Kennedy's observation that 'being poor and female makes for a very different experience'.[45] Although Sarah is initially portrayed as wealthy enough to travel abroad, her imprisonment and subsequent low-paid work as a server at weddings contrast sharply with her earlier economic status. Raif, being a male and from an affluent family, receives a one-year prison sentence. The novel's depiction of Sarah's experience highlights a form of societal marginalization. She encounters a metaphorical ghetto within the prison, inhabited by women who, like her, are relegated to the margins of society. This setting underscores the intersection of gender, class and imprisonment, illustrating the challenging realities faced by women in this context.

Not surprisingly, the novel serves as a powerful critique of a deeply entrenched gender bias that holds men and women to different expectations and standards. This is particularly evident in the scene where Sarah defies the religious clerics and refuses to sign her accusation papers. Her defiant statement 'I won't sign, I won't sign *ya sheikh*, I won't sign *ya* defender of Islam' marks a significant moment of resistance against the oppressive forces. This passage is notable for its unprecedented depiction of women confronting the religious clerics, reflecting a shift in how Saudi women challenge discriminating laws. Following Raunig's analysis, this 'new text' transforms the relationship between art and politics from merely instrumental to transversal, disrupting the traditional hierarchy that relegates art to supportive roles within a specific discourse.[46] Foucault's insights further illuminate how this connection between art and politics challenges the alienation imposed by power structures.[47] Women writers create a discourse of transversality that subverts the dominant-male narratives and values. By turning what Butler defines as the 'oral performativity' practices of oppression into texts of resistance, the novel highlights the cumulative nature of oppression. It critiques class and gender-based victimization and holds the clerics accountable for their discriminatory practices.

As part of the new rising discourse, al-Megrin openly challenges the discriminatory laws at the heart of the *saḥwa*, and succeeds in subverting the master narrative that had hitherto fostered misogyny. This text, to quote

Shereen Abouelnaga, stems from different positionalities 'banished for a long time in the margins, not only endowing it with power but also qualifying it to be a tool of analysis, capable of interpreting an important part of the sociopolitical situation'.[48] Al-Megrin's work brings marginalized voices to the forefront, providing a powerful critique of societal norms and contributing to a broader understanding of the complexities and injustices within the culture.

Notes

1 Henri Lefebvre, *Spatial Politics, Everyday Life and the Right to the City*, ed. Chris Butler (Routledge: London and New York, 2012), p. 15.
2 Suellen Diaconoff, *The Myth of the Silent Woman: Moroccan Woman Writers* (University of Toronto Press: Toronto, 2009), p. 150.
3 Susan Friedman, 'Introduction', in Friedman, *Mappings*.
4 Friedman, 'Introduction'.
5 Friedman, *Mappings*, p. 139.
6 Edward W. Said, 'Travelling Theory', in Said, *The World, the Text and the Critic* (Harvard University Press: Cambridge, MA, 1983), p. 226.
7 Friedman, *Mappings*, p. 113.
8 Omima al-Khamis, *al-Warefa* [The Leafy Tree] (Dar al-Mada: Damascus, 2008).
9 Monica Carol Miller, *Being Ugly: Southern Women Writers and Social Rebellion*, Southern Literary Studies (Louisiana State University Press: Baton Rouge), pp. 2–15.
10 Marilyn Booth, ' "The Muslim Woman" as Celebrity Author and the Politics of Translating Arabic: Girls of Riyadh Go on the Road', *Journal of Middle East Women's Studies*, Vol. 6, No. 3 (2010, Fall), p. 158.
11 Naomi Wolf, *The Beauty Myth: How Images of Beauty Are Used against Women* (Vintage: London, 1991).
12 Al-Khamis, *al-Warefa*, p. 10.
13 Gillian Whitlock, *Soft Weapons: Autobiography in Transit* (University of Chicago Press: Chicago, 2007), p. 67.
14 Edward Said, *Orientalism* (Penguin Random House: London, 2019).
15 Friedman, *Mappings*, p. 19.
16 Zaineb Hefny, *Nesā' 'End Khaṭ al-'Estewā'* [Women on the Equator] (Al-Mu'sassah al-Arabyya lilderasāt wa-Alnasher: Beirut, 1996), p. 2.
17 From a paper presented at the American University in Cairo in 2011, entitled 'Revolution in Saudi Women's Literature: Zaineb Hefny a role model'.
18 Zaineb Hefny, *Ahlāmy mā Zālat Tantather: Ru'yah Hayātyah* [My Dreams Are Still Waiting] (Cultural Ministry of Egypt: Cairo, 2016), p. 46.
19 Anzaldúa, *Borderlands/La Frontera*.
20 Zaineb Hefny, *Siqan Multawiah* [Twisted Legs] (Almu'assasa al'arabyya Lilderāsāt Wa-alnashr: Beirut, 2008), p. 51.
21 Hefny, *Siqan Multawiah*, pp. 103–4.
22 Theodor Adorno quoted in Caren Kaplan, *Questions of Travel: Postmodern Discourses of Displacement* (Duke University Press: Durham, NC, 1996), p. 101.
23 James Clifford, 'Notes on Theory and Travel', *Inscriptions* 5 (1989) – quoted in Kaplan, *Questions of Travel*, p. 137.

24 Booth, 'Celebrity Author', pp. 149–82.
25 Muhammad al-Abbas in private email interview with the author, 2012.
26 Margo Badran, 'The Course and Future of Islamic Feminism: Conversation with Yoginder Sikand', *Dialogues on Civilization*, 13 October 2010.
27 Anne McClintock cited in Abouelnaga, *Women in Revolutionary Egypt*, p. 38.
28 Munira al-Subai, *Bait al-Ṭa'ah* [The House of Obedience] (Al-Dar Al-Arabiah Lel'ulume: Lebanon, 2007).
29 Sara Matar, *Qabīlah Ismha Sara* [A Tribe Called Sara] (Faradis Publishers: Bahrain, 2008), p. 10.
30 Raja al-Sanea, *Banat al-Riyadh* [Girls of Riyadh] (Penguin Press: London, 2007).
31 Al-Sanea's webpage, subsequently taken down (voluntarily): http:www.rajaa.net
32 Al-Rasheed, *Most Masculine State*, p. 255.
33 Nizar Qabbani, *Journal of an Indifferent Woman* (Nizar Qabbani Publications: Lebanon, 1968).
34 Al-Sanea, *Banat al-Riyadh*, p. 169.
35 Malcolm Bradbury quoted in Kaplan, *Questions of Travel*, p. 29.
36 For further reading on the subject, please see Freeman, 'Moral Geographies and Women's Freedom'. Freeman explains how women's mobility is both constrained and enabled by cultural and religious practices and discourses, and by material circumstances. She notes that the Muslim world's anxieties about women's freedom have been related to the desire to control, socially and spatially, their sexuality in order to ensure their purity. She warns against the rigid private/public dichotomy of gender and segregation, arguing that the 'moral geographies' within which Muslim women are situated are open to interpretation.
37 Malcolm Cowley, in Kaplan, *Questions of Travel*, p. 47.
38 Al-Sanea, *Banat al-Riyadh*, p. 74.
39 Friedman, *Mappings*, p. 6.
40 Glover and Kaplan, *Genders*, pp. 73–9.
41 Al-Megrin, *Nesā' al-Munkar*, pp. 13–14.
42 Said, 'Travelling Theory', p. 227.
43 The *muṭaween* are religious scholars/vigilantes.
44 Clifford, 'Notes on Theory and Travel', pp. 177, 188.
45 Baroness Helena Kennedy at the International Gender Studies Centre 2013 Anniversary, Lady Margaret Hall, Oxford, 2013.
46 Raunig, *Art and Revolution*, p. 18.
47 Foucault, 'The Subject and Power', pp. 777–95.
48 Abouelnaga, *Women in Revolutionary Egypt*, p. 41.

6
PROTEST AND SELF-ORIENTALIZING TEXTS

If there is a single society that contemporary US readers see as encapsulating the mystery of the Islamic Orient, it is Saudi Arabia. Within that mystery, the mystery of mysteries remains the Arab Muslim woman, often homogenised and made to stand in for an entire society and history.[1]

This 'mystery' regarding the Muslim world was intensified by the events of 9/11 – more precisely, during the United States' subsequent 'war on terror' and Arabia's struggle with extremism. Paying attention to the historical context in which these works appeared explains the proliferation of self-orientalizing works that tend to confirm what the Western reader assumes about the veiled, enigmatic and oppressed women of Arabia. This 'mystery of all mysteries' has been unpacked now – more precisely, between the years 2005 and 2010 – by the new crop of Saudi women authors, who are breaking their predecessors' long silence; defying patriarchal tradition; and writing about almost everything, including the 'mother of all taboos', sexuality (something that their parents' generation would not think of discussing freely even behind closed doors). Like occupants of harems suddenly exposed to the outside world, Saudi women writers have become, as Madawi al-Rasheed observes, the authors of 'their own orientalist texts'.[2]

The spread of information technology has significantly influenced how these women connect with the world beyond their private spaces, and across national and linguistic boundaries. For many young Saudi authors, new technologies have both accelerated and complicated their lives. However, this also risks turning them into elite native informants of Orientalism, where writers might unintentionally reinforce an inferior image of the East.[3] Writers like Saba al-Herz, Warda Abdul Malik and Taif al-Hallaj (discussed below)

DOI: 10.4324/9781003539681-7

have chosen to hide their identities behind a pseudonym, offering their audiences 'literature of protest', to borrow the words of Miral al-Tahawy. Al-Tahawy notes that

> [t]he emergence of that writing exposes the strong relationship between excessive use of explicit language and tackling sexual taboos and the rise of the religious extremist discourse's influence in spreading ideas that emphasize the impurity of the female body and reduce it to genitalia. By now it has become clear that the more the conservative discourse reviles and oppresses the female body, the more extreme is women's reaction of using that body as an instrument of protest, in ways that the Arab world has never seen before.[4]

What is important here is not merely the profane images produced by these writers but how obscenity serves as an indicator of shifts in collective social attitudes. Obscenity is a fluid concept that, as David C. Rittenhouse notes, 'takes its fabric from the warp and the woof of the society in which it is spun'.[5] Marina Stagh further notes that obscenity, blasphemy and political dissent are intertwined with moral values and limits of tolerance, which evolve with public opinion.[6] Consequently, the use of obscene and blasphemous language by anonymous Saudi women writers aims to challenge and embarrass religious extremists and alter the dynamic of gender power.

By giving voice to the voiceless in society, these writers not only challenge the patriarchal structure of that society but also bring to the forefront transgressive female characters. Using the binary oppositions of good and bad, right and wrong, and the socially permissible and the criminalized, these writers seek to undermine social laws that, for example, condone prostitution under religious pretexts and justify 'marriages of convenience'. Al-Hallaj's *The Sacred Marriage* uses these contrasts to critique such practices. Meanwhile, Abdul Malik's *The Return* attempts to shame the extremist subculture by employing a Qur'anic tone and language to question and mock extremists and their societal representatives. Both Abdul Malik and al-Hallaj work to redefine the social and political structures of patriarchy, challenging the notion that Islamists represent 'political correctness' and virtue, while modernists are associated with corruption.

'Hell Is Other People': Saba al-Herz – *The Others*

Echoing Jean-Paul Sartre's famous statement 'Hell is other people', this self-orientalizing work reveals, right from the outset, the struggle between self and society, breaking taboos related to formal human relationships and religious and social codes of behaviour. This approach led Saudi critic Abd Allah al-Ghadhami and Muhammad al-Ali to dismiss it as not representative of the

Saudi novel. Their views, in turn, were criticized by many. For instance, Ahmad al-Wasil in 'Curtains and Sharp Pens' argued that both critics were unable to transcend their patriarchal cultural traditions. Consequently, they dismissed the novel as an exploration of private issues that are not bounded by place or time.[7] This dispute targeted claims by al-Ghadhami that acknowledged and praised *Girls of Riyadh* as representative of a certain social class, unlike *The Others*. Not surprisingly, the author's use of pseudonym enabled her to delve into controversial themes, such as lesbianism, without the fear of facing a direct backlash. By concealing her identity, she could explore topics of sexual identity and societal rebellion, addressing themes that would have been met with resistance or outright hostility from both critics and audience.

Throughout the novel, the protagonist is portrayed as a lost soul, rejecting both her femininity and her identity as a Muslim woman belonging to the Shi'i branch of Islam. The religious rhetoric that forbids any mingling between the men and women has shaped her rebellious character. Like many self-orientalizing novels mentioned in this chapter, *The Others* not only shakes the stable symbolic order that once governed meaning and power relations in Arabia but also rethinks and challenges the actual status quo, particularly regarding Shi'i culture and identity. Written in a memoir-like narrative structure, where the protagonist's perspective is deliberately linked with the collective view of society and the nation, the novel uses the female as a site to challenge, if not indict, socio-religious laws.

The protagonist's experience, including being a victim of child abuse and suffering from epileptic seizures, highlights the intersection of multiple oppression. I find that Friedman's discourse of multiple oppression (mentioned in the Introduction and in Chapter 2) is helpful in understanding the multifaceted character of al-Herz's protagonist because, to borrow Friedman's words, it emphasizes the differences among women and considers oppression as a core element of identity. This leads to the additive naming of various forms of victimization based on race, class, religion, gender, national origin, ableness and more.[8] For instance, the protagonist is a woman from a minority group, specifically a Saudi Shi'i woman. She is also a lesbian. She was abused as a child, making her an abused woman, and she suffers from epileptic seizures, making her an ill woman. Her identity, therefore, sits at the crossroads of numerous forms of powerlessness and multiple oppression. In Friedman's words, this discourse

> expresses a kind of interminable negativity evident in the pileup of oppressions, with its implicit hierarchization of suffering. But this discourse has also developed a dialectical analysis whereby the multiplication of oppression creates its antithesis, a multiple richness and power centered in difference.[9]

Narrated in the first person, *The Others* feels like it is sharing a secret with the reader. The protagonist's physical attractiveness is implicitly embedded in the textual world, with rare references like *ya ḥelwah* (pretty) that are countered throughout the novel by her masculine behaviour and way of dressing. She is frequently depicted wearing boyish trousers. The author negotiates cultural narratives of gender bias by turning these narratives into sites of contradictions, particularly by presenting a lesbian lifestyle as an alternative to the emotional emptiness and monotony of her protagonist's life.

The Others can be said to lack serious literary or artistic value; it nevertheless succeeded in the international market, and has been translated into English and sold internationally. This is not surprising because it largely served to validate stereotypes of the exotic and repressed woman through a girl's journey from homosexuality to straightness in the closed and segregated world of eastern Saudi Arabia. The covers of translated works such as *The Others* and *The Return* feature images of a man and a woman with intertwined hands, which triggers curiosity in Western readers. These images tap into a Western fantasy of Arabia, particularly appealing to those eager for information about the strictly gendered spaces of the Islamic world. Sanaz Fotouhi observes that

> [g]ender issues, particularly gender dichotomy in the Middle East, have shrouded Middle Eastern women's lives in mystery for the west. [...] Consequently, this has led to overexaggeration of the situation of Muslim women, and over centuries many have constructed the assumption that veiled women were necessarily more oppressed, more passive, more ignorant than unveiled women.[10]

The author effectively politicizes the female body within the context of a patriarchal, authoritarian society, using the fantasies of her protagonist as an expression of revolt and a means of reclaiming agency. Echoing Lévi-Strauss' expression 'I am the place in which something has occurred', the female protagonist is ensnared between absurd religious rhetoric and a compliant officialdom, both of which combine to enforce a form of gender discrimination. As a victim of child abuse, the protagonist's ambivalence is heightened. She is depicted as living in two conflicting worlds: one, as an active member of a religious charity, and the other within the clandestine realm of same-sex relationships. This duality culminates in her occasional epileptic seizures, which she hides out of fear that their disclosure would lead to her marginalization from social activities, work and marriage opportunities, much like the ostracism she would face if her homosexuality were revealed.

This constant fear over the disclosure of her secrets compounds her sense of alienation, which is so familiar to members of minority groups – be they ethnic or gender. When a grand mal seizure occurs, her body is metaphorically turned inside out and she cannot continue her work at the nursery, worrying that she might scare the children one day. The author, who is in control of the discourse, discloses to the reader the unnamed protagonist's struggle with epilepsy and fear of society in a direct, first-person narrative that lends certainty and truthfulness to her suffering:

> My illness had always been a secret, for long periods of time, even speaking about it was a disgraceful act that could trigger a scolding in our household. It was as if illness was a sin without possibility of forgiveness, a flow it was necessary to hide, a little scandal blemishing the family that must not get out beyond the most intimate circles. I understand the logic that equates illness with a bad reputation. No one is going to come forward promptly to pick this up and carry it for you; no one wants to take it to his bosom; no one will be in a hurry to procure such a thing for his sterling family tree.[11]

In this passage, the protagonist elucidates the agony of her occasional epileptic seizures – which strip her of her agency to control her body and voice, making her condition visible to the world. This pain is compounded by the fear of societal knowledge, where epilepsy is perceived as a 'sin', 'disgrace', 'blemishing', 'flaw' or 'scandal', reflecting a 'bad reputation'. The emphasis on the social stigma attached to such illnesses reveals a mirror-like consistency between the body and society. This narrative not only portrays the protagonist's suffering but also comments on broader human relations, including how such an illness might diminish her marriage prospects, as potential suitors may be deterred. This depiction of pain and its social implications serves as a tool for understanding societal perceptions of illness, resonating with Elaine Scarry's observations on how pain is articulated and often made to signify broader social contexts, 'or some dramatised surrogate of the world'.[12]

The protagonist's body serves as a metaphor for a suffering community, with her illness deeply intertwined with the social and religious facets of that community. Drawing on Mary Douglas' concept, the physical experience of the body is always influenced by social categories, which sustains specific societal views. This creates a continuous interplay between physical and social experiences, each reinforcing the other's categories.[13] While al-Herz grants the protagonist a narrative freedom to articulate her illness, her narration is imbued with a profound sense of shame.

In the context of Saudi women's discourses of resistance, the protagonist of al-Herz's narrative embodies metaphorical connotations of anger and destruction, reflecting resistance against cultural laws and the dismantling of outdated traditions. Her efforts to repress her anger result in frequent seizures, which exacerbate her shift from a sociable and lively girl to one who is uncommunicative and isolated. She expresses her struggle with her body: 'my body betrays me. It hurts – the unfaithfulness of a body that has always been neutral, even in the worst of its histories with me.'[14] She then adds, 'My body pains me, the kind of pain that Panadol pills do not take away, an ache that does not disappear when I try to ignore it.' She further articulates her feeling of despair when her illness flares up; she explains her struggle: 'Pain that is like heaviness, as if I am pushing forward with difficulty across a terrain of mud [...] pain that urges me to abandon the idea of life altogether.'[15] Al-Herz's detailed description of pain challenges what Virginia Woolf famously termed the 'poverty of language', and her observation that English, despite its capacity to articulate complex emotions and tragedies, often lacks adequate words to express the nuances of physical suffering.

The Marker of Identity Goes Anonymous: Warda Abdul Malik – *The Return*

Warda Abdul Malik, in *al-Awba* (The Return), was by no means the first Saudi female author to break taboos. Other women writers from the kingdom have been increasingly addressing taboo subjects, challenging traditional norms and exploring themes of gender, sexuality, identity and societal expectations. However, no one has approached these topics with Abdul Malik's level of crudeness, vulgarity and offensiveness, likely aiming to create a work that is explosive, scandalous and self-orientalizing. The author explores the religious-extremist subculture through her protagonist Sara, a young and lively girl who leaves school to marry the devout Abdulla. Abdulla is the brother of her school's social worker, Filwa, who is depicted as an agent of the *saḥwa*, who provides Sara with pious cassettes, guides her through the religious circles and teaches her how to be a submissive, domestic, reticent and docile wife to her brother.

For this, Sara is indoctrinated to believe that the path to paradise is through total submission to her husband and his marital desires. A stark example of this portrayal is found in Sara's terrified recollection of her wedding night: 'He started showering me with crazy kisses on my cheeks. He devoured my mouth, chewed my tongue, and ground my teeth against his [...] He did not leave me until the caller of prayer announced the early morning ritual.'[16] Her nightmarish memory of their wedding night emphasizes the oppressive and abusive dynamics she faces, highlighting the author's critical view of *saḥwa* and its impact on women.

The novel's excessive use of obscene and blasphemous language aims to disgrace the religious clique, shift the gender power struggle, and highlight gender inequality in the kingdom at the time. This effect is further intensified by employing Qur'anic tone and language to question divinity and ridicule the religious system and its representative society. Thus, the transformation of Sara's nightmare into what Dominick LaCapra describes as a narrative memory and total meaning or knowledge[17] allows the story to be communicated to the individual and collective knowledge of its readers. This narrative strategy opens up new possibilities,[18] particularly by turning the *saḥwa* and its repression of women into an unforgettable testimony.

When Abdulla falls ill, and starts hallucinating and cursing divinity, the narrative depicts a shocking scene of him being possessed by an infidel *jinn*. Filwa is depicted as unsurprised when Sara reports to her what has happened. She immediately goes to their house, barges into the bedroom, and shakes Abdulla, telling him to 'wake up' as if she had done this a thousand times before. The omniscient narrator describes how Sara, wanting to understand what had happened the previous night, asks Filwa, 'What's wrong with him?' Filwa responds with a wicked look, as if she does not know Sara at all, and shouts, 'Nothing, do you understand nothing, and don't go telling your family what […] happened.' She then continues manipulatively, saying, 'God has entrusted you with your husband, are you going to breach this trust?'[19] Abdulla's sister then decides to subject him to exorcism rituals, and brings in a group of sheikhs who spit on him and chant verses of the Qur'an in order to draw the *jinns* out of his body. Abdulla is subsequently depicted as shattered and depressed. The all-seeing narrator's horrific images of Abdulla's mental illness – the pornographic scenes that depict him lying in bed, impotent and passive, with Sara driven by satanic powers and subjecting him to lustful behavior – are meant to demean and subvert the nation's piety and patriarchal hierarchy.

Crucial to these accounts is the use of a first-person narrative, which allows readers to peek into the protagonist's stream of consciousness and observe the ideological shifts brewing within her. For instance, the many flashbacks that fuse the past and present in one scene appear to reveal Sara reaching a point where she can no longer recognize herself. She yearns for the good old days, and she asks herself, 'Where's Suri, as my grandmother would call me?' and 'Where's the apple, as my uncle would call me?' Her lacerating self-examination is also evident when she wonders, 'Where's Sara, who's been crushed a thousand times by their blessings, curses, piety, vices, lies and illnesses?'[20] The novel's subplots further incriminate radicalism, recalling the time when Sara – driven by her increasing piety – burned the only picture she had of her deceased father:

> while I was holding the only picture of my father, my hands shivered, it was an old picture of him taken in the mid sixties in front of the Umayyad grand mosque in Syria. I kissed it and in a matter of seconds it was dusty ash.[21]

This narrative strategy effectively deepens the reader's understanding of Sara's internal struggle and the societal pressure that shape her experiences. Through this intimate first-person perspective, the author vividly illustrates the protagonist's journey from subjugation to a quest for identity and freedom, underscoring the broader themes of resistance against oppressive ideologies and the search for self amidst societal constraints. The misery, rage and anger embedded in Abdul Malik's novel point the finger of blame at the *sahwa*, which has stolen the best years of Sara's life – a recurring theme, and one shared with the characters of Samar al-Megrin's *Women of Vice* (examined in Chapter 5). Both writers, in their different ways, mark the reverse shift in their protagonists' religious consciousness from extremism to moderation, regretting how radicalism has negatively impacted on their major decisions in life – including marriage.

After a psychological struggle, Sara embarks on a new chapter in her life that starkly contrasts with her previous existence. The anonymous author draws another self-orientalizing image – of Sara drifting into a life of decadence at home and abroad, dancing, drinking and enjoying casual encounters. However, anguished by her moral and psychological regression, she becomes ill and troubled. Like her ex-husband, she is taken to a sheikh who spits and chants over her – but also secretly subjects her to abuse. Her persistent thoughts of illness lead her to accept counselling with a female psychiatrist to treat her compulsive behaviour of repetitively washing herself. In this context, her illness acts as a signifier of a deeper social malaise. Abir Hamdar describes this as a 'counterpoint to prevailing political rhetoric, formations and ideology'.[22] This is hardly surprising, as the discourse on women's resistance implicitly links the narrator's perspective to the collective experience of women negatively impacted by the *sahwa*.

Given a new lease on life, Sara – accompanied by her brother, Omar – arrives in London, where she is portrayed as reborn. Relishing her new sense of agency and freedom. Enjoying a new chapter in her life, and falling in love with Mishari, her brother's friend, she is hopeful and joyous, declaring,

> I want to live every minute of my life, I want to love and be admired. I want to travel, dress and listen to music. I want to enjoy the company of others, read, and go to the movies. I want to sink in life's *halāl* and *harām* before it is over.[23]

No longer limited to the private space of her home, kitchen, prayer mat and marital bed, Sara is indeed reborn. The author effectively uses the female body as a narrative site of sin and redemption, embodying the tension between societal norms and personal liberation. In the novel, the protagonist's physical and emotional experience reflects broader social and religious conflict. The protagonist's body becomes a battleground where sin, in the form of imposed religious doctrine, clashes with the potential for redemption through self-awareness and resistance. Through explicit and often shocking depictions of her physical experiences, the narrative exposes the extent of her oppression, aiming to critique and dismantle the power dynamic at play. This use of the female body as a metaphorical site enables the story to transcend individual experiences, turning them into a powerful testimony against systemic injustice. It allows the reader to witness the protagonist's journey from subjugation to a potential for liberation, thus making a broader statement about the need for societal change and the reclamation of agency by women.

Selectivity in Patriarchal Discourse: Taif al-Hallaj – *The Sacred Marriage*

Taif al-Hallaj's *Al-Qaran al-Muqadas* (The Sacred Marriage) is an introspective narrative that calls for social and political changes and dares to use the figure of the prostitute in order to highlight societal and religious problems. Of course, prostitution has been a significant theme in women's novels, often serving as a lens to explore complex issues related to gender inequality, religion, power and societal norms. Using this framework, the author attempts to analyse broader patterns of domination and exploitation in male-dominated societies, often to draw the reader's attention to the larger context of women's exploitation. Like Abdul Malik's *The Return* and al-Herz's *the Others*, this novel breaks down the social and religious barriers that contribute to women's subordinate status in Arabia's society. It opens with the protagonist, Laila – who has recently lost her husband – in the car with her brother, Ibrahim, on their way to their aunt's house. Ibrahim, depicted as the patriarch of the family, drives at high speed but Laila is afraid to say a word, and they end up in an accident. Laila loses consciousness and starts recollecting her past life with the help of an illusory interlocutor named Ishtar. Ishtar, in this context, signifies a multifaceted deity whose influence spans love, fertility, war, power and transformation. It embodies the divine feminine; a lens through which the protagonist examines her fears and ambitions. This device explains the tedious narrative structure that is built on Laila's stream of consciousness and an abundant use of flashbacks, which makes the novel overly crowded and aesthetically flawed because it tries too hard to use introspection as a means of delivering ideas. This futility becomes evident when the author reveals at the end of the novel that there was, in fact, no accident and that Laila has actually experienced a protracted dream.

Nonetheless, al-Hallaj dares to break taboos in order to warn against the perils of sectarianism, foreign interventions and the troubles of unbalanced gender relations, power dynamics, and societal issues. For instance, Laila debates patriarchal double standards, particularly within her Shi'a community – first, with respect to the community's passivity in the face of political and sectarian challenges; second, for its approval of 'convenience/temporary marriage'. She points the finger of blame at the community's mullahs for misleading people and recruiting them to serve foreign agendas of expansion in the area. This, she argues, provokes instability and disorder. Laila stresses, 'The *mullahs* are trying to export their revolution to the rest of the Muslim world, in doing so, they are distracting their own people from looking into their own internal affairs.'[24]

Each chapter of *The Sacred Marriage* opens with a couple of lines from a poem, a famous proverb or a phrase written by the author herself. Most relevant to the current volume is the chapter entitled 'Al-Saqifah' (A Porch). It starts with the line, 'A women who fools around is perceived as [a] great sinner, one that shakes the thrones of heaven and earth, while the same sin is perceived as a sign of maturity and virility in men.'[25] In this novel, al-Hallaj scrutinizes the troubled relationship between patriarchy and the oldest profession in the world, prostitution. The narrator poses the questions 'What is prostitution?' and 'Why do people overlook those whom they pay?' Such probing is meant to subvert the male-dominant discourse, in which women have been sidelined and prostitutes portrayed mainly as victims of poverty and social and economic circumstances instead of being seen as symbols of hypocrisy and double standards that society imposes on women. This explains the author's view and her incessant attempts to transgress traditional male discourses:

> Real prostitution is what men are doing in this world [...] starting wars, demolishing houses and dividing families, killing people and committing genocide. Prostitution is when people are bought and sold in deals, when people die in prisons, when people every day suffer and die because of severe hunger, while [a] few squander public wealth; prostitution is when corruption is beautified.[26]

In this passage, the author draws a clear parallel between the exploitation of women in prostitution, and humans' lives in wars. If prostitution means the exploitation of women's bodies, initiating conflicts often comprises the exploitation of human lives for political, economic, or ideological gains. This metaphor implies that men's actions of initiating conflicts are in a way another form of 'prostitution' of human values and lives.

It is worth noting that Taif al-Hallaj – which is rumoured to be the pseudonym of a well-known feminist and women's-rights activist in eastern

Saudi Arabia – tries to be a voice for the voiceless yet becomes involved in a narrative that appears to further self-orientalization. Here, the author forms a creative alliance with Western stereotypes that represent Arabia's women as abused victims of patriarchal culture. This explains the anonymous author's tendency to humanize the figure of the prostitute and women involved in secret/temporary marriage, or *muta'a*.[27] This tendency crystallizes in her questioning of women's rights in such marriages through the character of Um al-Shaikh, a poor and ugly widow who was chosen for a marriage of convenience by a line of mullahs and sheikhs. Similarly, the many subplots in the novel attempt to demean the male figure – which includes Laila's brother, whom she dared not ask to slow down when he was driving crazily, and her father Abu Anwar, an old man who has married a young Lolita-like bride, Anisa, in order to satisfy his needs and compensate for his insecurities.

The setting of the 'road' in the chapter 'Al-Saqifah' enhances the process of rendering time material in the novel's space, with the protagonist primarily serving as an onlooker, standing on the road peering at Rabab's house from a distance. It is a scene that depict a moment of profound transformation for Laila, as she encounters a situation that challenges her values and beliefs. The use of an omniscient narrator allows the reader to see into Laila's thoughts. The details of Rabab being with a man, naked on the floor, eyes closed, suggests vulnerability or powerlessness. and Laila's shock implies that she is confronting something deeply unsettling. This scene, while verging on the explicit, is a pivotal point in Laila's personal journey, where her assumptions and views are forced to collide with unexpected reality. On a surface level, the narrator expresses her disgust at what she sees, calling Rabab a 'witch' (*ḥaizabūn*), but on a deeper level the narrator also attempts to humanize the prostitute – specifically, when describing her eyes, which in this context represent conscience or truth: having them 'closed' symbolizes Rabab's disavowal of what she is doing. By framing the scene in this way, the narrative taps into complex social responses to nudity and personal boundaries. The narrator's harsh tone might mirror cultural attitudes that cast judgment and shame on those who transgress norms, revealing how societal beliefs often influence personal perceptions and internal conflicts. For Laila, this incident serve as a catalyst that forces her to confront these external pressures and question the validity of such judgments. As such, staging Rabab as a 'prostitute' and a 'witch' the narrative leverages powerful, historically loaded archetypes that challenge patriarchal discourse and expose the limitations of Laila's and society's understanding of complex female identity.

This shift in the narrative marks a pivotal transformation in Rabab's character, reframing her as a dynamic almost heroic figure, who transcends the rigid geder boundaries imposed by society. By moving beyond the stereotypes of "prostitute" and "witch", Rabab evolves from a marginalised or vilified figure into a powerful symbol of agency and defiance. At a Shi'ite religious gathering, she is staged not only as powerful in the face of men but also as sickened by their cowardice; she shouts at them, 'I spit on this kind of man'.[28] Rabab's expression of disgust is, in a way, reflective of the author's feminist grievance towards hypocrisy in male-dominant societies.

> The victory of Rabab was something that she would achieve anyway, even if she doesn't attend that meeting, because she had the backing and support of powerful men, who were her clients. For this none of them dared to challenge her. They were all terrified of her dominance.[29]

The author intentionally draws a comparison between women involved in marriages of convenience, like the widow character in the novel, and Rabab, the prostitute, in order to incriminate selectivity in patriarchal laws. She concludes that Rabab and the widow are two sides of the same old coin: both are victims of an oppressive code of conduct. They sell their bodies for money under different pretexts; however, one is approved of by society while the other is shunned as illicit. Capturing the ugliness of the reality of illiteracy and poverty in both women, al-Hallaj paints a troubling picture of Arab women, who, in the absence of personal freedoms and equality, continue to be treated as subordinates. By incorporating prostitution into the narrative, the author draws the reader's attention to the fact that, despite the many pleasures allowed men in Islam – the four wives, for instance – prostitution also has a place in this ostensibly puritanical culture.

It is not surprising, however, to see that many Saudi writers dwell on the various levels of female prostitution: some of their characterizations, like that of Rabab, stress 'common-ness' and 'vulgarity' while others dwell on 'luxury prostitution' – as does the characterization of Salwa in al-Beshir's *The Swing* (discussed in Chapter 4). The metaphors of transgression found in both *The Sacred Marriage* and *The Swing* attempt to explore the relationship between a woman's stifled and silenced existence in society and the writers' expression of it through the politicized female body. Both levels of prostitution depicted by these authors are, in fact, *zina*: unlawful relationships between men and women who are not bound by an official marriage contract.

It is important to mention here that Saudi women writers each deal differently with the issue of prostitution but, like female authors from the wider Arab world, they all agree that in the absence of women's rights, good education and financial independence, women will continue to be in the lower spectrum of economic and social participation. Evelyne Accad notes in this regard,

> Images in Arabic literature of women in various relationships with men signify a deeper social rupture – the extreme degree to which the social status of Arab women is both male-centered and male-sanctioned. The condition of women being what it is in these societies, prostitution is only one further level of degradation.[30]

It is worth mentioning that, the figure of the prostitute is not new in Arabic literature. It has been employed since at least 1948, when it was used by the Noble Prize laureate Egyptian author Naguib Mahfouz in his *Midaq Alley*, by Nawal el-Sadawi (*Woman at Point Zero*), Salwa Baker (*The Golden Chariot*) and the Palestinian Sahar Khalifah in *Abbad al-Shams* (1980). The character of Ḥamida is blamed by the (male) author Mahfouz for taking a short cut to happiness, and being lured onto the slippery slope of prostitution. She is also depicted as a beautiful and bright woman who is able to manipulate (to a certain extent) Si-al-Sayed, the famous patriarchal figure in Mahfouz's Cairo Trilogy. In women's novels, by contrast, the prostitute is often depicted as a dynamic character who is capable of challenging outmoded taboos by means of adhering to their author's fundamental ideological beliefs. For example, Khalifah's protagonist Khadra is humanized through her brave and challenging stance against Israeli soldiers, reflecting the author's feminist views of women's heroic stand in the Palestinian struggle.

Notes

1. Booth, 'Celebrity Author', p. 157.
2. Al-Rasheed, *Most Masculine State*, p. 216.
3. Lisa Lau and Ana Christina Mendes (eds), *Re-orientalism and South Asian Identity Politics: The Oriental Other Within* (Routledge: London, 2011), p. 4.
4. Al-Tahawy, 'Writing the Body', p. 2.
5. David C. Rittenhouse, 'Obscenity and Social Statics', *William and Mary Law Review*, Vol. 1, No. 2 (1958). Available at scholarship.law.wm.edu/wmlr/vol1/iss2/4 (accessed 5 May 2022).
6. Marina Stagh, *The Limits of Freedom of Speech: Prose Literature and Prose Writers in Egypt under Nasser and Sadat* (Acta Universities: Stockholm, 1993), pp. 127–9.
7. Al-Wasil, 'Sat'ir wa aqlam sarikhah', p. 102.
8. Friedman, *Mappings*, p. 20.
9. Friedman.
10. Sanaz Fotouhi, 'Self-orientalisation and Reorientation: A Glimpse at Iranian Muslim Women's Memories', paper for the International Centre for Muslim and Non-Muslim Understanding, University of South Australia, 2012, p. 27.
11. Fotouhi, 'Self-orientalisation and Reorientation', p. 110.
12. Elaine Scarry, *The Body in Pain: The Making and Unmaking of the World* (Oxford University Press: New York and Oxford, 1985), p. 51.
13. Mary Douglas, *Natural Symbols: Explorations in Cosmology* (Routledge: London and New York, 1996), p. 68.
14. Saba Al-Herz, *Al-Akrūn* [The Others] (Seven Stories Press: New York, 2009), p. 253.
15. Al-Herz, *Al-Akrūn*.
16. Warda Abdul Malik, *Al-Awba* [The Return] (Saqi Books: Beirut, 2006), p. 19.
17. Dominick LaCapra, *History in Transit: Experience, Identity, Critical Theory* (Cornell University Press: Ithaca, NY), p. 120.

18 LaCapra, *History in Transit*.
19 Abdul Malik, *Al-Awba*, pp. 25–7.
20 Abdul Malik, p. 8.
21 Abdul Malik, p. 14.
22 Abir Hamdar, *The Female Suffering Body: Illness and Disability in Modern Arabic Literature* (Syracuse University Press: Syracuse, NY, 2014), p. 59.
23 Abdul Malik, *Al-Awba*, p. 66.
24 Taif al-Hallaj, *Al-Qaran al-Muqadas* [The Sacred Marriage] (Dar al-Faradīs Lilnasher: Beirut, 2007), p. 100.
25 Al-Hallaj, *Al-Qaran al-Muqadas*, p. 235.
26 Al-Hallaj, p. 242.
27 Robert Smith defines the practice thus: '*Muta'a* in short is simply the last remains of that type of marriage which corresponds to a law of mother-kinship, and Islam condemns it and makes it "the sister of harlotry" because it does not give the husband a legitimate offspring, i.e. an offspring that is reckoned to his own tribe and has right of inheritance within it.' From W. R. Smith, *Kinship and Marriage in Early Arabia* (Cambridge University Press: Cambridge, 1903), p. 85.
28 Taif al-Hallaj, *Al-Qaran al-Muqadas*, p. 243.
29 Al-Hallaj, p. 244.
30 Evelyne Accad, 'The Prostitute in Arab and North African Fiction', in Horn and Pringle (eds), *The Image of the Prostitute*, p. 66.

CONCLUSION

In today's Saudi Arabia, 'change', 'reform', 'transformation' and the 'woman question' cannot be read in isolation from an ideology such as *sahwa*. Indeed, this very point provided reason enough for me to examine it as a pillar in the shaping of both the public discourse and cultural identity at crucial points in these writers' 'historical' lives. It also led me to examine what Saddeka Arebi rightly dubs the 'double struggle' of Saudi Arabia's women writers, who continue to be torn between local and global discourses of power. On the one hand, the *sahwa* strengthened limiting definitions of women as both cultural markers of the nation and sole bearers of Islam, an enervating process that slowly but deliberately turned them into symbols of either shame or honour. This development has shaped an entire literary genre, affecting the various voices and themes that different generations of female authors chose in order to subvert the prevailing 'master narrative'. On the other hand, Western discourses have continued their intervention in the region under the pretext of 'promoting women's rights and democracy', igniting antagonism in Arabia towards anything coming from the West – especially incessant calls for women's rights.

For the sake of this argument, I found that defining the socio-religious shifts in Saudi women's writing was crucial in terms of how these have shaped women's discourse in the kingdom, leaving a marker on both the rhythm of their writing and the level of anger and literary activism that evolved with time into what amounted to a suffrage movement. Using the concept of cultural 'counter memory', drawn from Michel Foucault's *The Archaeology of Knowledge* (1972), I have examined how these female writers have used their small space of power and their so-called marginal discourse to subvert the dominant master narrative by exploring issues of widespread discrimination against women and the misogyny that is deeply embedded in their culture. This concept of counter memory has been a valuable analytical tool in understanding not only the evolution of Saudi women's discourse but also the accumulative impact on the dominant discourse of these writers' contributions to literature.

Examining Saudi women's texts as 'points of protest and resistance'[1] that generate a multitude of points corresponding to the ideas of 'power' and 'defiance', this book has attempted to chronicle and consolidate the twists and turns in their literary tradition. Such points, I have argued, are capable of transforming the status of women from that of 'symbolic' to 'active' and even 'revolutionary' – and of subsequently shifting the attributes of women's space from powerlessness to empowered and from silenced to voiced. Using this concept has allowed me to examine women's texts – including the handful of examples that have been deemed 'flagrant', such as Warda Abdul Malik's *The Return* (examined in Chapter 6) – as constituting an intersectional space of 'identity', 'power' and 'agency' capable of challenging, if not demolishing, traditional hierarchies. In so doing, the texts 'produce different forms of [collective] subjectivity that [break] down the oppositions between the individual and the group'.[2] This process has provided a reminder of what Paul Connerton defines as an 'act of transfer',[3] which creates a collective cultural memory capable of generating both discursive and non-discursive forms of resistance.

Of course, the study of 'power' and 'defiance' in women's fiction is not new. Elaine Showalter's book *A Literature of Their Own*, first published in 1977, was a milestone in feminist literary criticism. To me, as a woman coming from Arabia, Showalter's notion of the three phases of women's writing – the feminine, the feminist and the female – was simply fascinating. And I still remember how I was left pondering – at the time – over its sustainability in assessing the literary tradition of women in Arabia. It was not until I obtained my PhD and went to Oxford University – more precisely, to the Gender Studies Centre there – to undertake postdoctorate research that the idea for this book was born, and, with it, a focus on feminism or literary activism in Saudi women's fiction. I believed that Showalter's approach offered the best lens through which these women's agency and subjectivity could be viewed in order to identify moments of romanticism; frustration; anger; and, of course, the rare moment when a writer appears oblivious to the critical gender divide.

As the work for this book progressed, however, I found that locational/ intersectional feminism – that is, the geographical interplay of gender with multiple constituents of identity – offered a more comprehensive analysis. This is because, within it, women's writing was recognized as a multilayered discourse that varies in intensity and configuration. This allowed me to move beyond gender into the new 'geographies of identity' in terms of women's agency and subjectivity – especially within the context of shifting social, religious and political times. It offered another discourse, through which 'different aspects of identity move fluidly from the foreground to the background and from powerlessness to power, depending on changes in location and the situation of the subject'.[4] This meant that the portrayal of binaries such as self/other, East/West and traditional/global in women's texts operated according to relational positionalities in which 'power circulates in multifaceted ways instead of flowing unidirectionally',[5] as is the case in the fixed binary structures of gynocriticism.

Most importantly, locational feminism blended well with the politics of place and what Islamic feminists dub 'moral geographies', which are evident in the writers' level of adherence in their fiction to the Islamic concept of *'urf* (a set of verbal and non-verbal cultural boundaries). In fact, it has proven to be a great analytical tool in understanding the blind spots, fragmentations and dead-end texts found in hybrid narratives – especially among the work of the first crop of Saudi women writers like Samira Khashugji. For instance, Gloria Anzaldúa's 'invisible borders' in the new geographics of identity – and their analysis of comparisons between 'here' and 'there', 'self' and 'other' in literary texts – offered a profound, non-discursive narrative through which the literature of these writers could be understood. In the context of the aforementioned early authors' work, these 'borders' functioned as a space in which Saudi and Egyptian identities met, with each culture prevailing to varying degrees in the texts. Such comparisons in (often expatriate) Saudi women's texts questioned the culture 'back home', igniting the first sparks of feminism in Saudi Arabia. For this reason, I maintain that although this book is about the voices and agencies of Arabia's 'revolutionary generations', it cannot by any means ignore the achievements of the pioneering generation who inspired and paved the way for others to follow. Hence, the discussion of women's early contribution to Saudi literature is just as important as the present discourse because it highlights the main constructs that have influenced resistance in Saudi women's literature.

In Chapter 1, 'Saudi Women Writers: Sociopolitical and Literary Landscapes', I examined the circumstances that made it possible for women to write, often transcending the concept of 'art for art's sake', and to develop what I call *Khalījī* / Saudi feminism (with *khalījī* referring to the people of GCC states sharing a similar social, political and religious background). Exploring the diverse political and historical milieus that impacted on Saudi women's literary journeys, I drew a distinction between three phases of women's writing in the kingdom: the postcolonial era of 1960s Egypt, which gave birth to the first generation of Saudi women writers, who were raised and/or educated in Egypt rather than in their homeland; the era of the First Gulf War in 1990–91, which was a major turning point in the history of the Gulf states; and post-9/11 and the outbreak of the Second Gulf War in 2003, which saw persistent calls and pressure on GCC states to modernize and improve the status of women.

A parallel, underlying concept to which I have paid careful attention throughout this book is that of the *saḥwa*, which I have treated as a point of memory (reminiscent of Roland Barthes' famous 'punctum') that revived a time in history replete with layers of political and cultural significance. More precisely, in the first chapter I examined 'silence' and 'voice' as two aspects modified and codified in women's literary contributions that show the authors' dilemmas over taboo breaking and over what is or is not culturally and religiously permissible. Variations in these areas raised questions as to why women's fiction in Arabia began with only 'soft' calls for change and from writers such as Samira Khashugji and Huda al-Rasheed, among others. Although I have treated this aberration as the result of cultural exposure and hybridity, it nevertheless illuminates the fact that *saḥwa* was a transient ideology and a narrative that came and went. Furthermore, to understand the aforementioned variations in women's texts, I have looked at the different phases through which women passed in relation to the punctum of the *saḥwa*, examining how texts that came at various historical times and in various historical spaces reveal the process of change in social attitudes, and the resulting transformation in women's perspectives.

For instance, a glance at the works of Samira Khashugji, Qmasha al-Olayyan, Zaineb Hefny, Badriya al-Beshir, Saba al-Herz and Warda Abdul Malik among others revealed not only major shifts in socio-religious consciousness but also women's mounting anger and resistance, and the small space of power that these women writers collectively cultivate in order to subvert the 'master narrative' of the dominant male discourse. Hence, each chapter has attempted to chronicle the evolution of women's discourse as it passed through phases of colonialism or non-organic calls for equality (i.e. those arising somewhere other than their country of origin); the internalization of *saḥwa* values and their obliviousness to the 'woman question'; the disruption of *saḥwa*; and, later on, an organic call for equality and protest against the male-dominant discourse and *saḥwa* that included anonymous writers who obscenely challenged the *saḥwa* and its agents, the clerics, from behind the 'veil' of their pseudonyms. Clear examples of the last-named trend were provided in Chapter 6 – by Warda Abdul Malik's *The Return*, which uses a Qur'anic tone and language to question divinity and ridicule the religious system and its representatives in society, and by Taif al-Hallaj's *The Sacred Marriage*, which foregrounds transgressive female characters with the intention of critiquing patriarchal social laws that, for instance, allow prostitution in the name of 'marriages of convenience'.

I have to say that the new geographics of identity was also a valuable tool in understanding how authors chronicled and textualized both the discursive and non-discursive narratives of power and powerlessness within Arabia's sensitive gender power relations. For example, Nora al-Ghamdi uses relational discourses of positionality that, as Friedman puts it, 'stress the constantly shifting nature of identity through different points of reference and material conditions of history'.[6] The *Eid* scene in al-Ghamdi's *Compass Direction* shows how Saudi women carefully move between segregated male and female spaces. When the head of the al-Sabti family (a misogynist and oppressive character, discussed in the section on *Compass Direction* in Chapter 3 of this volume) enters the harem space to pass on his good wishes to female members of his family, his presence, the author notes, brings sublime joy to the women, who are portrayed as dashing to the door to see him. In that particular scene, a non-discursive narrative of power and powerlessness is carefully woven into the text, with women depicted as inhabiting the private and marginal space while men occupy the public and central space. Thus, unequal gender hierarchies are textualized by the author to further indict cultural laws that permit the likes of al-Sabti to wield unchecked power over the female members of his family.

Chapter 5, 'Travel, Women and the City', sought, through the examination of an array of novels, to understand the impact of globalization on identities and cultures and its role in instigating 'local agencies' and spreading 'global feminism',[7] to borrow the words of Susan Friedman. It closely examined how narratives that take place in Western cities give women writers the space and freedom to negotiate issues of identity and agency and to question, if not actively challenge, their home culture. Analysis of these many narrative texts revealed how globalization, travel, urban life and the West generate an introspective discourse that challenges socio-religious limitations 'back home'. These aspects also help in the process of deconstructing the figure of the silent and submissive female by creating another, bolder, savvier woman. Hence, Western cities such as London are portrayed not only as a window onto freedom and love but also as a space that provokes activism. A clear example of this trend is embodied by the protagonist Sarah in Samar al-Megrin's *Women of Vice*, who, while visiting London, goes through an introspective moment and realizes that the best years of her life had been stolen by an ideology that she nonetheless believed in at the time – an implicit reference to the *sahwa*. Sarah goes on to challenge the tyranny of the *mutaween* on her return to Saudi Arabia.

However, while Western metropolises invoke questions of freedom, the city of Riyadh and its people are fetishized through the eyes of a stranger in Omima al-Khamis' 2006 novel *Sea-wafted Women* (see Chapter 2), which explores the dilemma of the Levantine Bahijah who fails to assimilate into the Najdi clan of her husband Saleh. Despite having children with him, she is reminded by the family that she is still a foreigner. By reviving chunks of memory related to cultural and gender identity, this narrative in a way questions the dominant discourse. Al-Khamis subtly challenges the logic of power deeply embedded in Najdi discourse by adopting Bahijah and a 'chorus' of foreign women who live in Riyadh as her central characters. By doing so, the author instantly shifts this hitherto powerless minority group into a position of power merely by allowing them greater fictional space in which to express their difference, and through episodes that tend to subvert the dominant male discourse.

Other chapters have examined how women writers turn the female body into a site of knowledge and history capable of telling stories other than those of the master narrative. These writers have attempted to contextualize the female experience within the social limitations of their time – relying on symbolic order, metaphor and hermeneutic discourses to further challenge those limitations. For example, in Raja Alem's *Khatem* (whose multiple aspects are explored in Chapter 3), the author symbolically elides the female body in order to mock patriarchal societies for favouring males over females. Saba al-Herz, in *The Others* (examined in Chapter 6), turns the female body into a reactionary tool of patriarchal prejudice by portraying the protagonist as burdened by her sexual confusion and her illness – evidenced through her occasional epileptic seizures, which she conceals from others for fear that they would reduce her marriage chances. Similarly, Maha al-Jahni's *The Cloak* (Chapter 2) skilfully undermines the *'abaya* garment as a marker of women's gender identity in Arabia, turning it from a modesty symbol into a tool with functions such as mystery and wrongdoing. Hence, the women writers mentioned above each, in their own way, turn the female body into a site of conscious mimicry or an interrogation of the cultural ideas and ideals of both women and men.

In Chapter 4, subtitled 'Communicating Corporeal Anxieties', I examined how women writers have used the female body as a site of abuse and torture, which explains why the protagonists in most of the works chosen for this chapter are depicted as victims of patriarchal culture that not only relegate women to a subordinate status but also denies them the opportunity to take responsibility for their lives. Hence, I drew my analysis from Foucault's *Discipline and Punish*, which, in spite of it being gender neutral, has been a very influential work among feminists. This is because it underlines the way in which the torture and abuse of rebellious protagonists, often documented in the works of women writers, is seen as a means of disciplining and rehabilitating those women in order to fit back into the family's and society's codes of 'virtue'.

For this chapter, I selected Laila al-Juhani's *The Days of Ignorance*, Badriya al-Beshir's *The Swing* and Hana Hejazi's *Two Women* in order to highlight the recurrent tropes of rape, racism and violence in Saudi women's fiction. It is notable that al-Juhani, in *The Days of Ignorance*, questions – if not directly reproaches – the male-dominated culture for discrimination against minorities generally – that is, women and black people, both of whom are present via the novel's doomed love between the characters of Līn and Malek.

Surely al-Juhani and other writers cannot be labelled 'activists' despite their contribution to the discourse of power and influence. This contribution is evident not only in these authors' choice of themes and issues but also in the intensity with which these aspects are treated – which, in large part, cause their works to fall into the category of 'feminist novel'. This is a literary type that Judi Roller, in *The Politics Of The Feminist Novel*, identifies as having an 'anti-authoritarian perspective, a rejection of traditional sex roles and an end that involves death or escape'.[8] These writers have this by simply contextualizing their own struggle within the social constraints of their time, and raising questions around futile cultural laws – questions that have thus far been sidelined, if not ignored outright, by the male-dominant discourse. No longer 'bearers of the word', as Margaret Homans notes, Saudi women writers 'exist as "authors" and "agents" who forge a different relationship to language in the face of an ideology that would deny them access to the status of subject'.[9]

There could be no better time than the present for a book like this one. Despite the rapid pace of change and reform that we are witnessing in Arabia, I find that it is as important as ever to chronicle and recall the evolution of Saudi women's discourse, their persistent calls for equality and the various themes that they have explored in order to subvert the prevailing 'master narrative'. I trust that this volume testifies to the fact that over the span of almost 50 years – that is, from the late 1960s to 2015 – Saudi women writers have used their pens as weapons of change and proven highly capable of producing a body of writing that diligently questions futile cultural laws while pushing back at the old boundaries of *'awra* (the 'shameful') that have been ascribed solely to them. In this book, I have argued that, by virtue of their contribution to literature, these women writers have not only disrupted the patriarchal discourse or 'master narrative' but that they have also been capable of creating a 'counter memory' that is driving change in cultural and social attitudes, and values. Each chapter in this book has dealt with a certain aspect of Saudi women's struggle for rights within the family and society, revealing the gradual process of change in social attitudes in the kingdom and the transformation in female perspectives – a transformation that is mirrored by recent changes and reforms to improve women's status in Arabia's society.

Notes

1 Raunig, *Art and Revolution*, p. 49.
2 See Genosko, *Guattarri Reader*, pp. 14–16.
3 Paul Connerton, *How Modernity Forgets* (Cambridge University Press: New York, 2009), p. 39.

4 Friedman, *Mappings*, p. 90.
5 Friedman, p. 50.
6 Friedman, p. 23.
7 Friedman, pp. 111–12.
8 Roller, *Politics of the Feminist Novel*, p. 107.
9 Margaret Homans, in Friedman, *Mappings*, p. 197.

INDEX

al-Abbas, M. 6, 132
'Abath 20
'Abaya see Cloak, The
'abaya garment 67–73
Abbad al-Shams 157
Abdul Malik, W., 145, 160, 162;
    The Return 46, 150–153
Abdulrahman, W. 24–25
Al-'Abedin, S. Z. 35
Abouelnaga, S. 86
Abu Khaled, F. 37
Abu-Lughod, L., 32, 33, 104
Adorno, T. 131
'Afwan Ya'Adam 20
'Agīl, I. 20
Ahmad, L. 7
Ahmad, Q. 26
Al-Akrūn 83
Alarcon, N. 51
Alem, R., 17, 24, 93, 164;
    Khatem 77–85
al-Ali, M. 146
al-Ali, N. 40
alienation 1, 131, 149
Alsharekh, A. 2
Altorki, S. 8, 20, 34
Amin, Q. 33
al-'Amri, K. 2
al-'Anbar, S. 39
anonymous writers 34–38
al-Ansari, A. Q. 17
Anzaldúa, G. 1, 51–52, 130

Arab *Khalījī*/Saudi feminism 31–34
Archaeology of Knowledge, The, 35–36, 159
Arebi, S., 19, 40, 83, 159
Al Areqi, R. 18
Ashcroft, B. 39
al-Aswani, 'A. 68

Badran, M. 133–134
Baḥryāt see Sea-wafted Women
Bait al-Ṭa'ah see House of Obedience, The
Baker, S. 157
Bakhtine, M. 86–94
Bakhtine, M. 89
Banat al-Riyadh see Girls of Riyadh
Barīq 'Aynaik 19–20
Barren Paradise 2, 85–91, 97
Barthes, R., 89, 162
Beauty Myth, The 125
Bender, T. 10
al-Beshir, B., 95, 162, 164–165; *Hend and the Soldiers* 4, 31, 50, 61–67; *The Swing* 09–114, 156
Beyond the Clouds 9, 25, 38–42
Beyond the Dunes 17
Bhabha, H. 39
bin Abdulaziz, A. 23
bin Abdulaziz, S. 3, 26
bin Salman, M. 23
Bodies That Matter: On the Discursive Limits of Sex 79

Booth, M. 9, 132
'borderland' cultural identity 41–42
borderlands consciousness 51–52
Bridget Jones's Diary 135
Bushnell, C. 135
Butler, J. 35, 60, 65, 79, 107, 109; on oral performativity 142

censorship 35
Cixous, H., 92
Clément, C. 4
Clifford, J. 31, 141
Cloak, The 67–73, 164
Compass Direction 2–100, 163
Connerton, P. 160
Convention on Elimination of all forms of Discrimination Against Women (CEDAW) 3, 28
critical agency 58
cultural definitions, transcending 124–127
cultural encounters 122–123; in *Girls of Riyadh* 135–140; in *The Leafy Tree* 124–127; local agencies and 122; second-generation voices on 124–132; third-generation voices on 132–143; in *Twisted Legs* 130–132; in *Women of Vice* 140–143; in *Women on the Equator* 127–130
cultural memory 6–7

Da'iman Sayabqa al-Hubb 86
Damanhourī', H. 18
Days of Ignorance, The 104–109, 116, 164–165
d'Eaubonne, F. 112
de Beauvoir, S. 107
deconstructionism 10
Departure, The 4
Derrida, J. 104
Discipline and Punish 5, 107, 118, 164
displacement 21
Douglas, M. 15, 149
Doumato, E. 1
Dreams of Trespass 30

education of Saudi girls 21, 26
El Fadl, K. A. 110
el-Sadawi, N. 157
Emra'tān 62
Al Erjouḥah 95

Faisal, King 9, 26, 62
Fakhro, M. 31–32

Fayed, E. 20
Fayed, M. 20
feminizing history: in *Barren Paradise* 85–91; in *Compass Direction* 92–100; in *Khatem* 77–85
Al-Ferdūs al-Yabāb see *Barren Paradise*
fictional space of freedom 127–130
Fielding, H. 135
First Gulf War, 1990 1, 93
forced marriage 3, 99, 116, 119
40 Fi Ma'na an Akbar 86
Foucault, M., 9, 10, 34, 35–36, 37, 55, 103, 159; *Discipline and Punish* 5, 107, 118, 164; on disciplining of the female body 114–115; on docile bodies 61; theory of resistance 32; theory on subjection 65
Freud, S. 58
Friedman, S. 8, 54–55, 57, 98, 163; on cultural encounters 122–123; *Mappings* 9, 103, 110; on multiple oppression 58–59

gender construction 07–108, 163
Gender Trouble: Feminism and the Subversion of Identity 107
Gender Writing/Writing Gender 41
geographics of identity 22
Ghadan Ansā, 20
Ghadan Sa-yakūn Al-Khamīs, 20
al-Ghadeer, M. 104
al-Ghadhami, Abd A. 146–147
al-Ghamdi, N. 4, 163; *Compass Direction* 92–100
al-Ghothami, A. 93
Girls of Riyadh 7, 21, 132, 135–140
global celebrities 132
globalization 132
Glover, D. 139
Golden Chariot, The 157
al-Gosaibi, G. 2, 37, 138
Gramsci, A. 97
"Gulf Women and Islamic Law" 31–32
gynocriticism 8

Al-Hadātha fī Mīzān Al-Islām: Nazrāt Islāmyya fī Adab Alhadātha 2
Haikal, M. H. 18
Hall, D. 22
Hall, S., 53
al-Hallaj, T. 145; *The Sacred Marriage* 46, 153–157
al-Hamad, T. 2, 24, 138
Harem Histories 29

al-Hazimi, M. 18
Hefny, Z., 32, 162; *Twisted Legs* 130–132; *Women on the Equator* 2, 124–127
Hejazi, H. 2, 164–165; *Two Women* 114–119
Hemingway, E. 88
Hend and the Soldiers 4, 31, 50, 61–67
Hend we al-'Askar see Hend and the Soldiers
Henrique, J. 59–60
al-Herz, S., 83, 145, 162; *The Others* 46–150, 153
homosexuality 146–148
House of Obedience, The 134
human trafficking 80, 93–94

identity: anonymous 150–153; borderland 41–42; in fictional space of freedom 127–130; geographics of 160–161; lipstick feminism and 135–140; paradigm shift in 140–143; in temporary destinations 130–132; transcending the limitations of cultural definitions of 124–127
'Imarat Ya'qubyan 68
In the Land of Invisible Women 26

Jacob's Room 90
Jahiliyyah 5, 104
al-Jahni, M. 67–73
Jayyusi, S. 7, 86
jihad 4, 63
Journal of an Indifferent Woman 136–137
al-Juhani, L. 4, 36, 164–165; *Barren Paradise* 2, 85–91, 97; *The Days of Ignorance* 104–109, 116

Kaplan, C. 139
Kennedy, H. 142
Khal, A. 37
Khalifah, S. 157
al-Khamis, O., 24, 27, 29, 163–164; *The Leafy Tree* 124–127; *Sea-wafted Women* 50–57
Khashugji, A. 20
Khashugji, M. 20
Khashugji, S. 5, 26–28, 37–38, 161, 162; *Beyond the Clouds* 9, 25, 38–42
Khashugji, S., 17, 19–20
al-Khateeb, S. 33
Khatem 164; 'faulty bride' in 77–80; history, myth and feminism in 80–85

Kristeva, J., 86
Kristeva Reader, The 86

Lacan, J. 58
LaCapra, D. 151
Leafy Tree, The 124–127
Lefebvre, H. 122
Le Renard, A. 6, 28
Lévi-Strauss, C. 5, 148
lipstick feminism 32, 135–140
Literature of Their Own: British Women Writers from Charlotte Bronte to Doris Lessing, A, 160
local agencies 22, 126–127, 160–161
locational feminism 160–161

Mahfouz, N. 8, 157
Mappings 9, 103, 110
Marxism 10
Maṭar, S. 134
Mawāni' Belā 'Arṣefah 20
McClintock, A. 134
McClur, M. 86
McDowell, L. 90–91
McKee, E. 7
al-Megrin, S. 38, 140–143, 152
melancholia 8, 61
Mernissi, F. 30
Midaq Alley 157
Miller, M. C. 124
Millstone, A. 72
modernism 10
moral geographies and private sphere 29–31
Most Masculine State, A 34, 135
al-Mughni, H. 28
multiple oppression 9
*Munis*the 15th of Wail* 104
al-Musa'id, J. 5, 37

Namy, H. 7, 21–22
Neither East Nor West 39
Nesā' 'End Khaṭ al-'Estewā' see Women on the Equator
9/11 3, 145
'Notes on Theory and Travel' 131–132

obscenity 146
al-Olayyan, Q., 50, 162; *The Virgin Wife* 7–61, 124
Orientalism 26, 127
Others, The 146–150, 153
al-Othman, L. 4

patriarchal discourse 103–104, 135, 165; *The Cloak* and 67–73; *Hend and the Soldiers* and 61–67; *Sea-wafted Women* and 50–57; selectivity in 153–157; *The Virgin Wife* and 57–61
phases of Saudi women's fiction 19–25
Politics Of The Feminist Novel, The 165
positional identity 38–39
Powell, M. 81
Power and Knowledge 107
power-knowledge 9
prostitution 53–154, 156–157
protest and self-orientalizing texts 145–146; *The Others* as 146–150; *The Return* as 150–153; *The Sacred Marriage* as 153–157

Qabbani, N. 136–137
Qabīlah Ismha Sara see *Tribe Called Sara, A*
al-Qaran al-Muqadas see *Sacred Marriage, The*
al-Qarni, 'A. 2
Qaṭrat Min ad-Dumu 19

Raghabāt Shayṭānyah 24–25
Al-Raqs 'Alā al-Dufūf 22–23
al-Rasheed, H., 20, 38, 39, 162
al-Rasheed, M. 134, 135, 145
Raunig, G. 3
Return, The 46, 150–153, 160, 162
Rittenhouse, D. C. 146
al-Riyywaya al-Suū'dia: Wāqeuhā wataḥwolātahā 17
Roller, J. M. 1, 165
romanticism 21
Roper, L. 69

Sacred Marriage, The 46, 153–157, 162
saḥwa ideology 3, 18, 21, 67, 150–151, 152
Said, E. 23, 126, 127
al-Sanea, R. 5; *Girls of Riyadh* 7, 21, 132, 135–140
Sartre, J.-P. 146
Saudi literature 17–19; growth of women's novels in 21–22
Saudi women: education of 21, 26; struggle for rights of 25–29; travel by (see cultural encounters); violence against (see violence against women)
Saudi women's fiction: conceptual and theoretical framework 5–12; female as repository of memories and (see feminizing history); feminism in 31–34; locational feminism and 160–161; moral geographies and the private sphere and 29–31; narratives of violence in (see violence against women); power and defiance in 160; prominent writers of 17; protest and self-orientalizing (see protest and self-orientalizing texts); reconciling Western and local discourses on 1–3; rethinking the patriarchal discourse (see patriarchal discourse); as subversive 159–160; three phases of 19–25; transversality in 'new texts' of 3–5; veiling, silence and anonymous writer in 34–38
Saussure, F. d 86
Sea-wafted Women 57, 163–164
self-orientalizing texts see protest and self-orientalizing texts
Sex and the City 135
al-Shadawi, A. 82
Shands, K. W. 39
Shaṭā, A. 20
Shaṭā', A. 7
Showalter, E., 160
Siqan Multawiah see *Twisted Legs*
situationality 57
slavery 2, 70, 80, 93–94
Snows of Kilimanjaro, The 88
social control 125
social death 110
social order 110
Society of Young Women, A 6, 28
spatial encounters see cultural encounters
spiritual-spatial 'fourth' dimension 93
Stagh, M. 146
structuralism 10
al-Subai, M. 4, 134
Swing, The 09–114, 156, 164–165

al-Tahawy, M. 7, 146
takfeer 24
Tanner, L. 111
Tarawri, M. 4
Al-Ṭareeq ela al-Jannah 24
Al-Tau'amān 17
Ṭawq al-Ḥamama 17
temporal encounters see cultural encounters
Thaman al-Tatḥya 18
Thekrayāt Dām'ah 19

theory of resistance 32
theory of subjection 65
third space identity 1–52, 54
third-wave feminism 133
al-Thunayan, I. 26
transversality in women's 'new texts' 5, 134
travel *see* cultural encounters
Travelling Theory 123
Tribe Called Sara, A 134
Twisted Legs 130–132
Two Women 14–119, 164–165

veiling 34–38
violence against women 103–104; in *The Days of Ignorance* 104–109; in *The Swing* 109–114; in *Two Women* 114–119
Virgin Wife, The 7–61, 124

Wadda't Āmālī 7, 19
al-Wahabi, A. 23
Wallace, M. 53
Warā' al-Dabāb see Beyond the Clouds
al-Wasil, A. 5, 147

Al Watan 4
Weijhat al-Bouṣlah see Compass Direction
Western feminism 8, 33–34, 41
Willingham, B. 118
Wolf, N. 125
Woman at Point Zero 157
Women and Language 93
Women and Words in Saudi Arabia, 19, 40, 83
Women in Kuwait 28
Women in Saudi Arabia 34–35
Women of Vice 38, 140–143, 152
Women on the Equator 2, 127–130
women's rights, Saudi 25–29
Woolf, V., 31, 67, 90

Yacoubian Building 68
Yamani, M. 19

Zainab 18
al-Zawjah al-'Athra' see Virgin Wife, The
Zeidan, J. T., 32
Zeitoun, M.-L. 82
Zwissler, L. 69

www.ingramcontent.com/pod-product-compliance
Ingram Content Group UK Ltd.
Pitfield, Milton Keynes, MK11 3LW, UK
UKHW030807050225
454689UK00015B/252